CROSS-CURRICULAR TEACHING AND LEARNING IN THE SECONDARY SCHOOL

SCIENCE

Using a cross-curricular focus, this book brings together ongoing debates about personalised learning, creativity and ICT in education, and establishes a principled framework for cross-curricular teaching and learning in Science. It identifies a range of key issues and aims to strengthen in-school science practices by introducing ways of teaching rigorous science through, and alongside, other subjects.

This highly practical book draws on examples and case studies taken from innovative practices in different schools and subject areas, as well as summarising lessons from key pieces of research evidence. *Cross-Curricular Teaching and Learning in the Secondary School ... Science* also includes the following:

- Clear theoretical frameworks for cross-curricular processes of teaching and learning in science, including chapters on maths, ICT and technology, English, the humanities and the arts
- An analysis of the use of language, ICT and assessment as key components of a skilful pedagogical practice that affects how teaching is delivered and how pupils learn science in cross-curricular contexts
- A lively account of theoretical issues blended with engaging stories of current practice
- Practical tasks and questions for reflective practice

This timely textbook is essential reading for all students on Initial Teacher Training courses and PGCE courses as well as practising teachers looking to holistically introduce cross-curricular themes and practices in science.

Eleanor Byrne is a Research Fellow at the Centre for Science Education at Sheffield Hallam University. She specialises in cross-curricular teaching and learning in science and teacher-led continuing professional development. She has written and developed various cross-curricular classroom resources and has expertise in science education during the transition from primary to secondary school.

Marilyn Brodie is a Principal Lecturer in Science Education at the Centre for Science Education at Sheffield Hallam University. She has almost 40 years experience in science education having been a secondary school science teacher, a further and higher education lecturer and teacher educator. She has worked on a range of national and international curriculum development and education research projects.

Cross-Curricular Teaching and Learning in . . .
Series Editor – Jonathan Savage (Manchester Metropolitan University, UK)

The *Cross-Curricular* series, published by Routledge, argues for a cross-curricular approach to teaching and learning in secondary schools. It provides a justification for cross-curricularity across the Key Stages, exploring a range of theoretic and practical issues through case studies drawn from innovative practices across a range of schools. The books demonstrate the powerful nature of change that can result when teachers allow a cross-curricular 'disposition' to inspire their pedagogy. Working from a premise that there is no curriculum development without teacher development, the series argues for a serious re-engagement with cross-curricularity within the work of the individual subject teacher, before moving on to consider collaborative approaches for curriculum design and implementation through external curriculum links.

Cross-curricular approaches to teaching and learning can result in a powerful, new model of subject-based teaching and learning in the high school. This series places the teacher and their pedagogy at the centre of this innovation. The responses that schools, departments or teachers make to Government initiatives in this area may only be sustainable over the short term. For longer term change to occur, models of cross-curricular teaching and learning need to become embedded within the pedagogies of individual teachers and, from there, to inform and perhaps redefine the subject cultures within which they work. These books explore how this type of change can be initiated and sustained by teachers willing to raise their heads above their 'subject' parapet and develop a broader perspective and vision for education in the twenty-first century.

Currently available:

Cross-Curricular Teaching and Learning in the Secondary School
By Jonathan Savage

Cross-Curricular Teaching and Learning in the Secondary School ... English
By David Stevens

Cross-Curricular Teaching and Learning in the Secondary School ... Humanities
By Richard Harris, Simon Harrison and Richard McFahn

Cross-Curricular Teaching and Learning in the Secondary School ... Mathematics
By Robert Ward-Penny

Cross-Curricular Teaching and Learning in the Secondary School ... The Arts
By Martin Fautley

Cross-Curricular Teaching and Learning in the Secondary School ... Science
By Eleanor Byrne and Marilyn Brodie

Forthcoming titles in the series:

Cross-Curricular Teaching and Learning in the Secondary School ... Foreign Languages
By Gee Macrory, Cathy Brady and Sheila Anthony

Cross-Curricular Teaching and Learning in the Secondary School ... Using ICT
By Maurice Nyangon

CROSS-CURRICULAR TEACHING AND LEARNING IN THE SECONDARY SCHOOL

SCIENCE

Eleanor Byrne and Marilyn Brodie

Routledge
Taylor & Francis Group

LONDON AND NEW YORK

First published 2011
by Routledge
2 Park Square, Milton Park, Abingdon, Oxon OX14 4RN

Simultaneously published in the USA and Canada
by Routledge
711 Third Avenue, New York, NY 10017

Routledge is an imprint of the Taylor & Francis Group, an informa business

British Library Cataloguing in Publication Data
A catalogue record for this book is available from the British Library

Library of Congress Cataloging in Publication Data
Byrne, Eleanor.
Cross curricular teaching and learning in the secondary school–science/
Eleanor Byrne, Marilyn Brodie. –1st ed.
    p. cm.
1. Science–Study and teaching (Secondary)–Great Britain. 2. Science–
Curricula–Great Britain. 3. Interdisciplinary approach in education–Great
Britain. I. Brodie, Marilyn. II. Title.
Q181.B995 2012
507.1'241–dc23

ISBN: 978-0-415-66681-7 (hbk)
ISBN: 978-0-415-66682-4 (pbk)
ISBN: 978-0-203-81773-5 (ebk)

Typeset in Bembo
by Cenveo Publisher Services

MIX
Paper from
responsible sources
FSC® C004839

Printed and bound in Great Britain by
TJ International Ltd, Padstow, Cornwall

Contents

Illustrations

Figures

Tables

Abbreviations

AfL	Assessment for Learning
APP	Assessing Pupils' Progress
BECTA	British Educational Communications and Technology Agency
CERN	Conseil Européen pour la Recherche Nucléaire (European Organization for Nuclear Research)
CSE	Centre for Science Education
CTD	Collapsed Timetable Day
D&T	Design and Technology
DARTs	Directed Activities Related to Texts
DES	Department of Education and Science
DfES	Department for Education and Skills
FIRST	For Inspiration and Recognition of Science and Technology
GCSE	General Certificate of Secondary Education
HSW	How Science Works
ICT	Information and Communication Technology
IWB	Interactive White Board
KS3	Key Stage 3
LA	Local Authority
NACCCE	National Advisory Committee on Creative and Cultural Education
OFSTED	Office for Standards in Education, Children's Services and Skills
OpArt	Optical Art
PE	Physical Education
PLTS	Personal Learning and Thinking Skills
QCA	Qualifications and Curriculum Authority
QTS	Qualified Teacher Status
RE	Religious Education
SEN	Special Educational Needs
SMT	Senior Management Team
STEM	Science, Technology, Engineering and Mathematics
STS	Science, Technology and Society

Acknowledgements

Figures 4.1 to 4.8, 'Building for the Future', *Cre8ate Maths*, reproduced with permission of the Centre for Science Education (CSE) and the Mathematics Education Centre (MEC), of Sheffield Hallam University

Figures 4.11, 8.2, 8.12, 8.14, 8.15 and 8.16 purchased from iStockphoto®

Figures 7.3 to 7.18, 'Time Raiders' and 'A Blitz Mystery', *Double Crossed*, reproduced with permission of the Centre for Science Education (CSE), Sheffield Hallam University with special thanks to Brinsworth Comprehensive School, Eckington School and the Astra Zeneca Science Teaching Trust.

Introduction: the context for cross-curricular teaching and learning

Key objectives

By the end of this chapter, you will have:

- Explored what is meant by 'cross-curricular' teaching and learning
- Reflected on the ways in which a cross-curricular approach could benefit your teaching
- Considered the role of cross-curricular teaching and learning in the twenty-first century and its place within the National Curriculum
- Reflected on your reasons for undertaking cross-curricular work
- Explored the distinct characteristics of your own subject area

There is little doubt that the way we live our modern lives could be described as cross-curricular. Many of the skills we use in one area of life can be utilised and put to work in another without much planning or forethought. It is interesting therefore that as teachers we are, more often than not, required to teach in distinctly separate topics and themes. Artificial barriers can be created through a curriculum disconnect – barriers that do not realistically represent the nature of twenty-first-century life. However, by applying a theme across two (or more) disciplines we are able to allow pupils the opportunity to form meaningful connections between subjects that better reflect the real world. The formation of links between seemingly separate curriculum subjects can enhance pupil learning and impact upon both cognitive and meta-cognitive understanding. It can also have a major impact on the development of core and transferable skills, which become useful both for a learner and for an active social citizen. This approach is known as *cross-curricular teaching and learning* although it can also be described as *curriculum integration*.

Throughout this book the concept of cross-curricular teaching and learning and its potential pedagogical implications will be explored and the process will be illustrated by real-life case studies. This book stands as part of a series looking at cross-curricular teaching in a number of different curriculum subjects including mathematics, the arts, English and the humanities. This edition seeks to explore the ways in which **science** teaching can be enhanced and strengthened through cross-curricular endeavours within the school classroom. But what do we mean by *cross-curricular* teaching and learning?

Cross-curricular teaching and learning

As an educational philosophy or approach, cross-curricular pedagogical methods can be seen as a way of supporting the varied and diverse abilities of pupils. The process sees the combining of one or more subject area(s) and often the incorporation of a wide range of concepts. The identified subjects can be integrated using 'a central theme, issue, problem, process, topic or experience' (Hayes 2010: 382) and the aim of cross-curricular teaching is to enhance more than just subject knowledge. As a methodology the approach looks to develop general skills, cognitive understanding, creativity and flexibility (amongst other things!). The lengthy list of aims prescribed to the approach leads to varying definitions for the concept itself. As such cross-curricular teaching and learning does not boast one single identity and it can be defined differently when explored by different education commentators. This should not, however, provoke alarm as there are various other educational concepts for which no agreed collective definition exists such as 'creativity', 'special needs', 'non-fiction' and 'high expectations' (Hayes 2010: 383). The view taken in this book is one shared by the complete series and defines the cross-curricular method as the following:

> A cross-curricular approach to teaching is characterised by sensitivity towards, and a synthesis of, knowledge, skills and understandings from various subject areas. These inform an enriched pedagogy that promotes an approach to learning which embraces and explores this wider sensitivity through various methods.
>
> (Savage 2011: 8–9)

This concept of cross-curricular learning arises from a constructivist stand-point in which learning is achieved through *doing* or *experiencing*. This pedagogical approach can be undertaken using a plethora of different methods that all engage children's imaginations, encourage investigation and foster creativity. The methods applied are drawn from the differing subject areas and linked though identified themes, projects or topics:

> Cross-curricular learning: when the skills, knowledge and attitudes of a number of different disciplines are applied to a single experience, theme or idea.
>
> (Barnes 2007: 8)

While a theme/topic/idea is a great focus for any cross-curricular teaching that is not to suggest a return to the solely thematic and awkwardly broad topic work of the 1970s. The cross-curricular work put forward in this book straddles this tired 1970s model and the disconnected subject work undertaken throughout the 1990s under the guidance of the National Curriculum.

Why is cross-curricular teaching important?

The National Curriculum identifies both statutory and non-statutory, distinctly defined subject areas that must be taught in schools. As important as each of these separate subjects are, on their own they cannot guarantee young people leave school with adequate knowledge, skills and ingenuity to contribute as citizens in what is an ever changing and unpredictable global society. This concept emphasises the need to prepare young people for the next phase of their education as well as their future, all of which must take place alongside the provision of sound subject-based understanding. This is a big task for teachers, and the enormity of the challenge is not lost on the authors of this book. However, the aspirations of the curriculum are commendable if we are to prepare our younger generation to cope with a changeable and potentially volatile future.

So now let us consider some of ways in which cross-curricular teaching can support the development of both knowledge and skills.

Context-rich teaching

The integrated curriculum approach to teaching moves us away from the notion of the teacher as the *provider of facts*. Instead the emphasis is on pupil-led thinking and reasoning skills, creativity, investigation and communication. This emphasises a more social model of learning, which sees pupils learn from each other as well as the teacher. In his 1978 work, *Mind in Society* the Russian psychologist Vygotsky suggests that all higher thinking, in terms of processes and structures (such as scientific concepts), is first experienced by learners as they communicate with others. This information must then be internalised and understood by the individual learner in relation to their own existing notions and beliefs. As such, this Vygotskian model suggests social communication followed by internal reasoning is fundamental to the understanding of scientific concepts. This theoretical view emphasises the importance of the individual in the learning process as well as the social aspects of learning. Contexts for learning become important as a means through which scientific concepts can be better understood. Science offers learners a new and often daunting way of speaking and thinking. This new framework can sometimes clash with pupils' already existing everyday way of thinking and communicating, and as such contrived obstacles to scientific learning can be created. Real-world contexts can help overcome these barriers by providing a familiar context for the learning. This cross-curricular approach can support the progression and retention of new scientific knowledge.

Skills development

Approaching learning from a more holistic viewpoint allows cross-curricular teaching to explore skills in an ultimately beneficial way. As a teaching method, cross-curricular work aims to transfer learning across one or more subjects and in the process utilises skills and methods relevant to each separate subject together. By drawing together the approaches familiar to each distinct subject, advocates of the pedagogical technique argue that this method of teaching allows a transfer of learning from subject to subject that is not seen through discrete curriculum work. This cross-discipline approach aims to make learning more relevant and accessible to young people by eliminating artificial barriers so familiar to compartmentalised National Curriculum teaching. That is to say that, cross-curricular learning focuses on the development of transferable skills that can be used across multiple subject areas. Tate (1994) believes that this skills focus is important if we hope to provide young people with a well-rounded education:

> Is education a matter of accruing information? The knowledge and understanding that we expect school children to learn can be itemised and structured in subjects and levels, as in the National Curriculum. Or is education a matter of learning ways to process information, developing strategies, concepts and categories, developing what are sometimes called core or transferable skills?
>
> (Tate 1994: 1)

This latter concept fits with the notion of *developing the individual* though education. While schools are required to provide a rigorous education as set out by the National Curriculum, is there not also a need for schools to be 'a place where students come to find out about the world and about themselves in that world?' (Morrison 1994: v). Verma and Pumfrey (1993) identify six distinct, cross-curricular skills that can be developed through an integrated learning approach:

- Communication
- Numeracy
- Study skills
- Problem-solving
- Personal and social skills
- Information-technology skills

(Verma and Pumfrey 1993: 20)

Along with the numeracy skills identified by Verma and Pumfrey in the above list, literacy can also be improved through cross-curricular undertakings. From the science perspective this can mean a move away from an emphasis on scientific literacy (although obviously of huge importance) towards structured oral activities such as debates and reading from popular literature as well as textbooks. Numeracy and literacy are explored further in Chapters 4 and 6.

The societal perspective

To understand the strengths of the cross-curricular approach we must first explore the purpose of education. While exploring the full spectrum of this philosophical debate may be a little too much for the pages of this book, it is important to stress the rapidly changing nature of twenty-first-century life and the responsibilities this presents to the education community. Some argue that it is no longer enough for young people to leave school with just an *academic* education, they also need to know how to utilise and apply their knowledge to allow them to become 'active participants in society' (Morrison 1994: 1). With reference to science education there is a particular need to support and develop scientific literacy to ensure young people understand the nature of science. As citizens of an ever-changing global community, today's school-leavers need to be equipped to confidently interrogate scientific evidence, understand the wider issues surrounding scientific advancements and question the media's representation of science in the news. To do so, pupils need to be developing these skills while at school by investigating contemporary and contentious real-world science topics:

> Pupils should actively engage with topical science-based issues so that they feel more confident to access the relevant information and participate in discussion on science-related controversies. If we believe in a democratic society, it is desirable for all citizens to be both equipped and empowered to take an active role in science-based issues, and so education needs to consider seriously how these aspects of science can be incorporated into the curriculum.
>
> (Alexander *et al.* 2008: 25)

Alongside this science focus is the broader issue concerning the society in which young people are growing up. The often turbulent and ever-changing nature of modern living can mean education has a role to play in preparing pupils for life after school:

> [C]hildren are growing up in a world where moral and social boundaries are becoming increasingly blurred. We live in a time where communication opportunities abound, one result being that young people are faced by a bewildering kaleidoscope of ideas, opinions and pressures.
>
> (Hayes 2010: 386)

The rapid shifts in communication technology call for an increasingly holistic model of education that can help today's young people place their learning into a context that supports their development as active, independent *global* citizens. This concept of pupils requiring an education that provides a global perspective is not new. In 2004, the Department for Education and Skills (DfES) published the paper *Putting the World into World-Class Education*. The paper identified three inter-related key goals:

- ■ Equipping children and adults for a global society and economy.
- ■ Working with other nations and regions to their benefit and ours.
- ■ Maintaining an education system that can further our global economic objectives.

(Department for Education and Skills 2004: 6)

In this paper one suggested way in which the 'International Dimension' could be integrated into a school is through cross-curricular delivery. This approach would see a teacher take on the role of 'head of international studies' and oversee the inclusion of a global perspective across the curriculum with a cross-curricular brief to advise on the international dimension in all curriculum areas (DES 2004:15). This can, in turn, lead us back to the notion of context-driven teaching and the need for authenticity and meaning in the lessons we deliver. Barnes and Shirley (2007) suggest that *meaning* in education is key to the development of well-rounded citizens able to cope with global issues such as climate change, energy shortages, global inequities and cultural hostility:

> The researchers consider that an education which places each learner's personal quest for *meaning* at the heart of curricular and pedagogical decisions, is the one most likely to generate the resilient communities needed to face a future of unimaginable challenge and change.
>
> (Barnes and Shirley 2007: 163)

Preparing the workforce

Alongside the social issues young people face, there is also a need for school leavers to complete school ready for the work place. This is not a new concept but one which cross-curricular work can support. Through an integrated learning approach the development and progression of pupils' transferable skills can be bolstered. Meijer *et al.* (2001) identified seven cross-curricular skills that this kind of work can help support, all of which encourage workforce readiness. The seven skills are:

[a] Conducting observations
[b] Selecting and ordering information
[c] Summarising and drawing conclusions
[d] Forming opinions on social issues
[e] Recognising beliefs and values in opinions and actions of oneself and others
[f] Distinguishing opinions from facts
[g] Working together on assignments
[h] Evaluating the quality of one's own work

(Meijer *et al.* 2001: 84)

Each of the seven skills were identified for assessment as part of the research undertaken and they were chosen because they all developed as a consequence of instruction (not dependant solely on intelligence). As can be seen from the list, any cross-curricular activity that focuses on the development of *any* of these seven skills will not only increase workforce readiness but also impact on young people's growth as active and engaged citizens.

Teacher continuing professional development (CPD)

Along with benefits to pupil learning and skill development, cross-curricular teaching can benefit the teacher. In England, the network of National Science Learning Centres (www. sciencelearningcentres.org.uk) offers specific courses to teachers on developing their cross-curricular skills in science with a particular focus on creativity and innovation. The philosophy behind the courses is to increase teacher confidence in undertaking imaginative and resourceful, context-driven activities in the science classroom. By exploring cross-curricular work teachers are able to interrogate the characteristics of their subject and test new or *out-of-the ordinary* teaching methods in relation to different themes, ideas and experiences.

In addition, cross-curricular teaching can offer up the opportunity for cross-departmental partnerships. Teachers from two (or more) different subject areas can come together to create an integrated learning project or activity and in the process develop a new and fruitful working relationship. This kind of colleague interaction can see the sharing of knowledge and practices across departments.

Making links with other departments

One of the central concepts put forward by this book is the notion of cross-departmental teaching partnerships within schools. The conception and design of cross-curricular classroom activities can require a creative developmental process to ensure an appropriate balance between the subjects involved. There is a lot to be gained both professionally and personally from cross-departmental partnerships and creative cross-curricular planning, but there are a few things to consider at the outset. The development of teacher confidence can be one powerful side effect of cross-departmental partnering. While working with a teacher from a different department can open one's eyes to the techniques, content and approaches relevant to a different subject, it can also support the confidence of the teachers involved in relation to their own subject area. When sharing knowledge about their subject, teachers can demonstrate expertise and perspectives that others can utilise:

> Teachers collaborate enthusiastically in interdisciplinary teaching especially if they participate from the standpoint of their subject mastery and have the independence to plan learning according to their own judgment and knowledge of their students.
>
> (Alexander *et al*. 2008: 34)

One of the main things to consider at the start of any cross-curricular project is its size. Trying to keep things manageable is critical and planning an activity that will last for a clearly specified length of time (e.g. one lesson, one double period, one afternoon) will help from the start. This will minimise the likelihood of an ever-expanding activity when it comes to the *nitty-gritty* planning stage. Equally, it is important that all involved are aware of the amount of time they can *honestly* devote to the planning of the activity. As such it is vital to be aware of time-consuming factors such as topic research, lesson planning and cross-departmental meetings that will take place between the cross-departmental partnerships. This became apparent during a cross-departmental collaboration undertaken between a science and a history department in a South Yorkshire school:

> The main issue in planning our activities was time. It was really hard sometimes to find a time when we could all meet but it was worth it in the end, I really feel like we've achieved something with our activities.
>
> (Science Teacher, Brinsworth Comprehensive School, Rotherham)

Another crucial element to consider is enthusiasm. When it comes to cross-departmental meetings with members of staff who have perhaps not worked together before, it is always enthusiasm that drives ideas forward and forms strong and lasting partnerships:

> I've absolutely loved working with [the science teacher] throughout this whole process. I feel like I have a new colleague now and we'll definitely be working together again in the future.
>
> (History Teacher, Brinsworth Comprehensive School, Rotherham)

Practical task

Setting up your own cross-curricular collaborative partnership

To get the most out of this book you may wish to make links with another department at your school. Creating a cross-departmental partnership will strengthen any activity you develop and will be a new and exciting challenge for you to undertake outside of your own department.

To get started you will need to ensure you have a member of staff in your chosen department who is willing and able to help you with your activity. Time is precious in school and we are well aware that finding a spare minute in school to sit down with a member of staff from a different department can be difficult. However, it is important that you work across the two departments to establish a new working relationship you may not have considered before. Try to make time for this as working with a member of staff from a different department is a great way to build confidence and show professional progression.

While cross-departmental partnerships can add a sense of authenticity and a breadth of knowledge to an activity, it is by no means a requirement in the development of a cross-curricular resource. The similarities and differences between two subjects can be explored independently if done so with sensitivity. Using science and art & design as an example, both subjects can be defined as creative with an emphasis on cultural understanding: this can form a great starting place for cross-curricular work. Such comparative thinking can be useful in the early stages of an integrated activity design to help identify common ground on which various concepts and skills can be introduced and developed. Using a tool such as this one may help to form meaningful connections between subjects based on disciplinary similarities. This is an important aspect of the cross-curricular approach and ensures a project can have significant impact on pupil engagement and is not viewed as a fun activity aside from their *academic* learning.

The National Curriculum

As we have seen, cross-curricular projects, if designed appropriately, can support skill development alongside cognitive *and* meta-cognitive understanding. Meaningful impact is crucial to any integrated subject model not least because of the ever-present call of the National Curriculum and the requirements and standards that loom over all subject-based teaching.

The introduction of the National Curriculum in 1989 saw a shift in UK education away from general thematic teaching controlled by the teacher on the classroom level, to a new structured system where each subject is assigned specific targets and requirements which must be met through national testing. Artificial barriers were created around each subject and the introduction of the National Curriculum was also accompanied by an increase in monitoring and inspection through OFSTED, the publication of national testing and the use of resulting league tables. The 2010 Wellcome Trust report on the National Curriculum described a 'mistranslation of what was originally intended' resulting in:

- many teachers feeling disempowered to teach in a manner appropriate to their students and circumstances

- a strong sense of over-prescription in terms of the content of the curriculum

- increased pressures to 'teach to the test' at all levels

- frequent, apparently piecemeal, changes to the curriculum in order to fix shortcomings and meet top-down policy changes

- tests and examinations dominating not just what is taught but also how it is taught.

(Wellcome Trust 2010: 3)

It can be argued that government implementation of the National Curriculum in 1989 and the use of national testing in England has increased the 'technical element' of teaching and reduced professional ownership (Ball 1993). Classroom practice has gone through a process of standardisation and, to some degree, the level of control held by politicians has reduced teachers to 'unquestioning operatives' (Alexander 2010: 3). Government recommended Schemes of Work have eliminated the need for teachers to apply any abstract creativity. Hierarchies and league tables have produced a Foucaldian 'normalisation' (1977) of achievement and discouraged any innovative freedom in classroom practices creating a kind of 'legitimation of education through preformativity' (Lyotard 1984). Within this context the teacher is little more than an instrument through which a generalist, unsophisticated and state-controlled education can be delivered. This is a bleak diagnosis for the teaching profession. Understood in this light teacher autonomy and power are limited to classroom delivery (and even this is constantly under review through government inspection). Even knowledge is in question as lesson content is fed down through the Curriculum and Schemes of Work:

Throughout the National Curriculum's history, science teachers have perceived a shift towards prescribing how to teach rather than what to teach. This has caused a drop in teachers' professional confidence, with many teachers following schemes of work without much interpretation to suit local needs.

(Wellcome Trust 2010: 5)

This notion of teacher autonomy (or lack thereof) is, however, rather forlorn. While the top-down nature of education policy has to some degree created a sense of de-professionalisation, this is not to say that teachers are without any power to question and influence their own practice. Creative, dynamic and engaging teaching takes place across the country all of the time. In their review of the National Curriculum the Wellcome Trust also identified a number of significant improvements (particularly in relation to science education) brought about by its introduction:

- the first ever national entitlement to science education for all students from 5 to 16
- a raising of standards in many schools
- ensuring that students studied all the major scientific disciplines, in particular increasing the number of girls studying physics to the age of 16
- establishing science as an important core element of the primary curriculum
- improving the continuity and transferability when young people moved from one school to another, whether between phases or geographically.

(Wellcome Trust 2010: 3)

Changes were made to the National Curriculum in the latter part of the 1990s and have been rolled out into schools since 2008 (QCA 2007a). The changes hailed a new emphasis on integrated learning at Key Stage 3 with cross-curricular teaching explicitly drawn out as a *curriculum opportunity* in science. Teachers became required, as part of the curriculum, to 'make links between science and other subjects and areas of the curriculum' (Item 4k, p. 213). There was also a renewed emphasis on the use of 'creativity and innovation' (4f, p. 212) in the teaching of science as a means through which pupils can discover new things and think in new and exciting ways.

Skill development was also revived in the National Curriculum with the inclusion of Personal Learning and Thinking Skills (PLTS). PLTS are a framework of skills and qualities that must be developed in all young people while at school. They are broken down into six groups:

- Independent enquirers
- Creative thinkers
- Reflective learners
- Team workers
- Self-managers
- Effective participants

(QCA 2007a: 1)

These skills and qualities must be developed within all subject areas as set out by the National Curriculum. As presented earlier in this chapter, cross-curricular teaching can go some way to support effective and lasting skills development. Along with these PLTS, the National Curriculum also put forward the notion of Functional Skills. These are relevant specifically to English, Mathematics and ICT but are not limited to just these three subjects. Functional skills are defined as the abilities young people require 'to operate confidently, effectively and independently in life, their communities and work' (QCA 2007a). The list of skills is fairly broad and includes abilities relating to reading, writing, ICT, reasoning, judgement, analysis, and communication. It was suggested that the successful development of these skills requires their broad integration into the full curriculum and where possible, for them to be taught in relation to real world contexts. This has implications for cross-curricular teaching as the emphasis is on 'working across subjects' as well as within the boundaries of the three core functional subjects.

A mindful approach to cross-curricular teaching and learning

While cross-curricular approaches seem to offer teachers a hugely beneficial method by which skills and creativity can be encouraged alongside the development of cognitive understanding, the planning time required for this kind of work can often discourage widespread usage. Equally, those who are against cross-curricular teaching argue that 'learning needs the clearly delineated boundaries provided by single-subject teaching' (Hayes 2010: 384) and that cross-curricular learning lacks the required rigour to support the development of fundamental subject knowledge specific to each subject. Equally, cynics of the approach believe that cross-curricular teaching encourages subjects to be forced together often in spite of suitability, for example, while science and mathematics may be happy bed-fellows, the combination of music and science may have little or no classroom benefits. While this is obviously true one expects teachers to approach the planning of any cross-curricular endeavour with the same intelligence they would use in devising any lesson. As such, it is somewhat patronising to assume that a teacher would attempt to combine the teaching of two inappropriate subjects (or subject areas) under the misguided view that cross-curricular is always best!

Despite the obvious benefits of the cross-curricular approach there is one major aspect of the method that must be kept at the forefront of any practitioner's mind when undertaking work of this kind – that of subject identity. While combining two or more subject areas the teacher may wish to draw out a number of different skills and techniques typical to each of the individual subjects within the boundaries of a specified theme or project. It is important, however, that the individual subject disciplines do not become blurred and subsumed by the topic itself thereby losing the distinctive subject-specific content unique to the subjects. The subjects themselves must have their separate identities that can be identified separately but brought together for the purposes of a specific project. To use a scientific analogy, successful cross-curricular teaching is much like a chemical mixture – it combines two or more substances. The mixture does not form a new element or substances and can be easily separated by physical means back into its separate parts. In terms of teaching, the two (or more) subjects that are been integrated remain identifiable not as a whole, but as discrete fields of study. A more troublesome example of cross-curricular teaching can be compared to a chemical compound of two or more elements which cannot be separated back into their original substances by physical means. In this model the subjects being combined have merged within the theme or project and are no longer identifiable as distinct specialisms. This latter example illustrates an area of concern for opponents to the cross-curricular model. Subjects such as design & technology can become so deeply amalgamated with other areas of study such as science and art, that they no longer maintain their own sense of identity.

The temptation to conflate Design and Technology with other subjects, such as science and art, and the resulting loss of its identity, is an issue with potentially serious consequences.

(Barnes 2007: 24)

Having visited a number of schools as part of a cross-curricular science and history initiative (see Chapter 7) this is a sentiment that has also been felt by humanities teachers:

At first I wasn't sure if I wanted to get involved with a project that teaches history with science. I don't think history has the status it should have anyway so I was nervous about seeing it disappear into science. We're all a bit nervous and protective about our subjects.

(History Teacher, Sinfin Secondary School, Derby)

That is not, however, to say that an integrated curriculum should be avoided. Subject identity can be easily defended through careful planning and a sympathetic approach can maintain the distinct identity of each subject involved. Equally, by making links between some of the core subjects (for example English and mathematics) and non-core subjects (for example music, modern foreign languages and history) an increased emphasis can be placed on those subjects which can otherwise be seen as 'fringe'.

The case for science

To understand the importance of cross-curricular teaching in science education we must begin by exploring why science education is important in the first place.

In 1916, Alfred North Whitehead observed the significance of science education as a means by which to cope with the technological advances associated with 'modern' life:

In the conditions of modern life the rule is absolute: the race which does not value trained intelligence is doomed ... Today we maintain ourselves. Tomorrow, science will have moved forward yet one more step – and there will be no appeal from the judgment which will then be pronounced on the uneducated.

(Whitehead 1916, cited in NSF 1965: 1)

This sentiment was echoed almost ninety years later by the widely influential *Primary Horizons* report produced by the Wellcome Trust:

The United Kingdom has an enviable global position at the forefront of scientific research. In a society where scientific and technological advances are playing an increasing role in shaping our lives, the education of today's young people will be crucial in determining not only whether this position continues but also in ensuring that young people develop the skills that will help them to make informed decisions about the impacts of these developments on their lives.

(Murphy *et al.* 2005: 7)

At a UK-wide, economic level, the move away from heavy and light engineering towards a more service-industry led economy has meant much of our mass manufacturing has reduced and as a result we are more reliant than ever on the importation of goods. Despite this shift the importance of science to economic growth continues to be emphasised by politicians (DfES, 2006) and science education continues to be discussed by the press and politicians alike.

As a result, science educators find themselves under increasing pressure to produce tomorrow's scientists. A large number of initiatives and policy changes have been introduced over the last decade to engage the interest and enthusiasm of young people in science education, demonstrate the relevance of scientific knowledge and skills to everyday life, promote excitement about England's science and technology base, and highlight the range of careers it can offer (see STEM Directories http://www.stemdirectories.org.uk/). This extraordinary number of new and continuing initiatives from government, professional bodies, education–business partnerships and employers has sought to change the teaching and learning of science and promote the choice of science-based careers. These initiatives have produced mixed results – some proving highly successful with others having little (or no) lasting impact on engagement in science.

Reporting on data from a five-year UK-based longitudinal study, Archer *et al.* (2010) stated that students felt that school science bears little similarity to science practised professionally. Similarly, Osborne (2007) suggested that a lack of interest in school science could also be influenced by a 'mismatch' between scientific values, teaching approaches and the aspirations and developing identities of young people. In the Royal Society 2010 *State of the Nation* report the learning of science is defined as comprising three elements:

- knowledge of definitions
- facts and procedures
- competence with scientific processes

(Royal Society 2010: 59)

These elements are not, however, viewed as distinct. In fact the report suggests that science facts and procedures can be best learnt and remembered when provided with a conceptual basis and that the development of conceptual understanding is vital in supporting general cognitive advancement (see Piaget 1974):

> Although much current teaching practice emphasises the learning of facts and procedures, conceptual understanding lies at the core of scientific and mathematical understanding.

(Royal Society 2010: 59)

The relationship between science and cross-curricular approaches is explored further in Chapter 2 of this book.

Beginning to explore cross-curricular teaching

This brief introduction to cross-curricular teaching and learning seeks to present some of the key benefits of undertaking an integrated approach. That is not to say, however, that an integrated approach is relevant or applicable in all circumstances and in relation to every topic – far from it. Cross-curricular teaching can *and* should only be undertaken when of benefit to both the pupils and teacher involved.

Before undertaking any cross-curricular project it is important to begin by considering the reasoning behind this action. By exploring both aims and objectives a more rounded and fruitful cross-curricular project can be formed.

Complete the reflective task below in relation to cross-curricular teaching in general.

Reflective task

Objectives

Use the model below to consider your own personal, departmental and teaching objectives – why are you thinking about undertaking a cross-curricular project? You do not need to have a particular theme or topic in mind, or even have identified the subjects you are wishing to combine.

Personal objectives What objectives do you have personally?	Departmental objectives What objectives does your department have?	Teaching objectives What objectives do you have in relation to your teaching? What objectives do you have for your pupils' learning?

Subject audit

Cross-curricular teaching and learning can be an approach that not only looks to amalgamate subjects together for the sake of greater understanding of each individual subject, but also to make meaningful connections between subjects based on disciplinary similarities. This involves a deeper understanding of each subject's specific characteristics and from the teacher's point of view this can entail an in-depth dissection of one's own teaching based on experience, the knowledge of one's own subject, the work undertaken by colleagues and, of course, the content prescribed by the National Curriculum. By fully understanding one's own subject specialism a greater understanding of that subject's fundamental characteristics can be reached and in turn, the potential links with other subjects can become apparent, and common ground can be found. One such way to begin this process is to complete a reflective subject audit. This can be a lengthy process that requires a significant amount of time and thought. One such process is illustrated below.

Reflective task

Subject audit – stage 1

What does my subject mean to me?

Use the bubbles below to think through your feelings about your subject. Consider the following questions, but write down any thoughts or feelings that spring to mind:

- How do I feel about my subject?

- What emotions do I feel when I am teaching my subject?

- What emotions do I feel when I am exploring my subject outside of school (reading, in the media, on TV)?

- What does my subject mean to me?

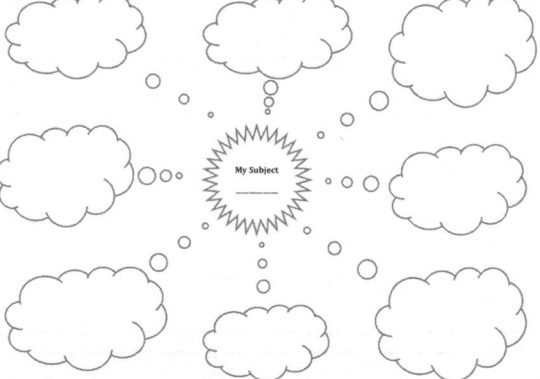

Figure 1.1 My subject.

Stage 1 of the subject audit should start to get teachers to consider their own views in relation to the subject they teach. Now it is time to identify the characteristics of the subject itself.

Reflective task

Subject audit – stage 2

The characteristics of my subject

Complete the table below thinking about the characteristics of your subject. Consider the following:

- How is my subject unique?
- What skills do I develop by studying my subject?
- What techniques or approaches do I use in my subject?
- What are the outcomes for my subject?

My subject characteristics

Finally what are the aims associated with the subject?

Reflective task

Subject audit – stage 3

The aims of my subject

Spend a little time thinking about what you hope to achieve when you teach
your subject. Think about the aims you have for your pupils, your school
and, of course, for yourself. Consider the following:

- Are there any specific skills that I am trying to develop in my pupils?
- Are there any topics I wish my pupils enjoyed more?
- Am I trying to reach a certain standard in my teaching?
- Do I have any specific career goals?
- Are there any specific topics about which my teaching could be
  improved?

Aims for my pupils	Aims for myself	Aims for my school

Each of the aims you have written above can help you begin thinking
about your cross-curricular work. If you have included a number of aims
relating to career progression at your school you may want to focus your
work on areas of your teaching that require improvement so as to
demonstrate professional development. Perhaps your aims are focused
mainly on pupil development; in which case this may help you identify an
area of the curriculum with which a number of your pupils struggle and
begin to creatively explore ways in which integrated learning could provide
support.

The reflective subject audit can be a powerful and insightful exercise. Done as an individual it can begin to highlight areas of teaching and learning that may benefit from an integrated subject approach. However, if cross-curricular work is being undertaken with two or more teachers across two or more different subject departments the reflective audit can become even more useful for identifying shared practices and common ground. Stage 2 of the process can immediately pinpoint one or more key aspects of each subject that may be shared. For example, a science teacher may describe their subject as 'investigative'; they may feel that this is a key and unique aspect in the study of science. The history teacher with whom they are working may also have written 'investigative' in reference to the way archaeologists and historians explore ruins or integrate primary source documentation. This is therefore a common characteristic shared by both subjects and a basis on which further work can begin.

Using this book

Along with the subject audit above, this book includes various short reflective and practical tasks that will enable you to begin your cross-curricular journey. You may wish to work through the book from start to finish or dip into the different chapters based on the subject links that interest you most. Chapter 2 of this book begins with a look at the wider, historical context of science and its place within education. By understanding the background of science education we can begin to explore the potential benefits of cross-curricular teaching as a means through which to encourage engagement and attainment in the sciences. Chapter 3 features three case studies of teachers currently undertaking cross-curricular activities in the sciences. These form a model of good practice but are drawn from three very different educational domains. The philosophy behind this book is to encourage cross-curricular practice but not by advocating a 'one size fits all' approach to this kind of teaching. The three case studies allow for different methods to be celebrated. Chapters 4, 5, 6, 7 and 8 all explore the relationship between science and mathematics, ICT and technology, English, humanities and the arts respectively. Each chapter emphasises the potential growth and development cross-curricular initiatives can have on individual teachers, departments and across the whole school. Chapter 9 investigates the potential mechanisms for assessment in relation to the content of the previous chapters looking at how cross-curricular science can benefit the classroom and how this can be formally and informally assessed. The concluding chapter draws together all of the pedagogical themes expressed in the previous chapters by emphasising the importance of cross-curricular teaching in the context of future curriculum development.

Understanding science and its place within the curriculum

Key objectives

By the end of this chapter you will have:

- Considered the place of science as a subject in the school curriculum
- Examined the affect pupils' attitudes can have on the 'popularity' of science in school
- Explored the cross-curricular possibilities for teaching and learning in science

Introduction

The 1988 Education Reform Act shaped the education systems of England, Wales and Northern Ireland. It paved the way for the first statutory National Curriculum together with national testing at 7, 11 and 14 years. The curriculum was first taught in schools from September 1989 and was set out to provide a shared framework for delivery while maintaining teacher autonomy:

> Legislation should leave full scope for professional judgement ... there must be space to accommodate the enterprise of teachers, offering them sufficient flexibility in choice of content to adapt what they teach to the needs of the individual pupils, to try out and develop new approaches and to develop in pupils those personal qualities which cannot be written into a programme of study or attainment target.
>
> (Department of Education and Science 1987)

During the years since its implementation the National Curriculum has undergone several revisions, has been the subject of much debate and has been used as a tool to achieve educational reform, the latest changes taking place over, for example, the review of 2011–14. The aims of this latest review are:

- to embody rigour and high standards and create coherence in what is taught in schools
- to ensure all children have the opportunity to acquire a core of essential knowledge in the key subject disciplines
- beyond that core, to allow teachers the freedom to use their professionalism and expertise to help children realise their potential.

To explore the position of science within current educational practice and policy we must first understand the nature of educational policy.

The creation and development of government educational policy is a 'sociopolitical endeavour' (Tamir 2010), which can be productively explored through Pierre Bourdieu's notion of the 'social field' (1985). According to this concept educational policy can be seen as a field in which agents are located hierarchically in relation to their social position. *Habitus*[1] determines social position and *capital* (social, cultural, symbolic and economic)[2] is possessed by the agent:

> In analytic terms, a field may be defined as a network, or configuration, of objective relations between positions. These positions are objectively defined, in their existence and in the determinations they impose upon their occupants, agents or institutions, by their present and potential situation (*situs*) in the structure of the distribution of species of power (or capita) whose possession commands access to the specific profits that are at stake in the field, as well as their objective relation to other positions (domination, subordination, homology, etc).
>
> (Bourdieu and Wacquant 1992: 97)

Agents within the field use and exploit their capital to enhance their power and it is through this power that they may be able to influence policy within the field. In the case of educational policy the agents include politicians, teachers unions, Local Authorities (LAs), teachers, parents, school management and governors, and pupils. Individuals (or agents) within the field are instinctively driven to reproduce the field through their behaviour and actions. As such they hope to maintain or advance their position within the field. The Bourdieuian field is not static, it is susceptible to shift and change which can create a conflict within and between fields.

Education policy since the arrival of the Education Act can be characterised by turbulence and centralisation. Educational reform during this period has taken place at an 'unprecedented' rate; much of it has been rushed through and 'piecemeal' (Royal Society 2010). Increased teacher accountability, managerial control in schools, a league table culture and significant reductions in the powers held by LAs have dominated policy during this period. Power has been taken out of the hands of teachers and local agents and placed under increasingly centralised state control. A greater emphasis on inspections, the introduction of a National Curriculum and a system of national assessment have transformed education provision at both a governmental and school level. Teachers have been expected to continuously adapt their practices in reaction to the unyielding flow of government policy changes. This has provided little overall stability for education professionals at the school level. To some degree this can be understood through an examination of the pressures faced by both the political and the economic fields. Both fields require high levels of education to maintain their *status quo*, and as such their requirements have implications on the education field. Thomson (2010) argues that inspections and greater accountability in schools have been implemented to harness education to meet the needs of the nation state. The political and economic fields can be seen as having implemented increased emphasis on public accountability to foster competition within the education field at the school level. This has produced a quasi-privatisation and 'performativisation' of the UK school system, which is to some degree maintained in order to meet the needs of the nation state:

> England's education system is now much more centralised than it used to be in as far as government and its agencies control what, in strictly educational terms matters most: curriculum, assessment, pedagogy, teacher training and inspection.
>
> (Alexander 2010: 462)

This issue is exacerbated further by the fact that government involvement in education does not just remain at the policy level. In 1991 the former Secretary of State Kenneth Clarke made decisive moves to directly influence classroom practices:

> I believe it is right for me to consider how the curriculum should be taught and how it is best organised in schools. Questions about how teachers teach, and the skills needed for them, are central to the success of the reforms in school.
>
> (Clarke 1991: 2)

Mr Clarke's report was intended as a starting point for an open and public debate on education reform and school practices. The report, however, provided little legitimate opportunity for teachers to respond. According to Ball (1993), it was in fact little more than an opportunity for greater governmental influence under the guise of open public discussion.

The introduction of the National Literacy and Numeracy Strategies in 1998 and 1999 also help to illustrate a significant example of governmentally determined 'pedagogical prescriptions' (Alexander 2004: 9). It can be argued that this turbulent and increasingly centralised state-led implementation of education policy has gone some way to question the power and autonomy of the classroom teacher.

Speaking in 2010, Michael Gove, the Minister for Education, discussed new changes to the National Curriculum based on this governmental over-prescription:

> I want to remove everything unnecessary from a curriculum that has been bent out of shape by the weight of material dumped there for political purposes. I want to prune the curriculum of over-prescriptive notions of how to teach and how to timetable. Instead I want to arrive at a simple core, informed by the best international practice, which can act as a benchmark against which schools can measure themselves and parents ask meaningful and informed questions about progress.
>
> (Gove 2010)

Reflective task

Jot down your own current thoughts on the National Curriculum.

How does it impact on your teaching? Do you think it supports or hinders creativity? Do you often deliver content from outside of the curriculum?

A brief history of science in school

Science became part of the school curriculum during the nineteenth century in Europe, in large part because of the urgings of scientists themselves, e.g. Thomas Huxley and Michael Faraday. This was not an easy job. The humanities were firmly entrenched as the subjects that were thought to lead to the most noble and worthy educational outcomes. Scientists had to be careful when arguing the utility of science not to present science as too materialistic and without higher virtue. So in addition to discussing the practical importance of science in a world that was becoming dominated by science and technology, they also said that science provided intellectual training at the highest level – not the deductive logic that characterised most formal education, but the inductive process of observing the natural world and drawing conclusions from it. Pupils in school would learn this way of thinking by carrying out independent inquiries and investigations in the laboratory. In 1898, Eliot summarised science education:

> Effective power in action is the true end of education, rather than the storing up of information ...The main object of education nowadays, is to give the pupil the power of

doing himself an endless variety of things which, uneducated, he could not do. An education which does not produce in the pupil the power of applying theory, or putting acquisitions into practice, and of personally using for productive ends his disciplined faculties, is an education which missed its main aim.

(Eliot 1898: 323–324)

Dewey (1916) also defended science as a legitimate intellectual study on the basis of the power it gave individuals to act independently, stating:

Whatever natural science may be for the specialist, for educational purposes it is knowledge of the conditions of human action.

(Dewey 1916: 228)

During the early years of the twentieth century, largely because of the influence of writers such as Dewey, science education, and education in general, was justified more and more on the basis of its relevance to contemporary life and its contribution to a shared understanding of the world on the part of all members of society.

By 1932, however, there was some concern that curriculum developers had gone too far in making subject matter 'relevant' and had forgotten the fundamental reason why science was being studied, which was to provide a broad understanding of the *natural world* and the way it affected people's personal and social lives. The challenge was to find the right balance between a broad intellectual understanding of the natural world and the scientific way of thinking on the one hand, and the utility of science for effective living on the other.

Practical task

What would those early educators think of today's curriculum?

Examine the Key Stage 3 Scheme of Work and highlight any topics that are taught as 'fact'. In another colour highlight those topics that are or could be taught on the basis of 'relevance'.

Concern about the public's attitudes toward science and their ability to serve as thoughtful critics of the role of science in society produced new reasons for teaching science. On the one hand, if there were risks associated with science, the public needed the knowledge and skills to make intelligent judgements about the risks. On the other hand, to the extent that science was a benevolent force in the world, it was hoped that citizens would be supportive of science. This support would come if they were familiar with the work that scientists did.

Pupils needed to be made aware of science as a social and cultural force and of the relationship between science and the rest of human knowledge. The aim of a Science, Technology and Society (STS) curriculum was to give pupils knowledge about the science/society interface and the ability to make decisions about science-related social issues. To many STS advocates, the highest goal of STS education was a social action, with pupils being able to identify science-related social issues, analyse the context in which the issues are played out in society, know the key individuals and groups involved in making decisions, investigate these science related issues themselves, develop an action plan, and implement that plan where appropriate. The major concern of STS critics was that science would lose out to technological issues and social analysis since technology would become the starting point for virtually all problems that had contemporary interest at the science–society interface. Others were concerned that the goals of STS would not be attainable since most real-world issues involving science and technology are complex and require either more knowledge of science that can be expected of school pupils or a more mature understanding of relevant political and economic forces than they possess.

Reflective task

Do you think that the science/technology debate exists in today's teaching of science as a social issue?

Do the main scientific issues of today remain too complex for pupils to understand? How could these be addressed?

See http://www.**upd8**.org.uk for an approach that translates the latest breakthroughs and science behind the news, into inspiring activities.

Clearly, the history of science education suggests a variety of goals for teaching and learning which include:

- Teaching and learning about science as a cultural force in the modern world
- Preparation for the world of work
- Teaching and learning about science that has direct application to everyday life
- Teaching pupils to be informed citizens
- Learning about science as a particular way of examining the natural world
- Understanding reports and discussions of science that appear in the popular media
- Learning about science for its aesthetic appeal
- Preparing citizens who are sympathetic to science
- Understanding the nature and importance of technology and the relationship between science and technology.

This still leaves a very important question about content. How do we deal with the facts and principles of science? With few exceptions, science content has formed the backbone of the science curriculum since its inception. This will most likely continue to be the case in the future since most of the goals of science require a basic understanding of the natural world. The challenge is to find a reasonable balance between science content and other important goals of science teaching. We know that the vast majority of what goes on in science lessons centres on prescribed curriculum content, conveying information about science. There is also the common perception on the part of teachers that they have to 'cover' a certain amount of content.

Even without targets and testing, the facts and principles of science will in most cases continue to form the basis of the science curriculum because this content provides an organisational structure that is understandable and recognisable. But teachers should also be free to balance and integrate the content of science that they select with the other goals that they choose to pursue. A cross-curricular teaching and learning strategy could begin to address the issue of making the content more appealing to pupils.

Science education's recent history

Education in England and Wales has seen considerable change since the 1960s. In the 1960s, the system of grammar, technical and secondary modern schools meant that most pupils were offered a science education of a general or vocational nature. The grammar school pupils, however, pursued more academic courses providing a more formal introduction to science and a preparation for further study at A-level. It is worth noting that, not unlike the current situation, biology classes were dominated by girls and physical sciences by boys.

The mid-1960s saw the 'comprehensivisation' of the schools and this now drew attention to the needs of the majority. Several science courses were developed which sought to provide an appropriate science education for all including the less academic pupil, e.g. 'Nuffield Secondary Science' in the late 1960s and 'Science at Work' in the 1970s. Other courses followed during the 1980s which sought to place more emphasis on the 'processes of science', e.g. 'Warwick Process Science' and 'Science in Process'.

During the 1980s, agreement was building within science education that all young people should have a 'broad and balanced' science education between these ages, occupying (for most pupils) 20% of curriculum time from age 14 to 16. This was supported by Her Majesty's Inspectorate in its policy statement *Science 5–16*. It was seen as necessary to ensure a broad, general curriculum for all and to eliminate the strong, gender-related affects in subject choice. As a result, in 1986 the GCSE as a single examination system for all pupils was introduced and resulted in a variety of science courses that included all three main sciences. These were intended to be suitable for all young people. There also followed a Double Award in science GCSE.

The National Curriculum, introduced in 1989, made science a 'core' subject of the curriculum from age 5 to 16. This led to the situation where – science was a feature of the curriculum for all pupils from age 5 to 16, and 80% of pupils studied a double science GCSE at age 16 in a programme covering all the major sciences. In 2008 the government introduced an entitlement for schools to offer a Triple Science course to students. Triple Award Science is the name for a course which delivers three separate GCSEs in biology, chemistry and physics. An increase in the number of students studying Triple Science GCSEs has been identified as one way to encourage more young people to take science subjects at A-level and to continue into science in higher education. 2008 saw a resurgence in the popularity of Triple Science with an increase of around 30% in the number of students taking GCSEs in biology, chemistry and physics. This continues to increase.

The current significance of science is reflected in the fact that it is considered, with literacy and numeracy, as the essential core of the primary curriculum and also a core subject of the 11–16 curriculum, along with English and mathematics. There has been a general acceptance that learning science involves more than simply knowing some facts and ideas about the natural world, and that a significant component of science curriculum time should be devoted to providing opportunities for personal inquiry.

Reflective task

Given that the curriculum is regularly reviewed, examine the current Key Stage 3 science curriculum, and write your own response to a hypothetical consultation of the National Curriculum.

Studying science

The future of the UK lies in knowledge. But our ability to generate new knowledge and use it innovatively depends upon having a scientifically literate population. And although people learn throughout their lives, good science education in schools is a vital preparation for scientific literacy later in life. But despite its importance, science education in schools is threatened from a number of directions, not least by a shortage of well-qualified science teachers.

(Diamond 2010)

There is widespread concern about the outcomes of science education at school. For example, the representatives of industry say that they need more high-grade scientists, technicians and engineers if the UK is to compete successfully in technology-intensive global markets. Whatever their career intentions, too few young people do much science in school once it ceases to be compulsory. This leads to fewer applications for science degrees and reduces the supply of science graduates. Just as importantly, the number entering non-graduate occupations involving science and technology is reduced, which leads to skill shortages in many sectors.

In the recent Royal Society *State of the Nation* report (2011) recommendation 7 makes a specific point of emphasising the importance of knowledge and skills education:

Recommendation 7
Science and mathematics curricula need to be inspiring and engaging for both boys and girls, whilst retaining rigorous development of subject-specific knowledge and skills.

Governments should work closely with experts from learned societies, the higher education sector and other key stakeholders to develop and maintain appropriate subject curricula.

(Royal Society 2011)

Practical task

Look at the Year 9 Scheme of Work and use Royal Society recommendation 7 to annotate it with areas where teaching could be enhanced by a cross-curricular approach.

'Science and mathematics curricula need to be inspiring and engaging for both boys and girls, whilst retaining rigorous development of subject-specific knowledge and skills.'

Pupil attitudes to science and the supply of future scientists

Pupils bring the legacy of their cultural backgrounds to their studies. They have all experienced science learning outside the classroom and form and express their own views. This means that they have their own attitude towards science education and this should not be ignored.

Unless school science explicitly engages with the enthusiasm and concerns of the many groupings that make up today's pupils, it will lose their interest. Accordingly, it needs to grapple with how it can respond positively to the wide diversity of student concerns. For example, it must think how to better address women, those who hold strong religious views, those who have little cultural capital and those whose current or recent roots lie outside Western societies. All too little is known systematically about these issues.

Many influences affect the attitudes to science that pupils develop. Research on attitudes towards school science shows that they become less positive from age 11 to 16 (Osborne *et al.* 2003). Research also suggests that the main factor determining attitudes towards school science is the quality of the educational experience provided by the teacher (Osborne *et al.* 2003). Part of the explanation for pupil attitudes toward school science may be a shortage of well-qualified science teachers capable of providing this positive experience.

A frequent aim of many science courses has been for them to provide a preparatory education for the small proportion of individuals who will become future scientists (in the commonly understood sense, as employed professionals). This aim has been widely critiqued on democratic grounds (e.g. Millar and Osborne 1998). Essentially, what of the great majority of school pupils who will not become scientists?

Nevertheless, there may be a danger that attempts to craft science courses so as to make them more relevant to *all* pupils will result in some of those who would previously have gone on to study science not doing so. It is possible that precisely those features that make certain science courses unpopular to the majority of pupils (impersonality, objectivity, the absence of value judgements) may make them attractive to those with a particular inclination for mainstream science (Reiss 2005).

Pupils' attitudes to school science decline progressively across the age range of secondary schooling. Declining numbers of pupils are choosing to study science (particularly the physical sciences) at higher levels and as a career (Bevins *et al.* 2005, 2011; Haste 2004; Sjøberg *et al.* 2004). For some time science educators have expressed concerns that current provision in schools (especially at ages 11–16) is all too often boring, irrelevant and outdated; and designed mainly to educate a minority of future scientists, rather than equipping the majority with the scientific understanding, reasoning and literacy they require to engage as citizens in the twenty-first century (e.g. Goodrum *et al.* 2001).

Practical task

Take one topic from the Key Stage 3 Scheme of Work and develop three lessons that use non-traditional approaches to teach that topic.

Teaching and learning science

There is now a significant body of knowledge about teaching and learning that has been developed through scholarship and empirical studies conducted in many countries around the world. All teachers know that what is taught by teachers is not the same as what is learnt by pupils. As in all acts of communication, learners have to make sense of what they hear, see and read in terms of what they already know. Teachers can make this easier or more difficult for pupils by the way that messages are put together, and the way pupils' questions are elicited and answered (Shulman 1986).

Significant work has also been conducted on the ways in which classroom communication, and particularly talk, can be used to support pupils in coming to understand scientific content (Ogborn *et al.* 1996; Mortimer and Scott 2003; Erduran *et al.* 2004). This evidence shows how teachers can use different patterns of talk for different teaching purposes. It can be used while working with individuals, small groups or whole classes and can help achieve aims such as introducing new ideas or supporting learners to use newly introduced content for themselves.

For teaching to be effective in promoting learning, it must involve interaction between teachers and pupils. One-way delivery from a teacher does not work for the majority of pupils. Assessment for Learning (a developed form of formative assessment – see Chapter 9) is a key to this interaction. A comprehensive review of the research literature has shown that there is very clear evidence that formative assessment leads to significant improvements in pupils' test scores, i.e. their attainment as measured by summative assessment (Black and William 1998).

If teachers are to communicate effectively with pupils they must set up activities and questions that help pupils to formulate and express their own ideas and then listen to what pupils say. On the basis of this assessment teachers must fashion the next steps, challenging pupils and leading them towards ideas which will be more fruitful. Such two-way interaction can happen several times during a lesson as learning progresses. A crucial aspect of such dialogue-based teaching is to give pupils a voice, and help them realise that their teacher wants to know what they think, so that they feel free to express even half-formed or confused ideas. By adopting a cross-curricular approach this can be made easier for both teacher and pupils as the remainder of this book will demonstrate.

Another approach requires interactive feedback on written work. Teachers have to annotate pupils' work with comments designed to guide them in making improvements, and then provide opportunities for them to use this guidance. Pupils then come to see their work as a step in improving their learning.

A further strategy is based on pupils working in small groups to assess each other's work. The point here is not to trust pupils with generating marks, but to help them to help each other so that they are better able to understand the aims of their work and the criteria by which its quality may be judged.

Practical task

Develop a lesson for a group of Year 9 pupils that involves using the types of pupil communication mentioned above, rather than 'teacher talk'.

Curriculum content and structure

Science educators have realised that major trends in twentieth-century scholarship on science itself, in particular the work of Popper and Kuhn, are important for science education. But much science teaching seems not to have absorbed this lesson. Some writing on science education has acknowledged that there is a tension between inducing pupils into a structure of agreed and essentially impersonal knowledge and the personal and social values associated with education and schooling. However, this has not influenced teaching significantly.

Changes in the UK science curriculum since the 1960s have largely reflected a growing acceptance that science is a subject for all pupils up to age 16 rather than one chosen by a minority as a preparation for more advanced study. Research and scholarship have made more important contributions to exploring the limitations of such trends and enthusiasms as 'guided discovery learning' and 'process science'. The worldwide growth in interest in Science, Technology and Society (STS) in the 1980s reflected continuing concerns about pupils' engagement with science. A review of the research (Bennett 2003) suggests that context-led courses lead to greater pupil interest, a greater appreciation of the relevance of learning to everyday life and no measurable decrease in pupil understanding of science content. What better, therefore, than to make these contexts such that a cross-curricular approach can be used? Pupils can see a relevance to their science but equally they can also see that it is not a subject in isolation.

More recent analyses have focused on the tension within the science curriculum between enhancing all pupils' scientific literacy and providing a foundation for more advanced study. It could be argued that different approaches are needed to do each of these effectively, and emerging evidence suggests that clearer links between school science and science as it is encountered out of school lead to greater pupil interest and involvement (Osborne *et al.* 2002).

Reforming science in the curriculum

In recent years reports from a range of sources in the UK have suggested that there are significant problems with science in the school curriculum, reflected most concretely in its relative unpopularity as a subject of study post-16 (e.g. Millar and Osborne 1998; Murray and Reiss 2003). Dr Ian Gibson, chair of the House of Commons Committee on Science and Technology in 2002, remarked: 'School science can be so boring it puts young people off science for life.'

Responses have been diverse from 'do more practical work' to 'make it fun and exciting'. These suggest that unless suitably staged, the study of science and scientific knowledge is 'boring'.

Donnelly (2005) raises the following issues when discussing the place of science in the curriculum:

■ Doubts about whether science is currently taught as coherently and effectively as it might be, and the means by which that effectiveness and coherence might be improved

■ The significance of science, especially under its philosophical and socio-political aspects, within contemporary life and collective and personal decision-making

■ The impact of proposed curricular shifts on the likely popularity of the study of science among the school population, both before and after the end of compulsory schooling

■ The interplay between all of these issues and the supposed distinction between pre-professional scientific education and a general education that includes science.

(Donnelly 2005: 294–295)

Cross-curricular and creative thinking

We are not preparing young people for the unpredictable realities of twenty-first-century life. A study involving 250 higher education staff across the UK concluded that Britain's 19-year-olds entering higher education often lacked the skills of independent thought and the ability to put ideas together, and tended to adopt a compartmentalised view of learning. Other studies (e.g. Goleman 1999; Csikszentmihalyi 2004) suggest that employers and universities seek emotionally intelligent, creative, flexible and independent thinkers as well as literate and numerate workers to operate in an uncertain and rapidly changing global future.

Practical example

Plants and animals – by the pupils for the pupils

Year 8 pupils have often had difficulty in studying plants and animals. This has historically been linked to the huge amount of 'information' that teachers have had to impart for this part of the curriculum. Very often in the form of lists that the pupils have had to learn! Not the most appealing way to learn, or to teach for that matter.

Therefore, it could be that a new approach could make this area of the curriculum more fun to teach and to learn. By using a range of cross-curricular links such as ICT, music or art the pupils can take a degree of ownership of their own learning.

Making the pupils the centre of the learning can also have a major influence on their learning. By combining these approaches lessons that have in the past often been rather dry and boring can come to life.

For example, groups of pupils can be given particular plants and animals to research and asked to develop some form of presentation for their peers. This could be the creation of a webpage, short animation or film, etc. They are told to approach this work in any way they wish incorporating art, music, etc as they wish. They must, however, ensure that they have included all the relevant facts.

The pupils take ownership of their work and immediately feel that their contribution to the class as a whole is of value. They are teaching each other. This can become even more powerful if assessment is given over to the pupils as well. The pupils develop new skills such as independent research, communication, active listening and speaking.

Science in a cross-curricular setting

A curriculum that motivates pupils, addresses real–life questions based on pupil interests and uses the disciplines as resources for answering those questions is an appealing notion for teachers and education reformers. Bean (1995), for example, advocates a curriculum that is generated from an integrated concept of knowledge that is whole and unified. Bean's vision reflects the knowledge we obtain in contexts outside school, rather than the fragmented knowledge gained in most school settings. This view suggests that a curriculum unbounded by the traditional constraints of discipline-based content has the potential to engage pupils in meaningful learning. The reality of learning in educational settings of today, however, is that the understanding of discipline-based concepts is important to success. This creates an apparent teaching and learning dilemma. Should teachers motivate pupils to learn in cross-curricular contexts or help them to learn traditional content knowledge to provide a grounding for disciplines-based future studies? What is not clear is whether these two approaches can co-exist:that is, whether pupils can understand and apply knowledge from the disciplines while working on cross-curricular tasks at the same time.

In Western Australia innovative teachers in a number of schools have attempted the integration of science, mathematics and ICT through diverse methods such as a thematic approach to curriculum, technology-based projects, competitions, integrated assignments, synchronised content and local community projects (Venville *et al.* 1998). On the one hand, teachers observed many benefits of integration for their pupils, including better understanding of mathematics and science concepts when applied to contextualised technology tasks. On the other hand, some teachers felt insecure when teaching outside their subject speciality and were concerned about pupil learning during integrated units of work because they felt their knowledge on content was weakened.

These issues are raised by Hargreaves *et al.* (2001: 103) who describe three tensions-filled implementation problems (for curriculum integration) as 'curriculum traditions', 'curriculum exceptions' and 'curriculum discontinuities'. They noted that curriculum traditions permeate not only what secondary teachers teach, but that their qualifications, departments and even their perceived identity and status are based in the discipline they teach. They also noted that teachers are often reluctant to move beyond their subject of specialisation and experiment with curriculum integration because they lack confidence with their content knowledge and because of the burden of additional preparation that would be required to familiarise themselves with new knowledge from other disciplines.

Science has been rated as one of the most frequently integrated subjects by Hargreaves *et al.* (2001). They concluded that the curriculum exceptions might better be taught in more specialised ways. The curriculum discontinuities discussed by Hargreaves *et al.* (2001) focused particularly on the transition from more integrated primary school settings to more discipline-based secondary school curriculum environments. Teachers in their study recognised that the strong subject focus in secondary school ran contrary to many primary school teachers' effort to integrate and develop cross-curricular skills in their pupils.

Reflective task

From a purely personal point of view, what do you see as your major concerns for implementing an approach as outlined above?

What would be the departmental/school issues?

Science and skills

Although there has been considerable debate about the meaning of the term *scientific literacy* (e.g. Hand *et al.* 2003), sufficient agreement exists about the term for it to be used profitably. Generally, scientific literacy is seen as a vehicle to help tomorrow's adults understand scientific issues (Gräber and Bolte 1997). The basic notion is that science education should aim to enhance understanding of key ideas about the nature and practice of science as well as some of the central conclusions reached by science.

Many designers of science courses hope that as a result of what is learnt pupils both now and in the future, as adults, will be able to benefit from them. At its most straightforward, this might be by entering paid employment that draws upon what has been learnt in science. Although most pupils do not embark on such careers, they too still benefit individually from their school science.

Another aspiration of school science is that it should equip the school leaver with a functional science to operate or understand technology, e.g. an understanding of how a computer, telephone or the domestic electricity system works, and so on.

Practical task (this can also be done with pupils)

Examine a range of newspapers – red tops, broadsheets, etc. – for articles about science. Analyse the language used in the headlines, article, etc. for understanding by the readership.

How can you use this to teach science?

Many in education are in favour of critical thinking where critical is taken to mean rigorous, analytical, logical, open-minded and penetrating, and thinking has elements of reflective scepticism. Oulton *et al.* (2004: 420) argue that science education needs both teachers and pupils to reflect: '[c]ritically on their own stance and recognise the need to avoid the prejudice that comes from a lack of critical reflection.' The issue of critical reflection is best seen in teaching controversial issues which can be an extremely valuable cross-curricular approach.

Practical and reflective task

You need to consider a range of issues when dealing with controversial issues, e.g. your own and your pupils' opinions.

Look at the points below and try to answer the questions while thinking about how these types of issues could be taught.

The challenges for teaching controversial topics

1. Pre-held beliefs

The pupil may enter the classroom with a lifetime of personal beliefs on a topic. These beliefs may extend from family, social experiences, church or other influences.

How can your teaching allow pupils to be open to these topics?

2. Biases and stereotypes

Unfortunately, many controversial topics are loaded with baggage. Biases may originate from media or political influences.

Does practising an environmentally conscious lifestyle make you a 'tree-hugger'? Is it true that only the wealthy drive hybrid cars?

3. All or nothing

Science is often thought of as a black and white, all-or-nothing proposition. Scientists are portrayed as purely logical with no personal feelings. Of course our pupils do not aspire to emulate that behaviour.

Can we show pupils that there is room for both emotion and science? In order to accept the science of evolution, must a pupil abandon all of their religious feelings on the topic?

4. Judgements

As teachers, we need to be careful not to preach or be judgemental about topics like evolution and environmental conservation. This may be a sure-fire way to irreparably turn pupils off. Worse yet, we may not even be aware when our word choice, attitude or body language may be broadcasting a judgemental tone.

How can we establish an open and non-judgemental learning environment?

Conclusion

Attempts to deal with the perceived problems of declining pupil interest in school science and low up-take of science in the post-compulsory phase have looked at such issues as the curriculum, pedagogy, pupil practical work and pupil discussion (Millar and Osborne 1998; Woolnough 1998; Mortimer and Scott 2003) and proposed changes. School science is generally too restrictive: for all the undoubted value of, and continued need for, school laboratories, they constrain activities that take place and fail to meet a number of current aims of school science education. As a representation of contemporary science, the mainly in-laboratory school model falls short. In the real world of science, laboratory time is expensive and costs must be justified. Scientists today are as likely to spend time reading, writing, working on computer models and simulations, in meetings and conferences, and doing field tests as they are in the laboratory:

> School science education should aim to produce a populace who are comfortable, competent and confident with scientific and technical matters and artefacts. The science curriculum should provide sufficient scientific knowledge and understanding to enable students to read simple newspaper articles about science, and to follow TV programmes on new advances in science with interest. Such an education should enable them to express an opinion on important social and ethical issues with which they will increasingly be confronted. It will also form a viable basis, should the need arise, for retraining in work related to science or technology in their later careers.
>
> (Millar and Osborne 1998: 13)

Furthermore, modern science is highly collaborative and multidisciplinary, so the way in which the current reliance on a mainly in-laboratory environment and solitary working methods of school science lead to a presentation of science that is less authentic as well as less motivating:

> Without such a mechanism for change, the failings of the science curriculum in meeting the needs of a modern society will lead to a growing disjunction between the aspirations of young people for a meaningful and relevant science education and that which is provided. The consequent alienation of science from society and of society from science is a price we cannot afford to pay.
>
> (Millar and Osborne 1998: 35)

In the twenty-first century adopting a more open and cross-curricular approach may go some way to answering these issues.

Other resources that could be useful

- *Triple Crossed* – a set of resources developed to make science learning more accessible, effective and enjoyable by using cross-curricular methods. Teachers of science, history and citizenship were brought together to develop the resources.
  http://extra.shu.ac.uk/cse/triplecrossed/resources.php

- *Opening Minds* – promotes innovative and integrated ways of thinking about education and the curriculum. Teachers design and develop a curriculum for their own schools based round the development of five key competences:
  1. Citizenship
  2. Learning
  3. Managing information
  4. Relating to people
  5. Managing situations

  http://www.thersa.org/projects/education/opening-minds

Professional standards for QTS

This chapter will help meet the following standards:

Q14	Have a secure knowledge and understanding of their subject/curriculum areas and related pedagogy to enable them to teach effectively across the age and ability range for which they are trained
Q15	Know and understand the relevant statutory and non-statutory curricula and frameworks for their subjects/curriculum areas. And other relevant initiatives applicable to the age and ability range for which they are trained

Professional standards for teachers

This chapter will help meet the following standards:

C15	Have a secure knowledge and understanding of their subjects/curriculum areas and related pedagogy including: the contribution that subjects/curriculum areas can make to cross-curricular learning; and relevant developments
C16	Know and understand the relevant statutory and non-statutory curricula and frameworks for their subjects/curriculum areas. And other relevant initiatives applicable to the age and ability range for which they are trained

Notes

1 *Habitus* can be defined as a system of acquired perceptions that determine thought and behaviour.
2 Social capital – associations and networks such as family, religious and cultural heritage; cultural capital – language, knowledge, taste and preferences; economic capital – money and assets; symbolic capital – things which represent the other forms of capital.

Tackling cross-curricular science teaching: three case studies of current teacher practice

Key objectives

By the end of this chapter you will have:

- Considered in depth a number of specific approaches to cross-curricular work both in the classroom and as enhancement activities
- Examined the differences in approach in the primary and secondary sectors and special needs education
- Begun to consider the cross-curricular possibilities for your own teaching in science

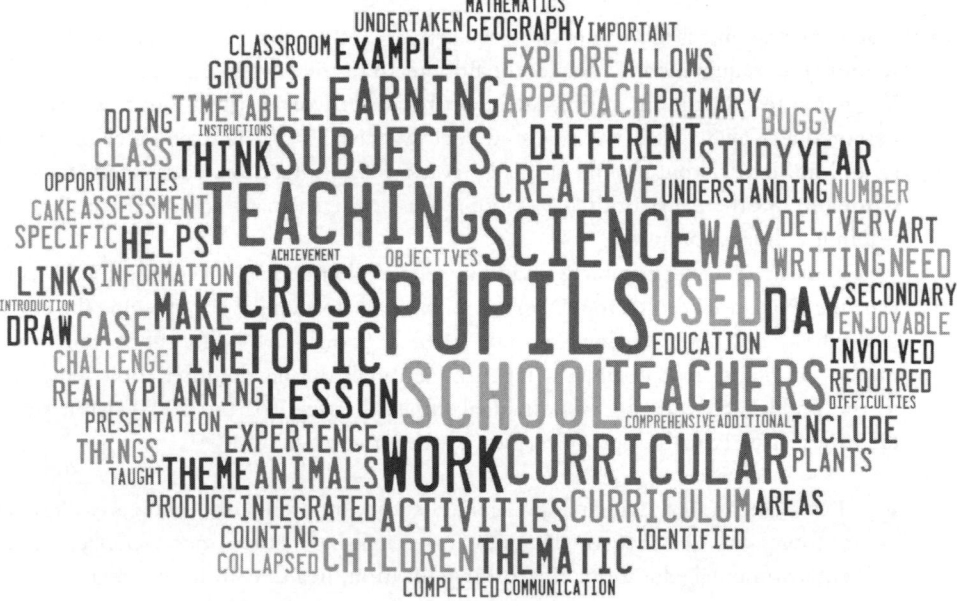

Introduction

This chapter explores some of the different ways cross-curricular approaches can enhance teaching and learning and uses current examples from schools. The previous two chapters have touched on the way integrated curricula can benefit education without much focus on specific modes of delivery. The case studies in this chapter go some way to begin to illustrate some of the different ways cross-curricular teaching can be undertaken. This includes a broad thematic approach, learner-focused work and challenge-based collapsed timetable days. The following case studies on subject links all draw upon lesson-specific activities to allow for a look at some of the ways integration can take place.

The first case study explores a thematic approach to teaching that integrates subjects where appropriate under broad topics. The study is based on the work done at a primary school in Sheffield. A case study of a special school is included to illustrate another area of education that utilises cross-curricular techniques on a daily basis. For the special education needs (SEN) environment differentiation is central to the way lessons are planned and delivered. The range of children within any one class calls for a diversity of teaching styles and techniques, to ensure all learners are fully participating and engaged. This is not, however, a concept solely associated with the SEN environment and will be familiar to any teacher working with mixed ability classes. The final case study explores the use of cross-curricular content during collapsed timetable days. This case study is drawn from a secondary school with extensive experience in running cross-curricular days. The identification of a specific challenge based around a broad theme is a useful illustration of the way cross-curricular teaching can be delivered as part of a manageable event.

Cross-curricular science in the primary school

Thematic teaching is more familiar to the primary setting than it is perhaps to the secondary school. The requirement to deliver the full breath of the curriculum at primary level makes integrated teaching more feasible and appropriate. However, this is not to say that it is not explored at Key Stage 3. The case study below draws upon the experience of one primary school in Sheffield but also includes observations and interviews conducted at a secondary school in Rotherham. Both have adopted a broad thematic approach to their science teaching where appropriate.

Thematic teaching combines and links several elements of different subjects to support learning around a specified topic. For some, thematic teaching is about seeing the curriculum as a whole and not as distinct, separate subjects (Yorks and Follo 1993). For others, this implies an inclusion of *all* subjects under the umbrella of one identified topic which can lead to the undesirable merging of individual subject barriers (Barnes 2007). Morrison (1994) identifies three types of topic in relation to thematic teaching:

- Type One: a topic which draws elements from different curriculum areas (for example a topic on *Ourselves* might draw on English, mathematics, science, geography, environmental education, citizenship education, health education, technology etc.)

- Type Two: a topic which, though it can make passing references to several curriculum areas, draws mostly from only two or three main curriculum areas (for example a topic on *Rivers* might make passing reference to mathematics and history but place much greater emphasis on geography, environmental education and science)

- Type Three: a topic which lies within a single subject area (for example a topic on *Shape* in mathematics, or a topic on *Sex Education* in health education)

(Morrison 1994: 63–64)

Barnes (2007) warns of a return to the 1970s and 1980s approach to thematic delivery, which saw teachers identifying the themes they used according to what they thought the children would enjoy. He uses the example of a *Pirates* theme. As part of this theme the children will complete pirate-themed mathematics, pirate-themed RE and, of course, pirate-themed literacy in the form of pirate poems! For Barnes this is a patronising approach to cross-curricular thematic teaching which will only succeed in switching children off. In the primary case study below the teachers have sought to avoid a return to the, often superficial, thematic work of the 1970s and 1980s by carefully identifying topics that offer a grounded context for learning. Broad topics such as *Rivers*, *Habitats* and *Plants* offer opportunities for an integrated approach but could also stand alone as meaningful subject areas in their own right. This strengthens the thematic approach and fits with Morrison's *Type Two* model of topic work. As such, meaningful thematic teaching often only draws on two or three different subject areas and the teacher is unafraid to temporarily abandon the theme to focus on other subjects that require teaching time. As such the thematic approach does not try to force together inappropriate and unsuitable subjects within the framework of a specific topic or theme. Figure 3.1 shows an example framework for a primary school

Class	Term 1	Term 2	Term 3
Reception class	Colours Sounds	My House My Family	The Emergency Services Weather
Year 1	Plants Antarctica	Animals My Body	Vehicles Playgrounds
Year 2	Power Clothes	Light and Dark Jungles and Woodland	Safety Pollution
Year 3	Forces Populations	Time Planet Earth	Italy and the Romans Sport
Year 4	Anglo-Saxon Britain Animals of Britain	Sugar and Sweets Fashion	The Tudors Music
Year 5	Electricity Exercise and the Olympics	Power and Fuel Local Habitats	Food Space
Year 6	Halloween Myths	World War Two Our Environment	The Ocean Transport

(Adapted from Morrison 1994: 64)

Figure 3.1 Example outline for full year (primary).

which covers all age groups over a full academic year. Each topic has a grounding within a specific curriculum subject such as science, history or geography but can draw upon two or three other subjects.

Reflective task

Take a look at Figure 3.1. What other subjects would you bring in to support each of these topic areas?

Remember, be creative!

Case Study 3.1: Grenoside Community Primary School, Sheffield

This case study is based on the cross-curricular teaching undertaken at Grenoside Primary School in Sheffield. The school has over 300 pupils aged 4–11. It is a mixed gender community school in the north of the city. In its most recent OFSTED inspection (2010) the school was judged *Outstanding* in terms of overall effectiveness and the school's capacity for sustained improvement. In the report it is stated that pupils 'of all abilities make excellent progress because of the high quality of teaching and the rich and exciting curriculum'. Staff morale at the school is understood to be 'very high' and the curriculum at the school is described as 'very imaginative'. The inspection report speaks very highly of the school's cross-curricular work:

> The outstanding curriculum brings learning to life for all groups of pupils. Extremely well planned programmes of work ensure rapid systematic progress in pupils' literacy and numeracy skills. Pupils' investigative and independent learning skills are very successfully promoted through many subjects and the excellent links made between them. In turn, these contribute to the very high standard in mathematics and science.
>
> (OFSTED report, Grenoside Primary School 2010)

Teacher 1 (T1) at the school puts much of this recent inspection success down to the creative way the curriculum is integrated at the school. A huge emphasis is placed on thematic teaching, which results in many of the lessons being strongly cross-curricular.

At the beginning of the school year the teachers at the school sit down together to identify the over-arching topics that will be explored during particular terms or half terms in relation to each year group. These broad themes tend to be either science or history/geography based which can mean that during the year any one year group will usually explore two science topics. One example of this is a *Plants* theme that had been undertaken earlier in the school year with a Year 5 group. The starting point for this teaching was the development of the thematic idea. From this, T1 built in as much cross-curricular activity as possible to strengthen and enhance the science topic. This included numeracy, literacy, art, D&T and PE:

> We start with the theme and that gives us the main focus for teaching – so in this case that was the science of plants – but then we bring in other subjects as much as we can.
>
> (T1)

As a way of developing literacy the pupils were asked to produce an information report based upon a specific plant. They investigated the way information reports were presented in books by exploring the layout of text, the language and the tools that non-fiction books use such as headings, labels and diagrams. The reports were used to create a classroom display to celebrate the work undertaken (see Figure 3.2).

Figure 3.2 Plants topic classroom display.

Along with the writing of information reports, the pupils dissected plants and produced detailed diagrams of the cross-section of a flower. This led them onto an artistic study of the shapes and colours of certain plants, seeds and flowers. The pupils learnt about shading as a way of adding dimension and emphasising specific features (see Figure 3.3)

We have been learning about the parts of a flower.

The flower contains the plant's reproductive parts.

Figure 3.3 Pupils' drawings of plants, flowers and seeds.

Along with plants the school ran a project looking at habitats that included a great deal of outdoor learning in and around the school grounds. The pupils explored the concept of mapping to demonstrate the whereabouts of different habitats. This drew heavily on a geographic understanding of maps with the pupils devising their own key system for identifying different habitats and locations. This activity included a wild flower survey in the school grounds that brought in a numeracy link through tally charts and counting. The concept of local habitats was closely linked with some geography work on climatic zones around the world to emphasise the links between both science and geography.

This creative approach to the curriculum has seen a great deal of success in both the OFSTED inspection and the pupils' engagement in learning. The school's decision to undertake thematic teaching and learning was originally taken with an aim to make the learning richer, to increase enjoyment and to make teaching less rigid. For T1 this cross-curricular approach allows a sense of creative freedom to develop lessons based on the best possible method of delivery:

> I think when you are teaching specific subjects it can get a bit boring, it's like 'Right let's just churn out a worksheet', rather than thinking what's the best possible activity for the topic. So now we take the topic and think 'What is the best possible way of teaching this?'. For example: it could be through writing, it could be through PE; it could be through drama, or it could be through doing experiments.
>
> (T1)

Part of the rationale for undertaking this thematic approach was to increase teachers' enjoyment and professional satisfaction. The creative freedoms associated with cross-curricular teaching can allow for a greater flexibility in both content and delivery:

> It gives us a lot more freedom to do what we want. There's not that idea of – you've got to do an hour of literacy every single day, and you've got to do an hour of numeracy every single day … We're not rigid and we have a loose timetable. For example I do try to do science after break on a Friday but if it doesn't fit then I might not do it. Equally I might have a day when I do science nearly all day because I want to get through a topic and the children are really engaged. This kind of flexibility is great because it makes my job more enjoyable.
>
> (T1)

At Grenoside Primary School this flexibility is encouraged through the support of the Senior Management Team (SMT). Providing that the main learning objectives for each year group are met, the school management continue to encourage this kind of creative thematic delivery. This is an interesting example of a highly supportive Senior Management Team who actively promote imaginative and inventive thematic teaching. It is a policy of the school to be as cross-curricular as possible. T1 believes that the school received its 'outstanding' grade at OFSTED, in part, because of the supportive relationship between management and teaching staff:

> The management team here simply let us get on with it; they're not monitoring us and checking up on us all of the time. We are not asked to constantly submit planning sheets or justify and evidence everything – this gives us more freedom and time to be creative.
>
> (T1)

Despite this emphasis on cross-curricular teaching, interdisciplinary links are not made needlessly and without serious thought and planning. Instead curriculum connections are made where appropriate and with a sympathetic approach to all subjects involved. T1 uses the example of a project on the *Ancient Greeks* to demonstrate this.

> We do an activity or exercise if it fits but otherwise we don't. It's about being creative as a teacher but not being silly with it. We try to make links throughout the curriculum but we don't force the links. We don't want to undermine the whole theme by putting things together that don't work. For example last term our topic was the Ancient Greeks and our science teaching at the same time was electricity, but we didn't try to fit these two areas together.
>
> (T1)

Despite being unable to fit electricity into the *Ancient Greeks* theme, the teaching of the science topic was still delivered using some creative cross-curricular techniques. The subject matter was linked with PE and D&T. The PE element involved the creation of electricity dances, while the D&T focused on model building with pupils producing their own models of a product, building or vehicle that communicates using flashing lights – for example traffic lights, a light house, a police car. They were asked to use their knowledge of electricity to produce circuits for their models while at the same time, being creative in designing the models themselves. T1 also recreated a fictional crime scene as part of the electricity theme with a school laptop having been stolen from the classroom. The pupils were asked to solve the mystery and design a burglar alarm that would be triggered by an intruder when placed under a doormat. Once again they had to put their knowledge of circuits into practice and try to answer the challenge.

The integrated curriculum at the school is introduced from Year 1 (5 and 6 year olds) with one recent topic exploring the rainforest by using science, geography and art to bring to life the wonder, beauty and sheer diversity of the rainforest for the youngest year group. For the Year 5/6 group (9, 10 and 11 year olds) the science topic was *Microorganisms*, which was linked with the main thematic teaching topic at the time – the *Tudors*. A gangrenous hunting wound endured by Henry VIII was the context for exploring the two topics together.

Alongside the thematic topics the teachers at the school spend much of their time developing pupils' skills for learning through science. This emphasises independent work, collaboration, communication, reflection and creativity. The school also does a lot of work using ICT in science. This is, in part, in response to observations of their pupils enjoying science but struggling with the writing that is so often involved. While the school teachers have not removed the key writing elements of their teaching, they have tried to find other ways of recording the work that the pupils have done. One such way is through ICT. The pupils produce PowerPoints and short films as a way of documenting their work while at the same time developing speaking, listening and literacy skills. Each pupil is required to write down what they are going to say on film or in a presentation, and as such the teachers at the school view this as a way of *covertly* encouraging writing and literacy skills. Both the filmmaking and the designing of a PowerPoint develop ICT skills and it is felt that communicating their findings in this way cements pupils' understanding of the science involved. The films use the same format as a written investigation so they are required to include an examination of the equipment used, the methodology, the results and any conclusions. This formal reporting is simply done verbally instead of on paper. As well as presenting on camera some of the pupils at the school have also produced animations of a scientific process or experiment using a simple animation package called 2animate (www.2simple. com/2animate/). The pupils can draw different images and use the software to create short cartoons. While this has had a big impact on enjoyment in science T1 does warn about the work introducing film and animation can involve.

> [Creating animations and films] can be a lot of work so you have to carefully choose what you have the time to do. Having said that, once you've got your head around what you're doing it can be more enjoyable to teach … and we all sit as a whole class to watch our creations, which everyone enjoys.
>
> (T1)

For T1 this kind of thematic, cross-curricular teaching helps her pupils to understand the subjects being explored, but perhaps more importantly it helps them to retain the information. This is in part due to the inventive way in which they ask pupils to share their work – through presentations, dramatisations, artwork and creative writing. This supports a more rounded and holistic form of education that draws on different talents in different circumstances. For T1 this helps those students who may not be quite so academic in the traditional sense while at the same time increasing confidence across the whole group:

> I think this kind of creative work encourages them to think a bit more and it gets them writing when they don't realise it. I think it's very beneficial for children who perhaps aren't so academic. If they do something practically, when it comes to having to write about it they find it a bit easier because they've got a bit more practical experience of it.
>
> (T1)

For the teachers themselves the emphasis on creative delivery can encourage new and exciting approaches to teaching. It is way of preventing professional stagnation and avoiding what T1 sees as the 'obvious' route for delivery:

> Thematic teaching helps you to stand back and think 'Which is really the best tool to use?' You can look at it a bit more objectively and not necessarily do what seemed obvious at first.
>
> (T1)

From the pupils' perspective the adoption of cross-curricular teaching methods at Grenoside Primary School has seen improvements in pupil engagement alongside a marked increase in pupils' information retention and skills development:

> I think this way of learning is far more enjoyable for the children and I believe they're developing far more skills. If, for example, they learn a lesson then churn out a worksheet, they can quickly forget what they've learnt and there is a risk that sometimes they're just regurgitating what the teacher has said. In contrast by trying to do presentations or present their work through art or drama, it helps the information to stick. I think a lot of the time something goes in one ear, they produce a piece of work, then it goes out of the other and they don't really retain what they've done.
>
> (T1)

While the context being explored here is a primary one there are many issues that resonate within the secondary sector. For T1 cross-curricular delivery can offer a great deal to pupils no matter what age:

> At Key Stage 3 they're [teachers] all specialists and they focus on their subject area and it's a real shame. There are so many areas they must miss out on. There are so many nice things you can do with topics. When we do the Ancient Greeks, which is a history topic, we do loads of D&T, literacy and art so they've made mazes and masks, drawn pictures of ancient Greek vases, studied the myths from the period and been asked to write their own Ancient Greek myths. Without a doubt, cross-curricular work helps the children to make these links in their minds and enables them to get a better understanding of a subject.
>
> (T1)

Within the secondary sector there are obviously more issues in implementing a broad thematic curriculum. That is not to say, however, it is impossible. Previous work with secondary schools in the South Yorkshire region has highlighted the way themes can be used at Key Stage 3. After working with its history department, the science department at Brinsworth Comprehensive School in Rotherham used the changes in the National Curriculum to introduce topic-based learning. The theme *Ancient Egypt* was used to influence much of their Year 7 teaching during one half term. This was to be rolled out across the full year after the initial pilot stage. Much like the experiences seen at Grenoside Primary School, this thematic approach involves a great deal of work at the beginning to design a new curriculum using appropriate and relevant activities that not only deliver the core subject matter, but also engage the pupils through multi-disciplinary creativity. It is important to consider that at secondary level there can be additional issues that teachers may encounter. For example, the older the pupils are, the more likely they can be to question the purpose of cross-curricular teaching, so once again it is crucial to consider the suitability of subjects when forming links. While an interdisciplinary theme may influence the content of your teaching for a half or full term, that doesn't mean that every lesson will fit neatly within this theme. To force links is to undermine the integrity of the thematic approach. T1 explains:

> It's so important that you don't go too over the top and try to force something to fit into your cross-curricular approach when it doesn't. There was no way in the world electricity was going to fit with Ancient Greeks so we didn't try to make it. At the moment we're doing a mini project on rivers but we're studying an author, so we're not going to try and fit the two together and that's OK – you need to be able to recognise that it is better to teach some subjects separately.
>
> (T1)

By sympathetically linking subjects certain topics and subject areas may be completely redesigned. This can mean a fairly comprehensive re-write of much of your teaching materials – a daunting and time consuming task for any teacher. In the case of Brinsworth Comprehensive the introduction of thematic Schemes of Work was a departmental decision and, as such, proposed changes were developed and designed by a teaching team and were not just the responsibility of one teacher alone. Regardless of this team approach, this kind of broad thematic planning requires confidence and, of course, time:

> Each year there are certain topics that we keep but equally we're not afraid to throw things out if we can think of a different area we want to do instead. It's a lot more work initially, you've got to throw out your old planning and bring new stuff in. But you shouldn't be afraid to do this. You'll be surprised how much more the children retain by doing something that they really enjoy.
>
> (T1)

For T1 the benefits of cross-curricular teaching outweigh the difficulties created by the initial planning time and effort involved. She uses the example of a *Human Body* topic to illustrate. As part of the topic she had asked the pupils to create accurate models of animal skeletons using art straws. They were then able to compare their models to the human body and as a result explore the reasons why bones are positioned where they are on both humans and animals. As an activity this was time consuming for the pupils but highly enjoyable and T1 saw increased understanding in comparison to standard revision lessons about the human skeleton:

> Perhaps some teachers might not see it as typically science and might think that it is going to take too long for their students to make animal skeletons out of art straws, but actually by making them they did really start to retain the information in a way I hadn't seen before when we'd just looked at

images of skeletons. So it's about trying new things because generally the benefits outweigh the risks.

(T1)

For T1 the practical and interactive side of integrated learning allows for better understanding and an increased retention of information. But the interactive side of this kind of delivery can sometimes make assessment difficult. Unlike marking written work, engaging cross-curricular activities can include dramatisation, film and artwork – all of which require a little more creativity when it comes to assessment. T1 suggests that this can include the use of photos, observation notes and team teaching. All of which help to build up an excellent picture of pupils' progress alongside the standard written work being produced:

> You can get great assessment information from these activities but it can be harder to obtain. It's much easier to assess a child's work if they've done a piece of writing but the opportunities are far richer from this cross-curricular approach. But you do have to think more carefully about how you plan and organise everything because it can be a lot more chaotic in your lessons so being organised is crucial. I sometimes assess work by focussing just on one group of children or I take some photos to remember what they've done. There is no denying that it's not as easy as when you've got a portfolio of writing but it can really help you to understand what your children are good at or what they're struggling with beyond their academic writing.
>
> One approach was to teach alongside another teacher. We delivered the lesson together and I observed and assessed the children while he was teaching and that was unbelievably beneficial.
>
> (T1)

There is no doubt that it is somewhat easier for the primary school teacher to justify the bringing together of certain subjects as they are committed to the teaching of all subjects. For example teaching art alongside science is a logical way to meet targets set by both curriculum subjects. For the secondary school teacher this becomes a little less black and white. How, for example, can a secondary science teacher set aside their own subject pressures and justify spending class time exploring art? For the teachers at Grenoside Primary School this is simple – the benefits outweigh any potential drawbacks and the recent OFSTED report stands as testament to their success.

What we can learn from the primary experience:

- Careful planning is crucial to successful delivery. When setting themes doing this alongside colleagues is helpful.

- Only link subjects with the theme when suitable. Do not try to force together subject areas for the sake of integration as by doing so the teaching will be undermined.

- Do not be afraid to temporarily abandon the thematic content when other subjects or skills need to be taught.

- Adopt informal assessment throughout the delivery to ensure the approach is impacting on knowledge and understanding.

- Be creative with delivery and assessment and explore different ways for the children to disseminate their work.

Cross-curricular science in Special Educational Needs (SEN)

With SEN we encounter different requirements that draw upon cross-curricular teaching in a different way. The engagement of the children in any one class relies upon the teacher's understanding of the range of ways in which their pupils learn. As such integrated learning allows for a more contextualised approach. Long-term thematic projects, as seen in the previous case study, can be inappropriate in the SEN environment as many children are unable to return to topics day after day. As such cross-curricular teaching is more focused and task specific. Activities such as baking a cake can be used to engage a class. For some pupils it is a creative cross-curricular way of teaching chemical reactions, whereas for others it is simply an enjoyable lesson in which they were able to bake a cake. The learning objectives are specific to the individual child based on ability, and the cross-curricular activities allow the child to meet those objectives. The classroom environment is also important in relation to SEN pupils. A report produced to review the implications of the National Curriculum on children with SEN stated that these pupils are more likely than other pupils to need 'a climate of warmth and support in which self-confidence and self-esteem can grow and in which all pupils feel valued and able to risk making mistakes as they learn, without fear of criticism' (NCC 1989: 8).

The following case study explores the work undertaken in the science department at one Special School in Knaresborough, North Yorkshire.

Case Study 3.2: The Forest School, Knaresborough

The Forest School in Knaresborough is a special educational needs school with around 130 pupils aged 3–16. Classes at the school are small and all pupils have a statement specifying the additional provision the school must provide in order to meet their specific learning or other needs. According to a 2008/9 OFSTED pilot inspection the school has a range of moderate and severe learning difficulties: some with physical or speech and communication difficulties and around a quarter with needs on the autism spectrum. In the pilot inspection the school was declared *Outstanding* in both overall effectiveness and in its capacity for sustained improvement. One area of recent improvement indentified in the report was the introduction of a more thematic approach at Key Stage 3. Teacher 2 (T2), the science teacher at the school, feels that surrounding his pupils with a theme or topic can help them with their understanding and development. At first glance this may seem like the pupils are working within a more limited curriculum but T2 feels that a more holistic form of delivery allows the information to be better retained by his pupils:

> If you were to look at our school curriculum I think you may at first think it is a little bit restricted. For example, we don't do history or geography – instead they have an hour and a half of humanities a week; we don't teach them a modern foreign language; and RE is taught as part of specific RE days. But there are lot of really good reasons for that. For our children, if you're going to introduce them to a religion such as Christianity or Sikhism it's much better to engross them in the religion. That can mean bringing people in from the Christian or Sikh community or visiting a church or temple. This can be better than trying to do it piecemeal because children forget and from week to week it's almost like every experience is new. So there are good reasons why our curriculum is designed the way that it is.
>
> (T2)

Despite this largely integrated approach, science is seen as a core subject by the school and, as such, every pupil receives at least an hour and a half of science every week. T2, as a science teacher, values the importance of making sure that the children have fun within a scientific context while at the same time ensuring that each child is learning some science skills, knowledge and understanding within the context of their individual ability:

> I want science lessons, first and foremost, to be fun and I want the children to experience science first hand.
>
> (T2)

The broad, mixed abilities in every class means that science lessons at the school almost always include mathematics as a means through which to embed numeracy and counting:

> I try to do everything I can in my lessons to bring in numeracy as a way of cementing learning. Even just handing things out in class can be utilised to practise counting. We were planting some sunflower seeds out in the garden last week and I had a Year 7 class so I asked one of the children how many seeds they thought we were going to need based on the number of children in the class. This meant they had to count out the number of pupils, count out the number of seeds and count out the number of pots. This is about constantly reinforcing essential numeracy skills and establishing some sense of number order and value.
>
> (T2)

T2 had recently run a lesson that integrated science, mathematics and food technology which focused on baking cakes as a context through which to teach chemical states, volume and numerical values:

> We used the lesson to make cakes, which was a great way to teach chemical changes. Baking a cake explores how some changes are reversible and some are irreversible. For example, if you're going to look at a reversible change you might melt some chocolate. You can melt the chocolate by putting it over warm water, and then if you leave it for a while it will go back to being solid chocolate. It's just like melting and refreezing an ice cube but chocolate's a good one because it then goes onto the cake and the kids can eat it. To demonstrate an irreversible change you can bake the cake itself. Once it is baked you cannot change the cake back into its original ingredients of eggs, flour, sugar, butter etc. Throughout the process you are also teaching quantity and mass by measuring out the ingredients; it's all mathematics even if it's not necessarily obvious that it's a maths lesson.
>
> (T2)

This kind of integrated approach to teaching science and mathematics can require careful planning, especially if it is to be undertaken with a large group or class. Some situations where cross-curricular teaching can be utilised can, however, be more spontaneous and undertaken in response to specific requests or needs expressed by the children. For some of the pupils at the Forest School (as is the case at many schools) major global events can be very unsettling. The earthquake in Japan in early 2011 called on a cross-curricular approach to ease fears. Some of the class were very frightened that a similar natural disaster would affect the UK. T2 used geography and science to alleviate pupils' anxieties and explore the reasons why Japan's location and geology makes it susceptible to earthquakes. In this way, cross-curricular delivery is spontaneous and responsive to pupils' needs.

Along with carefully planned activities and those which are more reactive in nature, T2 utilises the equipment, objects and animals in his lab to enhance his integrated curriculum. The science lab at the school has a number of different fish and animals including giant snails and bearded lizards. The animals feature regularly in T2's science lessons when teaching about living things, food chains and habitats. They are also used in a mathematical context to explore size and weight, which is linked with nutrition and food education. The feeding of the animals in lesson provides an opportunity for the pupils to practise counting. As has been seen before, for T2 almost every lesson offers an opportunity for counting. This may be a simple daily exercise of feeding locusts to the bearded lizards. Each locust needs to be counted out and the children must ensure each lizard receives the same number at feeding time. The food nutrition element comes in with the weighing of the animals:

> We recently did a lesson on comparing size by weighing the animals in my classroom. We started by looking at nutrition and the types of food each

animal likes to eat, for example meat or foliage. Then we went on to weigh them individually to see which one was heavier. This linked back into nutrition and food intake in relation to size, which can teach the children how important it is to eat. In the case of our snails they're both the same age, but one is much bigger than the other and so we can discuss why that might be and whether food might be a factor.

(T2)

The nature of the different learning abilities in the class determines a need for flexible and creative delivery. In the weighing of the animals digital scales can be easy to use but for some pupils using analogue scales can be better because the moving needle is more visual. In contrast, when measuring temperature it is easier for the pupils to use a digital thermometer that does not require them to have to read the bead, which many of them struggle to see. Issues such as these have led T2 to develop an innovative Velcro wall scale that can be used in a wide range of science lessons. Numbers are printed out and backed with Velcro and attached to the wall. This can then be used with the class to explore the numbers in a scale. For example, when doing an exothermic reaction such as metals in acid, the reaction will cause the temperature to rise. It may only go up by about 1.5 degrees, which can be difficult for some of the pupils to read. The Velcro scale can be started at any number so it can be set to the increments needed for example 1, 2, 3, 4 … or 25.1, 25.2, 25.3 … This allows the pupils to see if the number is going up or down, or if the next number is to the left or the right of the previous number allowing them to determine the direction of the scale. This can help the children to understand the direction of values even when the increment is very small.

As seen in the primary school case study above, recording and reporting work is done in a variety of ways and not simply through writing-up, which is often unfeasible for many of T2's pupils. One way is through art:

> We often use art to summarise a lesson, so the children might draw a picture rather than write an academic report. Some of our children really get a lot from using art as a way of summarising what they've done. For example, if we've done a lesson on nutrition with the context being feeding the animals they might draw one of the animals or what the animals have been eating. This can really cement an idea explored during a lesson so I feel strongly that you can use art a lot in science.
>
> (T2)

However, in the SEN classroom, art as a means by which to summarise an activity is not always a realistic option for all children:

> For some of our children the picture they draw won't really summarise the lesson because no matter what you've done they will always draw the same thing. We've got some pupils who will always draw tiny swirls that just

grow into bigger and bigger things and they'll do that no matter what you've taught.

(T2)

A major issue when teaching pupils with severe and moderate learning difficulties is that of assessment and recording. It is quite likely that much of the evidence of pupil achievement and progress will be ephemeral. T2 has found that using a digital camera in his lesson has helped to support assessment and offered an interesting way for the pupils to share their work. For T2, however, cameras can offer a range of opportunities within a lesson that can include:

- Catching the moment
- Starters and plenaries
- Sequencing
- Pupil centred reviews

Catching the moment

For T2 photographs can be used in class to capture a pupil's reaction to an experiment, as well as the experiment itself. This can be a record of the work undertaken and a way of assessing achievement and progress.

Starters and plenaries

Many classrooms have dedicated computers operating an interactive whiteboard. If the USB camera lead is left plugged in, it is a matter of a minute or two to transfer the pictures onto the computer so that they can be used to summarise the lesson, and to prompt pupil responses about what they have learnt. At the Forest School, the pupils usually enjoy seeing pictures of themselves, and seeing an aspect of the lesson again helps them to remember it.

Sequencing

Many experiments, particularly in chemistry, require several steps to be carried out in a particular order. To help enhance the pupils' learning, a visual record of the pupils carrying out those steps can be arrayed randomly, and the pupils asked to put them in the correct order.

A good example of this is the extraction of copper from copper carbonate. The green copper carbonate is put in a test tube. It is heated and it turns black (copper oxide) and the powder bubbles (carbon dioxide is driven off). This is thermal decomposition. It is left to cool, and sulphuric acid is added (neutralisation). It turns blue (copper sulphate solution). An iron nail is placed in the solution and it turns red/brown (displacement reaction). The pieces of copper can then be scraped off.

As can be seen, there is a lot of chemistry in this procedure. Anything that helps break it down into a logical sequence can only make it easier to follow and understand.

Photographs of certain experiments and processes can be ordered by some pupils and used as guidance by others.

Pupil-centred reviews

One of the main reasons that T2 frequently uses a camera in the classroom is in response to a need to record achievement. Pupils who find it difficult to write down, or even recall their experiences rely on the recollection of the adults in the class. When the pupil's work is reviewed, the outcomes can then be very one-sided and incomplete. Photographs are used during pupil reviews to show what the pupil can achieve, and to encourage pupils to talk about their work.

For T2 the use of digital images can also provide opportunities for raising self-esteem by celebrating the work the pupils have completed. It can be used for modelling good behaviour. A good role model for poorly behaving pupils can be the pupil themselves. By capturing the pupils doing something good, and displaying it in the classroom, T2 has seen pupils with behavioural difficulties adjust their behaviour as they are reminded that they can behave well and achieve positive outcomes. In lessons the photograph can be a way of sharing and reflecting on the work undertaken. Photos are also used in the classroom as wall displays to celebrate the science work undertaken during previous lessons. T2 keeps the photos on display for about a week before being given to the pupils for inclusion in their workbooks. By displaying the photos T2 hopes to provide the pupils with an identifiable connection to the room and to previous work completed.

> It's very important to us to display the children's work around the classroom. I want the children to come into the lab and they feel that it's *their* room. I think in a lot of secondary schools the dominating feature of the science classroom is that it's a science laboratory that includes gas taps, cupboards of equipment, and a demo bench at the front. In contrast I try to make my classroom much cosier so that the children feel comfortable and we able to sit around and talk about science. To be honest, my ideal scenario would be to have a living room somewhere in school that we could go to and sit around on couches talking about science. In that respect the physical environment can sometimes get in the way of what we want them to learn.
>
> (T2)

Cross-curricular teaching and learning within the Forest School science department draws upon a variety of subjects as a means by which to assess, share and celebrate the work being undertaken by the pupils. It is obvious that the nature of the teaching differs from that seen in mainstream schooling because the needs of the pupils are different, but it is not the aim of this case study to stress these differences. This case study is in fact about emphasising the creative, integrated approaches used at the Forest School which can be implemented across mainstream schooling including the use of wall displays, numeracy, hands-on practical science activities and contextualised teaching.

T2's work on photography was explored as part of the UK-based Science For All project which was funded by the Astra Zeneca Science Teaching Trust. For more information about the way the Forest School works with photography and utilises an integrated curriculum please visit the Astra Zeneca Science Teaching Trust website at www.azteachscience.co.uk or get in touch with the Science For All project at the Centre for Science Education, Sheffield Hallam University.

What we can learn from the SEN experience:

- Cross-curricular teaching can have multiple objectives which may be dependent on a child's abilities.

- Cross-curricular teaching can be spontaneous and in reaction to a specific event or a pupil's question.

- Cross-curricular teaching can enhance a diverse range of skills not always immediately obvious to the topic being taught.

Cross-curricular science in the secondary school

An alternative to the introduction of cross-curricular themes during subject-led timetabled teaching is a Collapsed Timetable Day (CTD). Otherwise known as *deep learning days*, *theme days* or *dropdown days*, CTDs offer fantastic opportunities for enriched cross-curricular learning. By suspending the timetable for a day pupils can focus on one specific question, topic or challenge and in the process develop skills and understanding. CTDs also provide a great opportunity for teachers to assess pupils' progress, comprehension and behaviour in a more informal setting.

CTDs often focus on a specific challenge based on a theme or topic, which allows pupils to work in small teams to answer puzzles and questions. The following case study is based on a CTD run at a comprehensive secondary school in Derbyshire. In contrast to the previous two case studies that summarise broad approaches to cross-curricular teaching, this case study offers an insight into one specific event.

Case Study 3.3: Eckington School, Derbyshire

Eckington School in Derbyshire is a mixed secondary for pupils aged 11–18. The school draws pupils from the surrounding region and across the Local Authority border. The school has specialist engineering status and for the past seven years it has been running a collapsed timetable, cross-curricular activity day with Year 8 (aged 12–13) pupils. The day is a solar buggy design challenge that incorporates science, engineering, technology, art, English and geography. The school runs six collapsed timetable days every year (one per half term) so the teachers are experienced in the planning, running and delivery of the days.

As part of the full day of activities the pupils are first put into groups of four. The teachers at Eckington choose to mix up friendship groups to get different pupils working together. Each pupil is given a name badge, which they must wear all day. The name badges allow all staff and pupils to be able to identify people they may not have worked with before.

The lesson is opened with a short teacher-led presentation that explores science, engineering and some environmental issues such as the global energy crisis. This five-minute presentation is interactive and asks the pupils to think about the ways in which science and engineering can help to solve issues around energy shortages. Once the topic area has been introduced the pupils are given an instruction sheet (see Figure 3.4) and told to work their way through the information.

The pupils are given a small buggy kit and instructions. They are then required to work in their groups to assemble the buggy. For the first thirty minutes of this assembly time the pupils are not allowed to ask for any help from the teacher. The groups are required to work together and solve any problems they encounter as a team.

Most groups try to ask for help at least once during this thirty-minute period. However, when they are told to work it out themselves nearly all groups are able to

---

Solar buggy challenge task sheet

- Decide what your team name is going to be and write it on your name labels.

- Design a logo for your team and draw that onto one piece of plain paper (colour in later if required).

- You are required to build a solar buggy and test how quickly it runs, you may need to change the gearing on the motor, you will then calculate the speed and produce reliable results, display them and reach a conclusion about your design.

- You will then research the different sources of energy that we can use to drive the buggy and produce a poster explaining the alternative sources and how they may be used in the future.

- You will then explain how the energy output of the solar cell is dependent on how much light comes from the Sun.

- Finally you will produce a PowerPoint presentation about energy sources and buggy design to present to parents and judges at the judging evening in July.

- You must now stand by your workstation to receive your buggy kit.

- Once you have received your buggy kit you must read through the challenge booklet and begin the challenge. For the first half hour you are not allowed to ask for help from staff.

Figure 3.4 Solar buggy instruction sheet.

work together to overcome whatever issue they had encountered and do so without any staff involvement. This seems to develop a sense of teamwork, ownership and pride within the groups.

The pupils' first challenge is to put together a short report on energy sources using the information booklet provided. The booklet covers a range of topics including renewable and non-renewable energy sources, solar cell technology and handling data. The next challenge is to build the solar powered, four wheel buggy. Each team builds one buggy using the equipment and instructions provided. The equipment includes:

> Solar cell with pinch terminals
> Front axle support
> Front wheels
> Rear wheels
> Rear axle
> Motor clip
> Motor and pinion gear
> Gearbox casing
> Double gears

Having built the buggy the teams must then measure its performance using the standard equation:

Speed = distance / time

They should measure the speed of their buggy at least three times and calculate the average speed. They then compare their buggy's performance with that of other teams' solar racers. By comparing their buggy with that of other groups they can then begin to analyse the reasons why the speeds may be different and what aspects of their racer they can adapt to increase speed. Pupils are then given time to make any changes they wish to their vehicle and the buggies are raced. The culmination of the day is the design of a team poster about solar energy and the work they have completed. The posters are accompanied by a five-minute group presentation, which must be based on research undertaken by the team. The presentations are delivered in front of parents and family members as well as other students and the teachers at a special evening.

The main focus of the day is within the boundaries of science and engineering. However, the inclusion of English, art and geography means that the day can be strengthened by the involvement of teachers from these other school departments. This allows for teachers to stretch their work and challenge themselves outside of their immediate comfort zone and, perhaps more importantly, it allows the pupils to make the connection between the subjects they are being taught. The cross-curricular nature of the activity is somewhat legitimised by the range of teachers involved. But this can mean that thorough briefing needs to take place prior to the day, which can be time consuming. The day itself is sometimes run during National Science and Engineering Week and the activity is undertaken with the whole year group of around ninety pupils so the careful planning of the activity is important. Appropriate rooms need to be found for the size of the group and additional teachers may need to be brought on board to help share the workload. The teacher in charge of the day's activities has experienced only slight resistance from a small number of teachers at the school who felt that senior management had forced the day's activities upon them. He felt that this mild opposition could be easily avoided through careful timetable planning and an assurance that all of the teachers involved are volunteers. As such, in organising the collapsed timetable day the teacher in charge cites a 'receptive and supportive SMT' as a crucial element of successful delivery.

As with most cross-curricular endeavours, the work undertaken as part of an integrated collapsed timetable day has an impact on both the teachers and the pupils involved, one of the main benefits to the staff identified by all teachers questioned was the creativity it requires. It allows the teaching staff to move away from national assessment criteria and demonstrate connections across curriculum subjects. The collapsed timetable format allows a natural flow throughout the day that is not stopped and started by the end of lessons. This allows the teachers to be more adventurous in their planning and allows them to visit topics in more depth and often across a larger number of subject areas:

> I really like these days because I get to let my hair down a bit and get creative with the pupils. We're not trying to meet standards or pass exams we're just having fun so it's fun for me too.
>
> (T3)

One of the benefits identified was the impact that this kind of day can have on the pupils' perceptions and they way that they view the staff:

> By getting involved in something like this you're viewed in a different light by the pupils. It helps them to see that it's not hard graft all of the time, they're not assessed or marked as such so it's more of a competition which means it's a day of fun.
>
> (T4)

For the pupils involved in the activities there was a sense of pride in the work they produced. They had been allowed to creatively experiment with the activities within their small groups without much teacher interaction.

> I really enjoyed today. I think we did really well and I'm pleased we got to work together. It was fun doing it without the teacher because we can say we did it. Even though it was hard at first.
>
> (Pupil 1 (P1))

One criticism often faced by cross-curricular activity is that it can be confusing to pupils who are so familiar with separate subject teaching. The mixing of subjects can lead to a blurring of the disciplines and pupils can be confused about what they are being taught. In the case of the collapsed timetable buggy challenge this was not apparent. When asked to identify the subjects they had encountered during the day they were able to distinguish each individual discipline from technology to art, science to ICT and English to geography. They were all very positive about the day's activities and the cross-curricular concept:

> I liked today because we got to do all of our favourite lessons together.
>
> (P2)

> It was really fun today because we got to do loads of subjects we wouldn't normally get to do. Not like this anyway.
>
> (P3)

Some of the pupils questioned also brought up the relevance of the cross-curricular day to working life and acknowledged the cross-curricular nature of the world of work:

> It's like when you get a job, that's got all of the different subjects as part of it. It's not just one subject on its own so it's good to do that at school.
>
> (P4)

What we can learn from the collapsed timetable experience:

■ Planning is paramount. The appropriate day, room and teachers need to be identified to make it a success. This includes people to set up the event and clear up afterwards.

■ Make sure the day is fun. While careful planning of the content will provide clear learning objectives, the main thrust of the day should be enjoyment and inspiration.

■ Involve parents and governors to disseminate and share the work.

■ Think about running a collapsed timetable day during an already existing event or celebration such as National Science and Engineering Week.

Conclusion

By exploring a number of different real-life case studies we can understand further the ways in which teachers approach cross-curricular planning and delivery. This book does not advocate a one-size-fits-all approach to integrated teaching. Mastering cross-curricular work is a personal experience that must be undertaken with individually identified goals and aims in mind. As such, what may feel right for one teacher may seem inappropriate for another. By drawing on three different teachers' experiences, from three different educational settings we are able to draw comparisons with our own teaching styles and aspirations. Despite the differences between the three case studies a number of shared issues have been highlighted in relation to cross-curricular teaching and learning. Notably:

- Creativity – this can be divided into two sub-categories
  - Teacher creativity – this includes creative objectives, creative planning, creative delivery and creative assessment
  - Pupil creativity – each case study looked to encourage pupil creativity in science

- Planning – all three case studies emphasise the importance of careful planning before undertaking any cross-curricular approaches
- Enjoyment – much like creativity, this can be split into two subcategories
  - Teacher enjoyment – for teaching
  - Pupil enjoyment – in learning

Cross-curricular practice: science and mathematics

Key objectives

By the end of this chapter, you will have:

- Examined some links between science and mathematics in the secondary school curricula
- Developed an audit tool to enable more cross-curricular working in science and mathematics
- Devised at least one new cross-curricular science–mathematics classroom activity

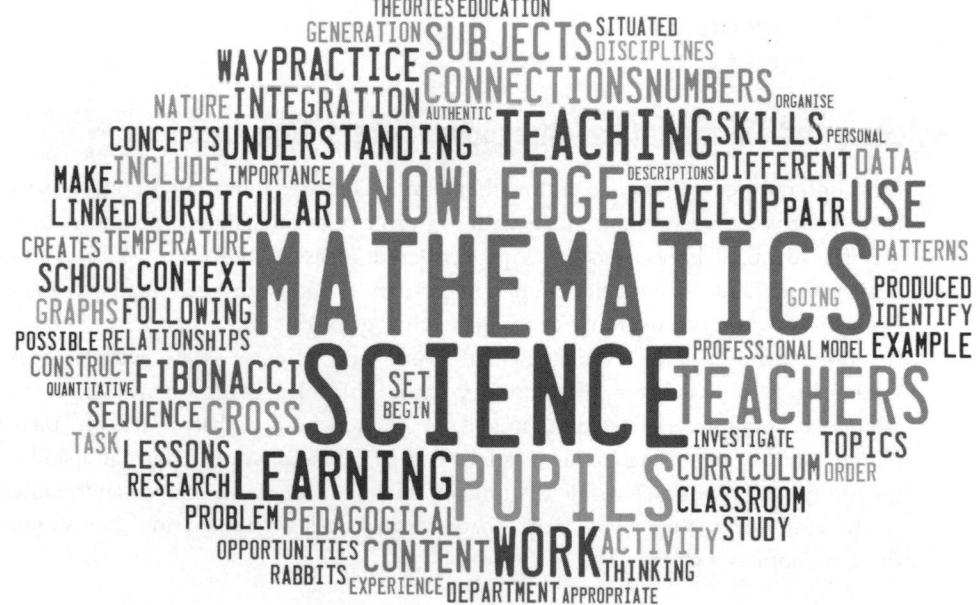

Introduction

In 1902, E. H. Moore delivered a presidential address to the American Mathematics Society in which he stated:

> Engineers tell us that in school algebra is taught in one water-tight component, geometry in another and physics in another, and that the student learns to appreciate (if ever) only very late the absolutely close connection between these different subjects, and then, if he credits the fraternity of teachers with knowing the closeness of this relation, he blames them most heartily for their unaccountability stupid way of teaching him.

Moore went on to advocate reforms in school science and mathematics that would prompt a more coherent organisation of the two subjects, including the overlap between them. Now, over a century later, is the educational establishment still running the risk of being in the words of Moore, 'unaccountably stupid' in the ways in which teachers are prepared to integrate science and mathematics?

For a science teacher it can be very frustrating to hear pupils moan that 'this is a science lesson, why are we doing maths?' or exclaim that they 'don't need maths to do science'. It is true that very often the introductory parts of science often focus on vocabulary development and 'recipe' practical investigations and the constraints of time and curriculum can limit many lessons. However, by using more data analysis, data logging and other sophisticated data collection techniques it is possible for pupils (and teachers) to see and develop further the close association that exists between science and mathematics. The subjects are by no means mutually exclusive and the skills developed in each subject could and should be both transferable and exploited.

This chapter examines this interdisciplinary relationship and interdependency and offers some suggestions for integrating science and mathematics further in the classroom and across the whole school.

Science and mathematics – the closest of relationships?

How intertwined are science and mathematics? Consider how much conceptual overlap there is between science and mathematics in primary school. Pupils learn to count, order, classify, identify shapes, recognise patterns and measure objects – skills common to both science and mathematics. Pupils in primary schools are encouraged to make their scientific descriptions quantitative by answering questions 'how many?' or 'how much?' In short, primary pupils learn essential foundation science skills, even as they learn mathematics, and vice versa. In secondary school this relationship often disappears and the science curriculum, rich with examples of science lessons that seamlessly incorporate mathematics by requiring pupils to apply related mathematics concepts and skills, would go a long way in making visible the fundamental bond between science and mathematics. In the real world, science and mathematics are intrinsically linked and they should be in the classroom as well.

Reflective task

Carry out a Key Stage 3 science curriculum audit and identify as many examples as possible where maths can be highlighted when pupils are doing their science work.

To what extent do you emphasise the importance of maths when you teach these topics?

Draw up a plan to increase maths awareness in your science teaching.

Brodsky's (2008) study of nine mathematics and science teachers highlighted a number of areas of concern. The message that emerged from interviews with the teachers was that of a distinct separation of mathematics and science in school. This was evident in the way the teachers discussed the lack of co-ordination and communication between departments and in the more implicit descriptions of the school disciplines as separate, independent subjects. As a consequence of this separation the teachers described differences in the style and in the terminology that was used in mathematics and science classes. The teachers acknowledged that these inconsistencies created potential barriers to understanding between mathematics and science for their pupils. Teachers also noted that their pupils saw science and mathematics lessons as being independent and, therefore, had certain expectations for each lesson that could affect their performance when mathematics concepts did arise in a science lesson. All the teachers agreed that there was a lack of formal dialogue between the science and mathematics departments. Each department had its own agenda and the need to meet and co-ordinate within the department was prioritised over inter-departmental communication. Most of the teachers did, however, think that a formal dialogue could be beneficial, particularly in terms of co-ordinating specific topics between departments. In addition to the concern about co-ordinating topics, co-ordinating terminology and even teaching styles came up as well.

Practical task

Cross-reference the science and mathematics schemes of work for Key Stage 3 and, using two different colours, highlight terms, concepts, etc. that, in the one case are used in the same way in the two subjects, and in the second, how the same concept, term etc. is referred to differently.

Together with a colleague from the mathematics department try to develop a 'common' list or at least a strategy to ensure that the pupils are made aware that two terms actually mean that same thing. Maybe devise a Maths–Science Glossary.

The need to assign topics to either mathematics or science is something that Bernstein (1971) discussed in terms of classification in school. He claimed that classification creates boundaries between disciplines and insulates them as specialised subjects. He argued that this creates a socialised 'subject loyalty' for both teachers and pupils as they hold on to the identity as given by their specialised subject. One of Brodsky's teachers summed it up when he said 'in maths we do it this way', drawing a difference between mathematics and science that indicates that even where there might be an overlap in content, there is still a distinct way that scientists and mathematicians do things. Furthermore, maintaining these boundaries, creates the need to assign certain topics or applications to one discipline or the other rather than allowing for connections between the two subjects.

Practical task

Ask a colleague in the mathematics department for a copy of their Key Stage 3 Scheme of Work and with the science Scheme of Work highlight areas where the same topic or concept is taught and list those places where there is a mismatch in timing.

Organise a meeting of the mathematics and science departments and feedback your findings.

Creating the separation

The classification as described above can be created or maintained, at least in part, by the testing-driven nature of mathematics and science teaching and of the set curriculum. The fact that teachers see particular topics as being their responsibility and others as being the responsibility of teachers in other subjects is facilitated by the demands of testing. In Brodsky's (2008) study some of the science teachers mentioned the need to review mathematics topics in their lessons in order for pupils to 'get to the science'. However, they were often reluctant to spend time on these subjects, teaching only algorithmic, functional mathematics, as they felt these topics should really be covered in the mathematics classroom. With the need to cover the science material in their lessons, many felt that there was no time to teach mathematics concepts in science.

Alongside testing the National Curriculum helps to create division between mathematics and science. It is generally assumed that anything mathematical should be taught in mathematics lessons in order to be used as a tool in science and when a mathematical concept arises in science first it is seen as the responsibility of the mathematics department to teach for an understanding of the mathematics. Another issue which arose in Brodsky's (2008) study was linked with setting in science and mathematics. Because pupils in one teacher's science classes might be in different sets in mathematics, some pupils might have covered a particular mathematics topic before it occurred in science while others might not.

The separation of disciplines stemming from testing and the curriculum is consistent with difficulties that pupils have with learning and making connections across the subjects.

Interpreting and applying

One aspect that makes the use of mathematics in science lessons difficult is the lack of understanding of the meaning of the mathematics the pupils come across. The compartmentalising of mathematics topics and rote teaching techniques make it difficult for pupils to apply their mathematics. For example, for a given problem in science, pupils might have difficulty first with the interpretation of the problem and then in deciding the appropriate technique to use to answer the question.

Many teachers feel that the teaching of concepts as individual topics as opposed to having

---

Reflective task

Look at your own lessons and highlight any areas where you *assume* that the pupils will already understand the mathematical operations you are asking them to perform.

---

more continuity between topics creates barriers for pupils and makes it difficult for them to remember concepts from 'different' topics that have been covered earlier in the lessons or in other lessons. One of the teachers in Brodsky's (2008) study talked about the teaching of isolated mathematics in mathematics lessons and he claimed that concepts such as gradient were taught without a context, and so when graphing occurs in science the pupils did not look for applications or see the relevance of the techniques they had learned in their mathematics lessons. He explained:

> You know just moving across from mathematics class to the science class, they just switch off from maths, and they do not expect to come and meet mathematics again. And that's one big problem. They do not understand the cross-curricular factor in their learning.

Conceptual framework for connecting science and mathematics

What follows is a conceptual framework for connecting science and mathematics. It describes the ways in which contemporary theories of situated cognition in science and mathematics provide the notion of situativity as it applies to *teacher* learning. It also examines the role pedagogical context knowledge plays in fostering integrated instruction in science and mathematics. Each will be examined in turn:

1. Learning in context – situativity
2. Integration and context knowledge

3. Towards a new conceptual framework for connected science and mathematics teaching

4. Issues of content knowledge and pedagogical content knowledge.

1. Learning in context – situativity

Constructivist theories guiding reforms in science and mathematics education have suggested a major shift from learning science and mathematics as an accumulation of rote facts and procedures to learning science and mathematics in authentic contexts – as socially negotiated constructions and explanations used to make sense of the world (Cobb 2000; Putnam and Borko 2000; Cobb and Bowers 1999; Roth and McGinn 1998). Much of the debate about school science and mathematics, therefore, has revolved around the differences between traditional classroom practice and the ways in which science and mathematics are used in authentic settings (Roth and McGinn 1998). Emphasising the importance of situated uses of mathematics in everyday life, Lave and Wenger's (1991) notion of situated learning has become a guiding theory for thinking about the authenticity of experience as a catalyst for growth and learning.

Other studies have extended the idea of situativity to the teaching of science and mathematics (e.g. Putnam and Borko 2000; Cobb *et al.* 1997; Yackel and Cobb 1996; Roth and Bowen 1994). It has been recognised that the knowledge and skills that *teachers* acquire are fundamentally linked to the contexts within which those attributes are introduced and developed (Barnett and Hodson 2001). Furthermore, as Shulman (1986) argued, these contextually developed knowledge structures are centrally connected to the ways teachers develop and practise their craft. It follows, therefore, that if science and mathematics teachers are expected to develop expertise in fostering cross-curricular learning opportunities for their pupils, then a significant part of their preparation experiences should be contextually based. As Putnam and Borko (2000) have suggested:

> How a person learns a particular set of knowledge and skills, and the situation in which a person learns, become a fundamental part of what is learned.
>
> (Putnam and Borko 2000: 4)

A focus for teacher development, therefore, should be:

> … interactive systems that include individuals as participants, interacting with each other as well as materials and representational systems.
>
> (Cobb and Bowers 1999 in Putnam and Borko 2000: 4)

As an example from a situative perspective, in their 1998 study, Roth and McGinn advocated the importance of providing a context for learning both science and mathematics. In their study, pupils participated in a ten-week ecology project in which they researched a $40m^2$ plot, or ecozone, in the school grounds. The researchers analysed the pupil-generated writings that illustrated the relationships between biotic and abiotic variables on a graph. Similar to scientists, Roth and McGinn contended the pupils were engaged in the social practice of negotiating the science and the mathematical interpretation of their data.

> ## Practical task
>
> Outline the teaching approach you would use to demonstrate the cross-curricular nature of science and mathematics from the suggestions 1–3 below:
>
> 1. Pupils compare the efficiency of washing powders by measuring the amount of light that passed through dirty and cleaned fabrics.
>
> 2. Pupils investigate the factors affecting the height to which a ball bounced.
>
> 3. Pupils use a motion sensor linked to a graphical calculator to explore how their motion produced graphs on the screen.

2. Integration and context knowledge

The example above of cross-curricular working leads to a question. What kinds of knowledge structures are necessary for this kind of teaching?

Barnett and Hobson (2001) articulated their own theory that promoted the study of teachers' pedagogical knowledge as a means for understanding what science teachers know and how they use that knowledge for teaching. This theory included four overlapping dimensions that provide a context for teachers' development:

■ Pedagogical content knowledge

■ Professional knowledge

■ Classroom knowledge

■ Academic and research knowledge.

Two of these dimensions – pedagogical content knowledge and academic and research knowledge – are common elements of many frameworks for teacher development. Specifically, pedagogical content knowledge includes:

> … such things as knowing how to set teaching goals, organise a sequence of lessons into a coherent course, conduct lessons, introduce particular topics and allocate time for satisfactory treatment of all significant concepts.
>
> (Barnett and Hodson 2001: 438)

Academic and research knowledge for teachers refers to content knowledge in the subject, including the nature of science. The other two dimensions – professional knowledge and classroom knowledge – are instrumental concepts in more recent and emerging frameworks that support a situative approach for teacher development. Professional knowledge refers to 'teacher lore' or knowledge about schools and curriculum passed from experienced practitioners to novice practitioners. The professional knowledge of teachers, field tested in the classroom, often avoids the academic knowledge of educational research. Classroom knowledge is the situational 'craft knowledge' teachers have of their own classroom and pupils. Thus, pedagogical *context knowledge* embraces situated science teaching and learning in authentic contexts. When and under what conditions do teachers develop this kind of context knowledge for teaching? Barnett and Hodson (2001) suggested that:

> … there are three kinds of 'places' where knowledge is acquired, constructed, rationalised and deployed: private, semiprivate and public.
>
> (Barnett and Hodson 2001: 436)

As they described, the teacher's personal reflections and cognitive activity is, of course, private and safe. Once teachers begin sharing the contents of their 'private' knowledge, however, they enter a zone where:

> … collective theories and values are constructed and where teacher lore is formulated. It is here that teachers' networks sometimes flourish and action research occurs … Moving comfortably between and among these places requires an ability to switch quickly and effectively between different elements of pedagogical knowledge, pedagogical content knowledge and classroom knowledge.
>
> (Barnett and Hodson 2001: 437)

Reflective task

Examine your own teaching approaches and identify those strategies and curriculum content that lend themselves to a science-maths cross-curricular approach.

---

3. Towards a new conceptual model for connected science and mathematics teaching

The following framework is based on the previous combination of theories about teacher learning. Specifically, by definition, the integration of science and mathematics is necessarily situative. That is, in terms of a pupil's construction of knowledge, in terms of curricular innovation and in terms of teachers' pedagogical practices, fostering understanding of the relationships and connections between science and mathematics is contextually based.

From integration to connections

The language used to discuss the relationship between science and mathematics must be carefully selected in order to promote different perceptions of and practices for science and mathematics teaching. There has been much debate in the research literature about the definitions of terms such as *cross-curricular* and *integrated*, and the implications of those definitions for practice (Berlin and White 1995; Berlin 1991). The Berlin–White Integrated

Science and Mathematics Model has been recognised in both the mathematics and science education communities (Berlin and White 1994, 1995, 1998).

This model includes six aspects:

3.1 *Ways of learning.* Integration can be based on how pupils experience, organise and think about science and mathematics. Based on a constructivist perspective or rationale, pupils must do science and mathematics and be actively involved in the learning process.

3.2 *Ways of knowing.* Integrated school science and mathematics can reinforce the cyclical relationships between inductive-deductive and qualitative-quantitative views of the world. In science and mathematics new knowledge is often produced through a combination of induction and deduction. For this discussion, induction means looking at numerous examples to find a pattern (qualitative) that can be translated into a rule (quantitative). The application of this rule in a new context is deduction.

3.3 *Content knowledge.* Science and mathematics can be integrated in terms of content that is overlapping or analogous. Big ideas or themes such as change, conservation, models, patterns, scale, symmetry and systems can be found in both science and mathematics. The examination of concepts, principles, laws and theories of science and mathematics reveal ideas that are unique to each discipline and ideas that overlap or are analogous, e.g. the fulcrum of a lever and the mean of a distribution.

3.4 *Process and thinking skills.* Cross-curricular science and mathematics can develop processes and skills related to enquiry, problem-solving and higher-order thinking skills. Integration of science and mathematics can focus on ways of collecting and using information gathered by investigation, exploration, experimentation and problem-solving. Skills such as classifying, collecting and organising data, communicating, controlling variables, developing models, estimating, experimenting, graphing, hypothesising, inferring, interpreting data, measuring, observing, predicting and recognising patterns are representative of this aspect.

3.5 *Attitudes and perceptions.* Integration can be viewed from what pupils believe about science and mathematics, their involvement and their confidence in their ability to do science and mathematics. Similarities and differences related to scientific and mathematical attitudes/perceptions or 'habits of mind' can be identified. The values, attitudes and ways of shared thinking between science and mathematics education include accepting the changing nature of science and mathematics; basing decisions and actions on data; a desire for knowledge; a healthy degree of scepticism, honesty and objectivity; relying on logical reasoning; willingness to consider other explanations and working together to achieve better understanding.

3.6 *Teaching strategies.* Integration can be viewed from the teaching methods valued by both science and mathematics educators. Cross-curricular science and mathematics teaching should include a broad range of content, provide time for enquiry-based learning and problem-solving, provide opportunities to use laboratory instruments and other tools, provide appropriate technologies (e.g. calculators and computers), encourage co-operative learning, embed assessment within teaching and maximise opportunities for successful connections between science and mathematics.

Practical task

Game example 1

Sometimes a good reinforcement activity is needed to help pupils with understanding. This can often be in the form of starter or plenary activities or homework. To add more fun to these activities games and quizzes can be used:

<u>Game example 1</u>

This can be used while working with pupils on cell division and/or biological communities.

The Game of Life
John Horton Conway was born 26 December 1937 and is a creative mathematician who is known by many for the invention of the *Game of Life*. His early investigations for the *Game* were done with pen and paper, as this was before personal computers existed. The Game can still be played using pencil and paper but more often than not is now played on a computer. The Game is played on a 2-D grid (see below).

For example see, http://www.bitstorm.org/gameoflife/.

Put simply, the game simulates a primitive form of life on a grid of squares similar to a chessboard. The squares are not black and white and there is no limit on the number of squares.

Blank Grid:

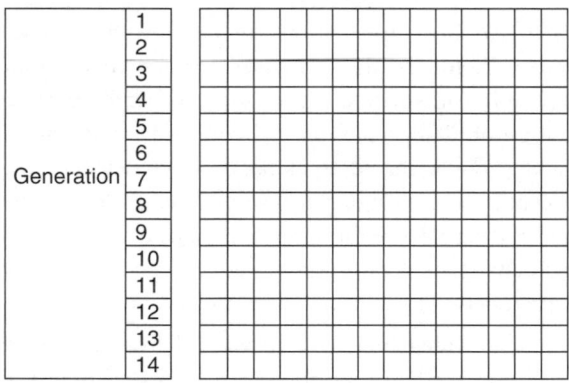

Each square can be occupied by a live 'cell' or it can be empty. Simple rules then determine which cells will die and which empty squares will go on to give birth to new cells. In the *Game* all births and deaths take place together, followed by a pause before the next cycle of life and death takes place. As the game progresses, the pattern of cells changes, sometimes growing, sometimes dying away.

Pupils can start to set challenges for each other by making up their own rules and investigate the effects on the *Game*.

For more information about Conway see http://en.wikipedia.or/wiki/John_Horton_Conway

---

Practical task

Cre8ate Maths – linking science and maths in the classroom

Using materials designed by the Cre8ate Maths project, this set of activities looks at the rigidity needed in constructing structures such as bridges and buildings.

Figure 4.1 Rigid structures.

Pupils are encouraged to experiment with what makes a rigid, load-bearing structure using simple materials. The resource includes images of structures to act as stimulus material but the pupils are encouraged to research more rigid structures.

The pupils then experiment by testing rigidity. They are encouraged to hypothesise and then test their theories practically.

A second investigation examines bracing as a way of enhancing rigidity

The mathematics involved is around shapes such as polygons and triangles and measurement of length and angles.

The science examines materials and their strength.

There is extension work that uses two web-based activities around bridge design and investigating their structural properties. The activities include choice and thickness of materials and once it is built it can be tested by driving a lorry over it. The activity allows pupils to refine their ideas as they experiment and encourages teamwork as well as thinking skills such as reasoning. There is an obvious second subject link here to D&T.

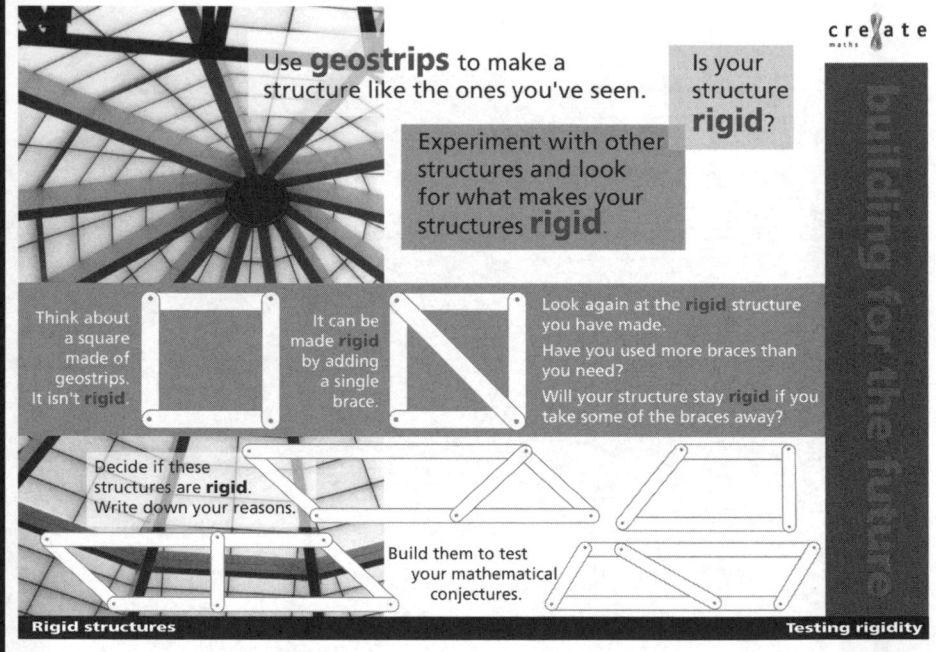

Figure 4.2 Using rigid structures 1.

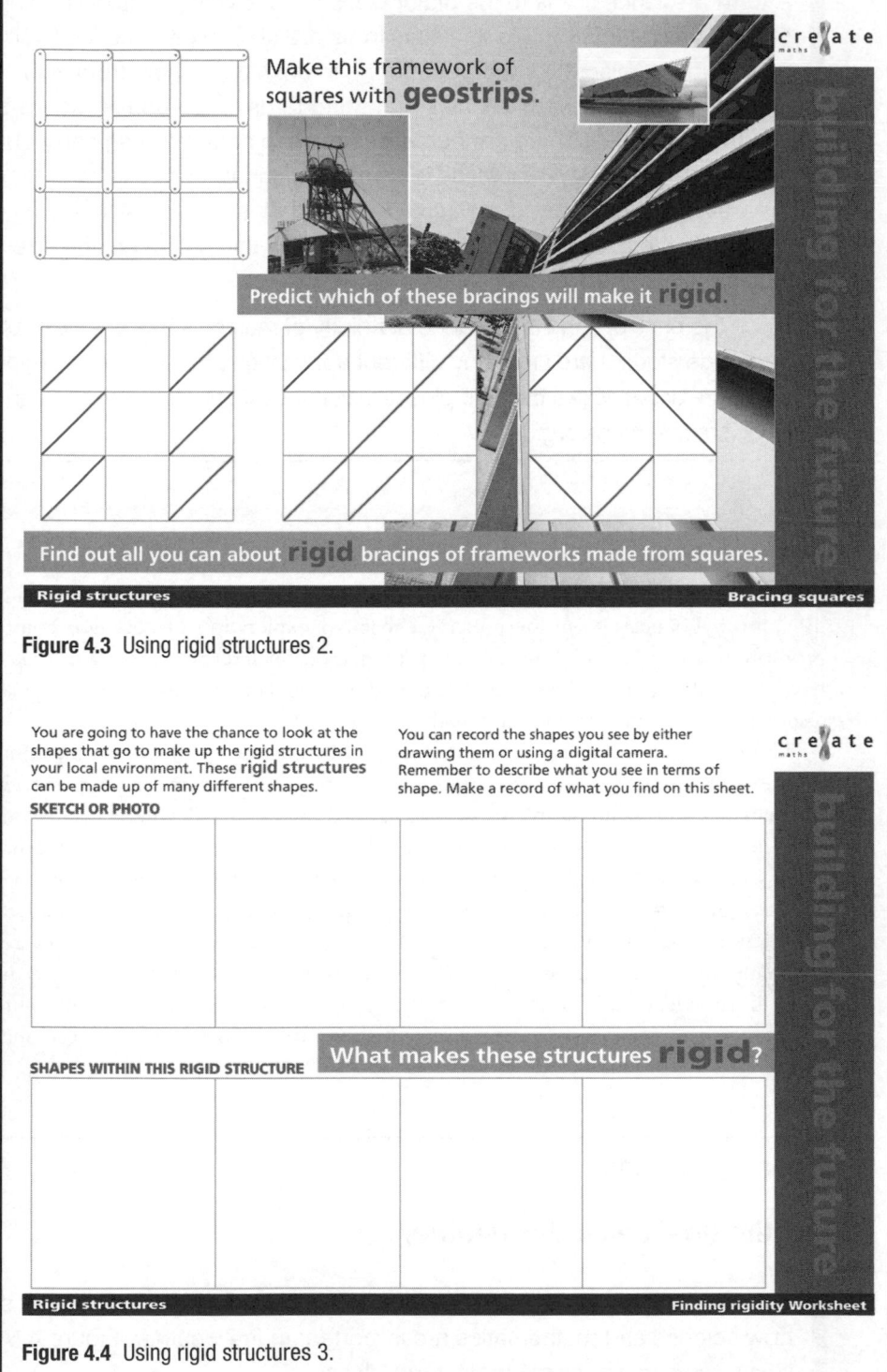

Figure 4.3 Using rigid structures 2.

Figure 4.4 Using rigid structures 3.

A further science link is to the biological sciences with pupils examining the strength of materials in plants – why trees are able to grow so tall (wood is very rigid) but also the structure of bone in animals ranging from very lightweight bone in birds such as humming birds to the denser bones they find in themselves. There are numerous experiments they can carry out to investigate the strength of these biological materials. There is an extensive discussion around why some animals have their support mechanisms on the outside, e.g. in insects, crabs, etc. and how this can affect the size to which they can grow.

Once the principle and importance of rigidity of materials has been established and understood there are many different applications that can be examined. For more activities like this one please visit the Cre8ate Maths website at www.cre8atemaths.org.uk

Making connections

Various definitions of cross-curricular teaching include the assumption that the integrity of disciplinary boundaries will be preserved through exploration of common contexts that promote learning of both science and mathematics. Such a view predicates that teachers have both the content knowledge and pedagogical content knowledge to teach two disciplines successfully, science and mathematics.

This can be unrealistic for beginning teachers who are usually still developing competence in one field. Similarly, common definitions of 'integrated' teaching imply that science and mathematics can blend seamlessly so that it is difficult to tell where science stops and mathematics begins. This view of integration has its own demands and challenges as well.

In what may be a more realistic approach, Frykholm and Glasson (2005) advocate the use of terminology that includes the notion of *connections* between science and mathematics – connections that are situated authentically in the respective practices of each subject discipline and in the common experiences of learners. Although teachers may not have enough knowledge to 'integrate' teaching, or are not able (i.e. lack of time, curriculum constraints, etc.) to work collaboratively toward fully cross-curricular teaching, many

Practical task

Stimulus ideas: the weather

Start by brainstorming with the pupils any areas they can think of that show how science and mathematics are important in the weather. Figure 4.5 illustrates some possible brainstorm ideas.

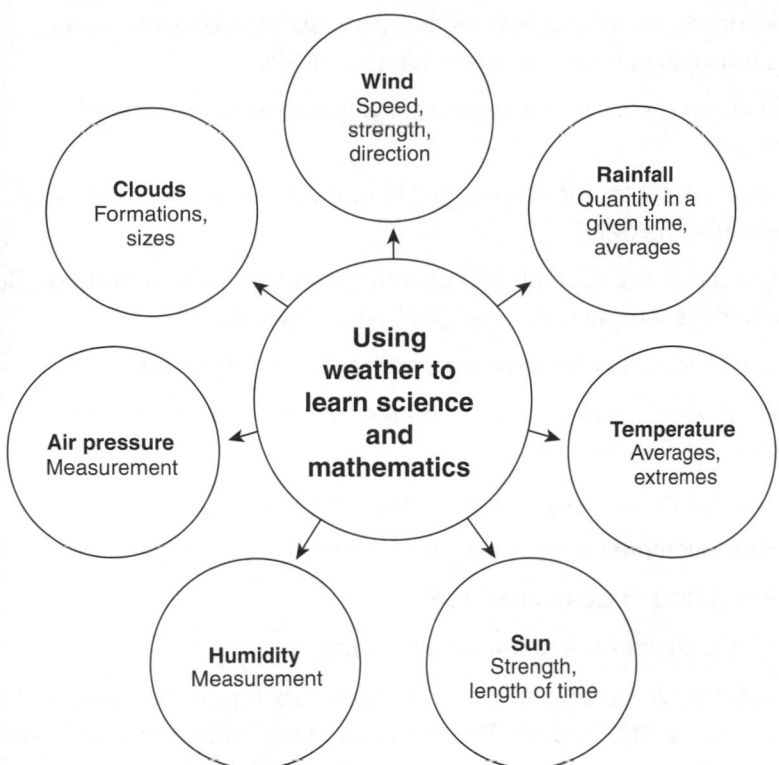

Figure 4.5 Weather brainstorm.

Science and mathematics can be taught together in each of the areas. This is also an opportunity for project work that could also link with the geography department.

Links to mathematics include drawing graphs, sampling, working with percentages and averages and in science understanding of pressure, formation of clouds, converting temperatures, the science and use of radar in weather prediction.

Practical task

Temperature

This activity will give you some information about pupils' current knowledge and understanding of temperature. It will also tell you something about what pupils do not know and how well they are able to pose interesting questions that can be answered mathematically.

In small groups the pupils begin by trying to answer the following questions:

1. Who collects temperature data? How do they do it? How do they describe the data?

2. How much attention do you personally pay to the temperature? Do you care if the temperature changes? Why or why not?

3. How much does the temperature change in a day? In a year?

4. When does the temperature change? Where does it change? What causes it to change?

This can be followed by a whole-class discussion:

1. What is temperature?

2. How is temperature measured?

3. The thermometer and temperature scales.

The activity can include keeping a temperature log of the classroom over a day, week and/or month. These can be plotted on graphs and averages can be calculated.

The pupils can learn about Fahrenheit and Celsius scales and how the two can be converted one to the other.

Other aspects of the weather can be studied in a similar way and the whole activity could be put together as class presentations, posters, etc.

teachers are able to recognise and build upon various connections between science and mathematics that they see as intuitive and relevant. Rather than resting primarily within the constructs of each discipline, these science and mathematics connections tend to emerge from the prerequisite knowledge bases and experience of teachers.

Pedagogical context knowledge

The conceptual shift toward *connected* science and mathematics teaching provides a new way to interpret the knowledge bases that teachers bring to the classroom. Specifically, though the idea of pedagogical knowledge is fundamental to good teaching of any kind, one essential construct for connected science and mathematics teaching is the ideas of pedagogical context knowledge (Barnett and Hodson 2001). That is, given the situativity of connected science and mathematics curriculum and learning, it is important that teachers understand contexts that hold potentially significant science and mathematics connections. That is, if one subscribes to situative perspectives on learning – that pupils and teachers construct meaningful knowledge of science and mathematics through interaction – then rich contexts become essential in order to promote deep thinking and learning and the recognition of a symbiotic relationship between science and mathematics. Hence, pedagogical context knowledge must be a starting point for teachers' growth and development with respect to promoting cross curricular teaching.

Reflective task

Make a list of more science and mathematics contexts where cross-curricular teaching could occur. Highlight common words and terms.

How could you improve your use of mathematics in your science teaching?

---

4. Issues of content knowledge and pedagogical content knowledge

To teach in a way that allows pupils to construct meaningful knowledge structures, teachers must possess richly connected understandings and content knowledge in their subject (Ball 1990). Yet, as Shulman (1986) suggested, content knowledge alone is inadequate unless novice teachers have also acquired pedagogical content knowledge – the ways of 'representing and formulating the subject that make it comprehensible to others' (Shulman 1986: 9).

Despite the many calls for rich content and pedagogical content knowledge for teachers, there is a considerable body of research suggesting that novice teachers often do not possess the content and pedagogical knowledge to teach understanding in the respective disciplines (e.g. Adams and Krockover 1997). Research findings confirm that knowledge gaps exist in mathematics (Frykholm 1998; Ball 1990) as well as in science (Lederman *et al.* 1994).

These deficits in content and pedagogical content knowledge are significant, considering the ways in which prospective teachers tend to rely heavily on previous knowledge and experiences when making teaching decisions (Lumpe *et al.* 2000; Frykholm 1998).

In their research into the connections between science and mathematics, Fryholm and Glasser (2005) found, for example, that trainee teachers:

> Almost without exception, the participants conveyed strong convictions about the importance of connecting mathematics and science instruction … one individual in science who noted that he was 'not willing to teach either mathematics or science without integrating them with the rest of the curriculum'.
>
> (Frykholm and Glasser 2005: 132)

The research went on to describe how the participants also indicated repeatedly that connecting the two subjects was not only important, but also possible. The very idea of linking science and mathematics seemed intuitively obvious to many participants, as a future science teacher stated:

> It is almost impossible not to combine mathematics and science … After all, mathematics is just as integral and a part of chemistry and biology as the scientific theories themselves.
>
> (Frykholm and Glasser 2005:132)

Many of Frykholm and Glasser's (2005) participants commented about the natural overlaps in science, mathematics and real world events. Despite these positive comments many had not experienced these connections in their own educational experience were, not surprisingly, concerned about how they would put this into practice themselves:

> I feel I would need to do a lot of research and preparing in order to connect mathematics and science in a meaningful way.

(Frykholm and Glasser 2005: 133)

Practical task

Architects and cells

This activity looks at the skills an architect uses to interpret ideas from clients when describing their ideas.

The activity invites one pupil to build a hidden shape and then describe it for a partner who listens to the description and then tries to build it themselves. Pupils can work in pairs or small groups.

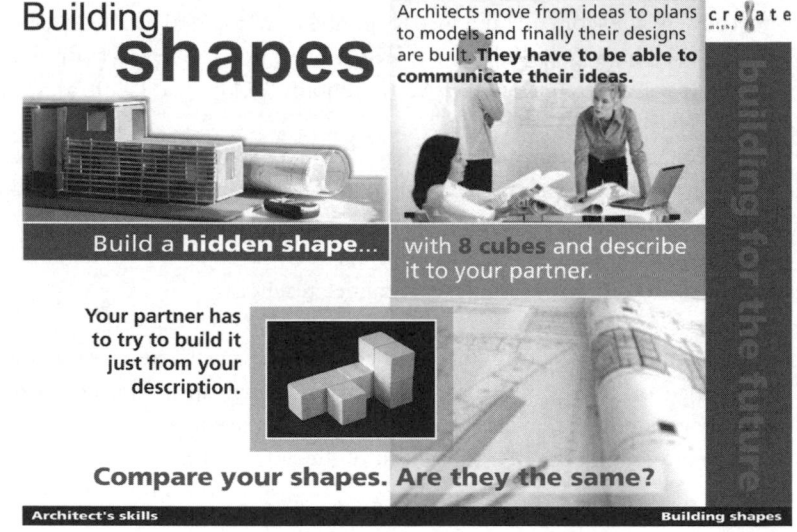

Figure 4.6 An architect's skills 1.

The builder's task is to describe their shape using words only – no hand gestures! This develops the accurate use of language to convey mathematical ideas. Comparison of the two shapes offers lots of opportunity for discussion.

These activities develop the process skills involved in understanding and making sense of mathematical information and depending on the shape can involve discussions about dimensions and shapes such as triangles, etc.

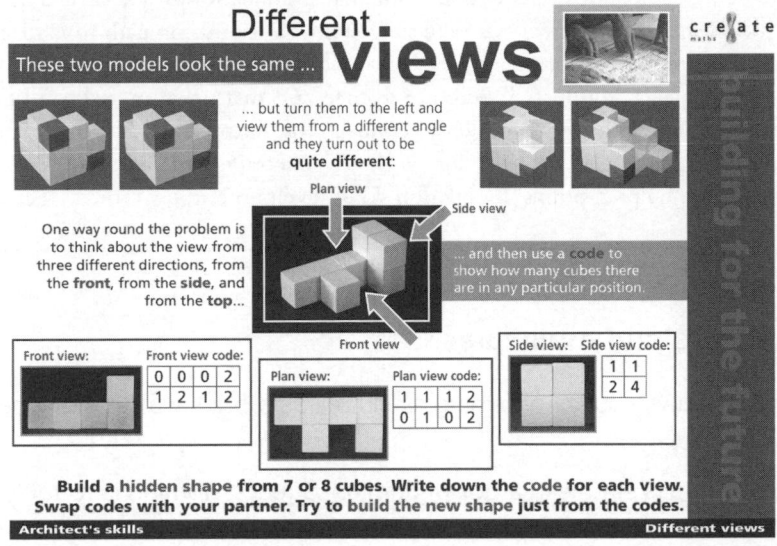

Figure 4.7 An architect's skills 2.

The size, shape and structure of cells is an ideal scientific application of this activity with pupils describing particular cells for their partners to draw and try to identify.

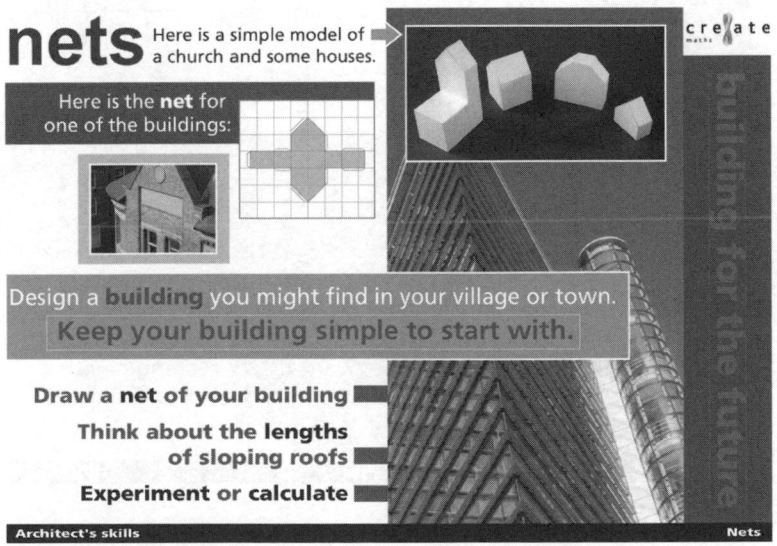

Figure 4.8 An architect's skills 3.

For more activities like this one please visit the Cre8ate Maths website at www.cre8atemaths.org.uk

Making more of the science–mathematics connection

The field of integrated science and mathematics education is not new. Since the beginning of the twentieth century it has been suggested as a promising path towards improved pupil understanding of, performance in and attitude towards both subject areas.

The subjects 'connected' here are science and mathematics and at primary level most would agree that there are numerous connections. Many activities require pupils to include numbers, quantities, etc., in their work. By encouraging this type of learning, primary teachers are helping pupils' foundation skills development.

Practical task

Bricks and molecules

This activity uses something as simple as a brick wall to examine strength of structures.

The pupils start with a box of dominoes (each domino is roughly the same dimension as a brick) and the task is to avoid lines of weakness either horizontally or vertically, e.g.

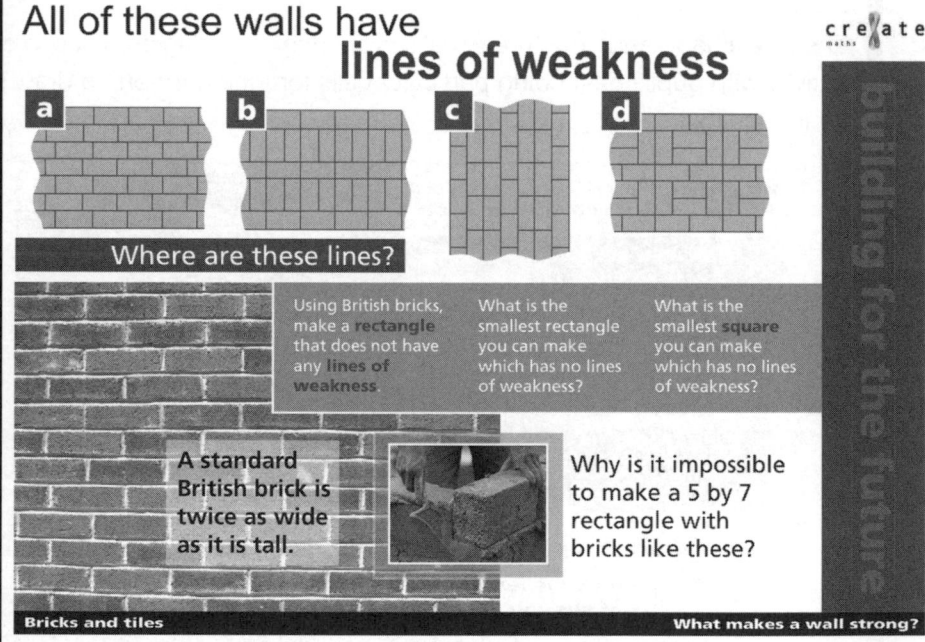

Figure 4.9 Lines of weakness in a wall.

Pupils will be surprised at how difficult it is to avoid such lines. The smallest rectangular solution is a 6 by 5 rectangle. It can be shown using proof by exhaustion that this is the smallest rectangle: this is a challenge to complete. Thinking about odd by odd rectangles will help eliminate some possibilities. One way to prove that no odd rectangle can be made is to note that the product of any two odd numbers is another odd number. Since each brick covers 2 squares, the number of squares covered by any set of 2 by 1 bricks will always be an even number:

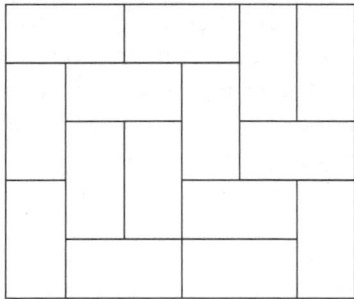

This activity helps to develop skills involved in solving problems in both science and mathematics.

Related directly to science, it can be used to examine the kinetic theory and the structure of molecules.

For more activities like this one please visit the Cre8ate Maths website at www.cre8atemaths.org.uk

Fibonacci – an example of science and mathematics working together

An interesting and very informative way of linking mathematics and science for pupils is to develop some classroom activities based on the work of Fibonacci. It not only introduces the pupils to number sequences but also shows them how the natural world and mathematics are linked in a very demonstrable way. By working with a colleague in the mathematics department a range of activities and projects can be developed that demonstrate to the pupils that the two subjects can be learned together.

A little background

Throughout his life Fibonacci was mainly known as a wealthy merchant with an intense interest in numbers. He was educated in Algeria, where his father worked as a customs officer. In his youth, while staying with his father in Bugia (now Bejaia), Algeria, Fibonacci was first exposed to Arabic numerals (1, 2, 3, 4, 5, 6, 7, 8, 9 and 0), which we of course use today. He quickly mastered the idea and continued employing them after his return to Italy. In 1202 he completed his work, *Liber abaci* (Book of Calculation) in which he explained how to use Arabic numerals and also noted their advantages.

The following problem was written in his book called *Liber abaci*:

A certain man put a pair of rabbits in a place surrounded on all sides by a wall. How many pairs of rabbits can be produced from that pair in a year if it is supposed that every month each pair begets a new pair, which from the second month on becomes productive?

It was this problem that led Fibonacci to the introduction of the Fibonacci numbers and the Fibonacci sequence which is what he remains famous for to this day. The sequence is 1, 1, 2, 3, 5, 8, 13, 21, 34, 55 … This sequence shows that each number is the sum of the two preceding numbers. It is a sequence that is seen and used in many different areas of mathematics and science. The sequence is an example of a recursive sequence. The Fibonacci sequence defines the curvature of naturally occurring spirals, such as snail shells and even the pattern of seeds in flowering plants. The Fibonacci sequence was actually given the name by a French mathematician Edouard Lucas in the 1870s.

Practical task

This activity illustrates the Fibonacci sequence, its origins and how Fibonacci explained it himself.

Numbers in nature

Give a brief overview of Fibonacci's work and outline the problem the pupils are going to solve. This is the problem that appeared in Fibonacci's book about the rabbits. In developing the problem, he made the following assumptions:

- Begin with one male and one female rabbit. Rabbits can mate at the age of one month, so by the end of the second month, each female can produce another pair of rabbits.

- The rabbits never die.

- The female produces one male and one female each month.

Fibonacci asked how many *pairs* of rabbits would be produced in one year.

Work with the pupils to see whether they can develop the sequence themselves. Remind them that they are counting pairs of rabbits, not individuals. You may want to talk them through the first few months of the problem:

a. You begin with one pair of rabbits (1)

b. At the end of the first month, there is still only one pair (1).

c. At the end of the second month, the female has produced a second pair, so there are two pairs (2).

d. At the end of the third month, the original female has produced another pairs, so now there are 3 pairs (3).

e. At the end of the fourth month, the original female has produced yet another pair, and the female born two months earlier has produced her first pair, making a total of 5 pairs (5).

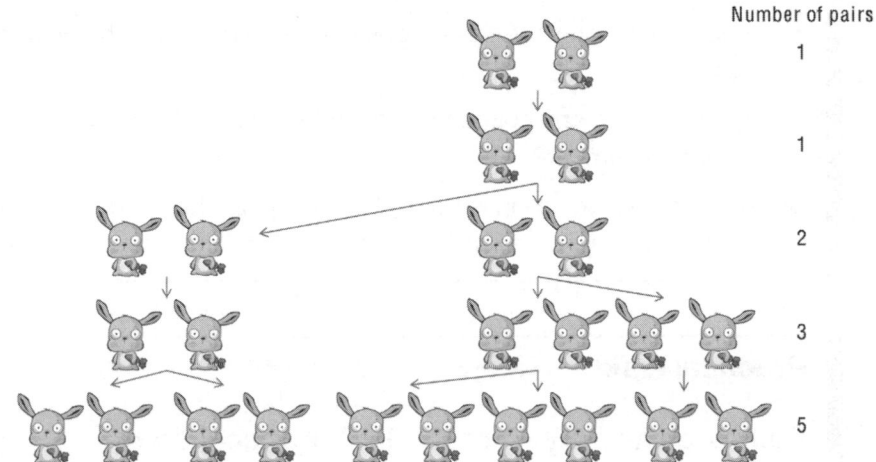

Figure 4.10 Fibonacci's sequence.

Write the pattern that has emerged on the board: 1, 1, 2, 3, 5, 8, 13, 21, 34, 55, 89, 144, 233.

Discuss what 'rule' is being followed to get from one number to the next. Help the pupils understand that to get the next number in the sequence, you have to add the previous two numbers. Explain that this is known as the Fibonacci sequence and as a class continue to produce a few more numbers in the sequence.

Explain that mathematicians have noticed that the numbers in the sequence appear in many different patterns in nature and that they are going to look for these numbers in pictures from the natural world.

Set up a set of stations around the room with pictures (or real samples if possible) of a range of flowers (calla lily – 1 petal; iris – 3 petals; buttercup – 5 petals, etc.), seed heads (e.g. sunflower), a cauliflower, a pine cone, a pineapple and an apple (cut in two horizontally).

The pupils work in pairs and at each station carry out the activity:

*   Flowers – count the petals. Are they Fibonacci numbers?
*   Seed head – examine the seed head for spirals. Start at the centre and find a spiral going to the right. How many seed heads can you count in that spiral? Do the same going left. Are they Fibonacci numbers?

- Cauliflower florets – find the centre of the head of cauliflower. Count the florets that make up a spiral going right and again going left. Are they Fibonacci numbers?

- Pine cone – look at the bottom of the pine cone. Count as many seed cases going in left and right spirals. Are they Fibonacci numbers?

- Pineapple – count the spirals going left and right. Are they Fibonacci numbers?

- Apple – how many points does the 'star' of seed have? Is this is a Fibonacci number?

Discuss with the whole class how often the spiral shape seems to appear in nature, e.g. snail and sea shells, the arrangement of petals in a rose.

Practical task

Follow-on activity – creating a Fibonacci spiral

Using the sheet shown the pupils follow the instructions and begin to see when they join up the sections how Fibonacci numbers can lead to a familiar shape in nature:

```
G G G G G G G G G G G G G
G G G G G G G G G G G G G
G G G G G G G G G G G G G
G G G G G G G G G G G G G
G G G G G G G G G G G G G
G G G G G G G G G G G G G
G G G G G G G G G G G G G
G G G G G G G G G G G G G
G G G G G G G G G G G G G
G G G G G G G G G G G G G
G G G G G G G G G G G G G
G G G G G G G G G G G G G
G G G G G G G G G G G G G
F F F F F F F F C C D D D
F F F F F F F F C C D D D
F F F F F F F F B A D D D
F F F F F F F F E E E E E
F F F F F F F F E E E E E
F F F F F F F F E E E E E
F F F F F F F F E E E E E
F F F F F F F F E E E E E
```

- Starting with square B, shade the sets of squares in different colours ending with the set marked G.

- Starting at the top right corner of square A draw a diagonal line to the bottom left, then up to the top left of B, bottom left to top right of set C and so on across all the sets.

Pictures such as shells, pine cones, pineapples and roses can show pupils examples of the spiral in the natural world:

Figure 4.11 A Fibonacci spiral.

Possible extension work

The pupils can discover what happens when instead of adding two numbers in the sequence, they divide them, e.g. 8÷5, or 13÷8 and so on. They find that they always get the same answer – around 1.6. This is called the Golden Ratio or Golden Number and can be found in art, music, architecture, technology and history. There is scope for an extensive piece of project work (for a more detailed look at the Golden Ratio please see Chapter 8).

Practical task

Talk to colleagues from across the school and look into the possibility of a collapsed timetable day for a Key Stage 3 year group and run a Fibonacci day. The pupils' activities will all be underpinned by Fibonacci's work but the pupils will see all the connections between subjects.

This could take place during National Science and Engineering week.

Game example 2

The game with no rules

This is a very simple card game. It has no rules except those that the pupils devise as they are playing. It ends when one player works out the rules. It is a simple way of demonstrating how scientists test hypotheses by carrying out experiments before reaching conclusions.

Playing the game

1. The game is played in small groups of 4–6 pupils and all that is needed is a pack of ordinary playing cards for each group (see Figure 4.12).
2. The joker cards are removed from the pack and all of the cards are dealt out around the group so that each pupil has the same number of cards. Any cards left over are discarded. The players can see all the cards in their hands.
3. One pupil then thinks of a rule. For example, every red even numbered card has to be followed by an odd numbered black card.

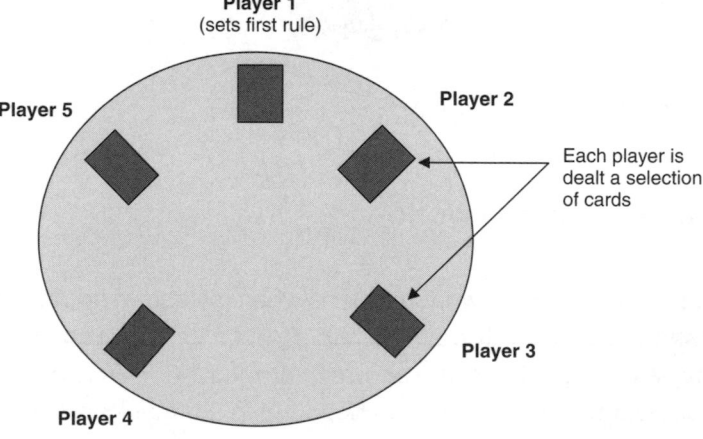

Figure 4.12 The arrangement of players.

Note – the aces in the pack equal 1.

4. The pupil who has thought of the rule lays down the first card in the middle of the table.
5. Each pupil takes it in turn to lay down a card next to the previous card and the person who has set the rule states if the card if right or wrong. If it is correct it stays where it is but if it is wrong the player must take the card back (see Figure 4.13).
6. The game continues until someone thinks they know the rule and they can have a guess when it is their turn. If they are correct they can now set the rule and the game is played again.
7. Each player in the group can take a turn at setting the rule.
8. At the end of the game the class can then discuss how this simple card game can be used to demonstrate the way in which scientists carry out investigations.

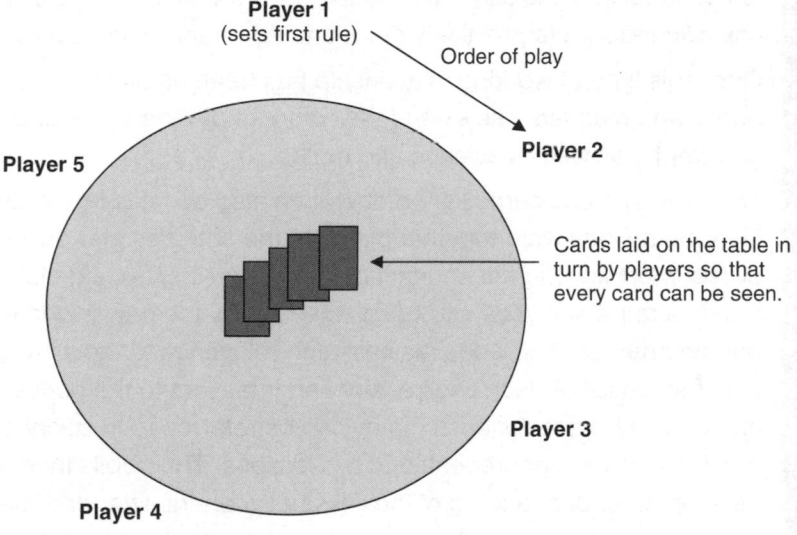

Figure 4.13 Playing the game.

It encourages pupils to be creative with the rules they devise and many incorporate quite involved maths operations to try and defeat the members of their group.

Practical Example
Cross-curricular work in mathematics and science

It is possible to use the data from scientific sources that can help pupils with their maths skills. This type of work can take place in one school or it can be shared across a number of schools. It can be particularly effective if a school is part of a cluster that regularly works together. It can be all from the same sector or can include, for example, a secondary school and some of its feeder primary schools. In the latter case it can be an activity that encourages Year 7 pupils and teachers to work with Year 6 pupils and teachers in developing particular maths skills.

For example, this type of activity would be some form of field work such as measuring changes in temperature in a particular environment like a school playground or playing fields. This would be done over time and in different schools and could involve the older pupils instructing the younger pupils in using data logging equipment and the interpretation of data records. The younger pupils learn new skills and the older pupils enhance their understanding of the use of the equipment. Together the pupils can complete any calculation, interpret the findings and agree on the conclusions.

Once this type of working relationship has been established the teams of pupils and teachers can extend their work to other areas that could include geography as well as science and maths.

This type of cross-curricular co-operation also benefits the teachers involved as they work together planning the activities and develop their own subject knowledge and that of other subjects. For example, in maths the data to be analysed had been collected by the pupils who then carry out the analysis. This adds realness and relevance to the activity that in the past has possible been seen as dry and irrelevant to the pupils. The analysis techniques used in maths can be referred to in science meaning that the activity is not repeated in two lessons. The pupils themselves develop an understanding of the links between the two (or more) subjects. In working with younger pupils the Year 7 pupils develop more independence and as a transition approach for the Year 6 pupils and their teachers, it demonstrates co-operation across sectors.

Practical task

Look at the science scheme of work for Year 7 and identity any fieldwork opportunities where Year 7 pupils could work with Year 6 pupils from one of your feeder schools. Discuss this with a colleague from the maths department and together approach a Year 6 teacher from a feeder school to plan an activity similar to the one described above.

Conclusion

The advocates of cross-curricular studies refer to mathematics as the language of science and develop taxonomies to support linkages between science and mathematics. These taxonomies include skills that direct pupil learning in problem solving, reasoning, information manipulating, information management and symbolic representation skills. Pupils (and teachers) are required to examine and understand concepts, principles and theories of science and mathematics for successful cross-curricular work. Topics shared by science and mathematics curricula include the study of measurements, patterns and relationships, probability, special relationships and variables. Only when these mathematical skills are directly involved in the science curriculum can there be true cross-curricular teaching and learning. Hollenbeck (2007) observed that when there is not a clear relationship between mathematics and science lessons this is lost.

The mathematics that pupils use in solving mathematics-based questions in science must be used as they have been learned in their mathematics lessons. This connection between theory and application helps reinforce the new material and creates relevancy for the learner. The mathematics used in the science lesson should be transparent and applicable.

Mathematics used in the science classroom should reinforce the perspective of investigation, exploration and experimentation in science. The applied mathematics provides quantitative evidence to the science work, taking it beyond just descriptions.

For science, mathematics underscores the importance of careful observations, data collection, logical thinking and modelling as part of the science method.

Recommendations

According to Hollenbeck (2007):

- If there is a desire to improve the learning of pupils in science and mathematics, good mathematics teachers should have the freedom to develop strategies that will allow pupils to construct their understanding in their mental frames of reference.

- Likewise, science teachers should be able to connect the appropriate mathematics links in their schemes of work. Effective use of mathematics in science will strengthen each discipline and allow the learners to link for themselves the language and description of the universe (p 80).

Other resources that could be useful

- http://www.cre8atemaths.org.uk/resources
  This project has developed engaging resources for Key Stage 3 mathematics. All the resources are free and can be downloaded from the website. The first unit 'Building for the Future' can be accessed without registration.
- STEM Subject Choice and Careers (http://digitalstorecupboard.tintisha-web.co.uk/)

This is a set of resources for Key Stage 3 pupils which have been designed to highlight the cross-curricular links between all STEM subjects but also possible careers. Of particular interest are the following units:

1. Working internationally
2. Taking a risk
3. Carbon footprints
4. Packaging design
5. Dispensing
6. Working in tourism
7. Artistic triangles
8. More artistic triangles
9. Pentagon patterns
10. Logistics.

Professional standards for QTS

This chapter will help meet the following standards:

Q6   Have a commitment to collaboration and co-operative working

Q7   (a) Reflect on and improve their practice, and take responsibility for identifying and meeting their developing professional needs

Q8   Have a creative and constructively critical approach towards innovation, being prepared to adapt their practice where benefits and improvements are identified

Q10   Have a knowledge and understanding of a range of teaching, learning and behaviour management strategies and know how to use and adapt them, including how to personalise learning and provide opportunities for all learners to achieve their potential

Q14   Have a secure knowledge and understanding of their subject/curriculum areas and related pedagogy to enable them to teach effectively across the age and ability range for which they are trained

Q17   Know how to use skills in literacy, numeracy and ICT to support their teaching and wider professional activities

Q23   Design opportunities for learners to develop their literacy, numeracy and ICT skills

Q24   Plan homework or other out-of-class work to sustain learners' progress and to extend and consolidate their learning

Q32   Work as a team member and identify opportunities for working with colleagues, sharing the development of effective practice with them

Q33   Ensure that colleagues working with them are appropriately involved in supporting learning and understand the roles they are expected to fulfil

Professional standards for teachers

This chapter will help meet the following standards:

C6   Have a commitment to collaboration and co-operative working where appropriate

C8   Have a creative and constructively critical approach towards innovation, being prepared to adapt their practice where benefits and improvements are identified

C15   Have a secure knowledge and understanding of their subject/curriculum areas and related pedagogy including: the contribution that their subjects/curriculum areas can make to cross-curricular learning; and recent relevant developments

C17   Know how to use skills in literacy, numeracy and ICT to support their teaching and wider professional activities

C27   Design opportunities for learners to develop their literacy, numeracy and ICT and thinking and learning skills appropriate within their phase and context

C40   Work as a team member and identify opportunities for working with colleagues, managing their work where appropriate and sharing the development of effective practice with them

Pupils' Personal, Learning and Thinking Skills (PLTS)

This chapter will help meet the following skills:

Independent enquirers   ■ Identify questions to answer and problems to resolve

Creative thinkers   ■ Generate ideas and explore possibilities

5

Cross-curricular practice: science, ICT and technology

Key objectives

By the end of this chapter you will have:

■ Identified topics/areas in the Key Stage 3 science curriculum that can be enhanced by the use of ICT and/or an integration with technology

■ Adapted the Key Stage 3 Scheme of Work to make use of ICT tools

■ Developed a set of lessons to be taught using a range of ICT tools

Introduction

New technologies, particularly information and communications technologies (ICT), have caused profound changes throughout society. A generation of children is emerging already immersed in a multimedia data storm. Their understandings and expectations of the world happen through their experiences of multimedia and ICT and these differ from those of preceding generations nurtured on linear technologies. Educating these children using models of teaching and learning that are grounded in concepts of knowing and understanding that are linear and finite will not help them succeed in a technological, global future where multi-disciplinary, holistic approaches predominate.

The term ICT encompasses the range of hardware (desktop computers, tablets, PCs, projection technology, calculators, data-logging, smart phones and digital-recording equipment), software applications (generic software, multimedia resources) and information systems (Intranet, Internet) available in schools. Pupils' access to technology at school and at home has increased astronomically over the last few years.

Living in a technological age

Modern technology offers many means of improving teaching and learning in the classroom. Dawes (2001) is of the view that new technologies have the potential to support education across the curriculum and provide opportunities for effective communication between teachers and pupils in ways that have not been possible before. ICT in education has the potential to be influential in bringing about changes in ways of teaching. However, this potential may not easily be realised, as Dawes (2001) underlined when he stated:

> Problems arise when teachers are expected to implement changes in what may well be adverse circumstances.
>
> (Dawes 2001: 61)

Practical task

Carry out a Key Stage 3 science curriculum audit and identify as many examples as possible where ICT can be used when pupils are doing their science work.

To what extent do you use/emphasise the importance of ICT when you teach these topics?

Draw up a plan to increase the use of various ICT tools in your science teaching.

Where does ICT fit in teaching science?

Many studies have been conducted to investigate barriers to the integration of ICT in education and in particular in science education (e.g. Özden 2007; Al-Alwani 2005;

Osborne and Hennessy 2003). Several studies argue that the use of new technologies in the classroom is essential for providing opportunities for pupils to learn to operate in an information age. It is evident, as Yelland (2011) argued, that traditional educational environments do not seem to be suitable for preparing learners to function or be productive in the workplaces of today's society. She claimed that schools that do not incorporate the use of new technologies across the curriculum cannot seriously claim to prepare their pupils for life in the twenty-first century.

ICT can play various roles in the learning and teaching processes. According to Bransford *et al.* (2000), several studies have reviewed the literature on ICT and learning and have concluded that it has great potential to enhance pupil achievement and teacher learning. Wong *et al.* (2006) point out that ICT can play a part in supporting face-to-face teaching and learning in the classroom. Many researchers and theorists assert that the use of computers can help pupils to become knowledgeable, reduce the amount of direct instruction given to them and give teachers an opportunity to help those pupils with particular needs (Iding *et al.* 2002; Shamatha *et al.* 2004; Romeo 2006).

While new technologies can help teachers enhance their pedagogical practice, they can also assist pupils in their learning. According to Grabe and Grabe (2007), ICT can play a role in pupil skills, motivation and knowledge. They claim that ICT can be used to present information to pupils and help them complete learning tasks. According to BECTA (2003: 10), five factors influence the likelihood that good ICT learning opportunities will develop in schools:

1. ICT resourcing
2. ICT leadership
3. ICT teaching
4. School leadership
5. General teaching

BECTA (2003) also indicated that the success of the integration of new technology into education varies from curriculum to curriculum, place to place and class to class, depending on the ways in which it is applied. In science education, there are some areas where ICT has been shown to have a positive impact.

Practical task

Examine the school-wide use of various types of ICT including teaching and learning across various departments and in school administration.

Highlight areas of good practice and areas where changes could be made.

Science education and ICT

'In the past few decades the science curriculum has changed to match the new aims of science education, and it will continue to change' (Osborne and Hennessy 2003). Osborne and Hennessy (2003) state that the latest move towards:

[t]eaching about science rather than teaching its content will require a significant change in its mode of teaching and an improved knowledge and understanding in teachers ...

(Osborne and Hennessy 2003: 4)

They emphasise that along with the changes in views on the nature of science and the role of science education, the increase in the use of ICT offers a challenge to science teaching and learning.

Practical task

Use the following headings to examine your Key Stage 3 teaching and add comments as appropriate.

Year group	Topic	ICT currently used	Teaching & learning benefits	Teaching & learning constraints	Possible new ICT approaches
Y7					
Y8					
Y9					

The last column can be completed as you work through this chapter.

Potential benefits from the use of ICT for science learning have been reported in several research studies. One of these potential benefits is the encouragement of communication and collaboration in science research activities. According to Gillespie (2006), new technologies can be used in science education to enable pupils to collect science information and interact with resources, such as images and videos, and encourage communication and collaboration. New technologies may also help to increase pupil motivation (Osborne and Collins 2000), facilitate clearer thinking and develop interpretation skills with data (Newton and Rogers 2003).

Another benefit from using ICT in science education is that it expands the pedagogical resources available to science teachers (Al-Alwani 2005). Pickersgill (2003) explored effective ways of utilising the Internet when teaching science. He found that the ease of Internet access allows teachers to help pupils to become experts at searching for information rather than receiving facts. He claimed that it could:

[i]ncrease their [pupils] awareness of the importance of the world around them, of citizenship and of a scientifically literate community.

(Pickersgill 2003: 86).

While ICT cannot replace normal classroom teaching, it can be a positive force in the science classroom for a deeper understanding of the principles and concepts of science and could be used to provide new, authentic, interesting, motivating and successful educational activities. There are other potential benefits as tools for enhancing teaching and learning in schools (Skinner and Preece 2003). These tools include those for data capture, multimedia software for simulation, publishing and presentation tools, digital recording equipment, computer projection technology and computer–controlled microscopes (Osborne and Hennessy 2003).

Reflective task

Take some time to examine your own ICT skills and identify areas of confidence and areas where you would like some CPD.

Practical project suggestion

Listening to music on an MP3 player is now standard behaviour for most young people and the Apple iPod is perhaps the most popular version of this equipment. Most people use their iPod for downloading and listening to music only but many have facilities such as video recording. Smartphone users have these facilities on their phones and so the suggested work can be carried out using them in the same way.

The facilities can be used by teachers to work creatively with their pupils using a device that the pupils are extremely familiar with.

They can be used with pupils for activities such as revision, homework, notes, and presentations. The pupils can develop tasks for themselves but also to share with their peers and teachers. Teachers can develop activities that pupils can access easily and anywhere.

By using a piece of equipment that most pupils have at their disposal in a unique way, pupils who might not normally be engaged with their science lessons can be newly enthused about their studies.

To find out more and look at a Case Study developed by a teacher in Warwickshire go to http://www.vital.ac.uk and enter 'Hard to teach case studies' in the search box or simply type 'Using ICT on hard-to-teach topics in science' in your web browser.

Barriers to integrating ICT

The act of integrating ICT into teaching and learning is a complex one and one that may encounter a number of difficulties or barriers.

Teacher-level barriers

- Lack of teacher confidence or fear of failure. Balnaskat *et al.* (2006) found that limitations in teachers' ICT knowledge makes them feel anxious about using ICT in the classroom and thus not confident to use it in their teaching.

- Much research into the barriers to the integration of ICT into education suggests that teachers' attitudes and an inherent resistance to change is a significant barrier (e.g. Gomes 2005; Schoepp 2005). BECTA (2004) claimed that one key area of teachers' attitudes towards the use of technologies is their understanding of how these technologies will benefit their teaching and pupils' learning.

School-level barriers

- Many teachers have competence and confidence in using computers in the classroom, but they still make little use of technologies because they do not have enough time, e.g. to plan technology-based lessons, explore the different Internet sites and look at various aspects of educational software.

- Research by Gomes (2005) relating to science education concluded that a barrier was lack of training in digital literacy, lack of pedagogic and didactic training in how to use ICT in the classroom, and a lack of training concerning the use of technologies in science specific areas were obstacles to using new technologies in classroom practice.

- Several research studies indicate that lack of access to resources, including home access, is another complex barrier that discourages teachers from integrating new technologies into education and particularly into science education.

- In science education, several studies indicated that lack of technical support was a main barrier to using technologies. According to Gomes (2005), ICT integration in science teaching needs a technician and if one is not available the lack of technical support can be an obstacle.

One can see that it is much easier to remove barriers by resolving and reducing the reasons for the occurrence of these barriers. Educators, teachers and school leaders need to collaborate to overcome any of the obstacles and break down the barriers to the meaningful integration of ICT into teaching and learning.

Self-review framework

The following provides a structure for reviewing your school's use of ICT. The framework is divided into six elements which support and challenge. These are displayed in Table 5.1.

Table 5.1 Framework for reviewing your school's use of ICT.

1. Leadership and management	• Develop and communicate a shared vision of ICT • Plan a sustainable ICT strategy • Develop an effective information management strategy
2. Planning	• Plan for the development of pupils' ICT capability • Plan the use of ICT to support the curriculum and respond to new technologies • Identify and evaluate the impact of ICT on learning and teaching
3. Learning	• Plan the use of ICT to enhance learning and teaching • Meet pupils' expectations for the use of ICT • Consider the impact of ICT on learning
4. Assessment of ICT capability	• Assess ICT of pupils to support their learning • Use assessment evidence and data in planning learning and teaching across the whole curriculum • Assess the learning in specific subjects when ICT has been used
5. Professional development	• Identify and address the ICT training needs of school and individual staff • Provide quality support and training activities for all staff in the use of ICT, sharing effective practice • Review, monitor and evaluate professional development as an integral part of school development
6. Resources	• Ensure learning and teaching environments use ICT effectively and in line with strategic needs • Purchase, deploy and review appropriate ICT resources that reflect school improvement strategy • Manage technical support effectively for the benefit of pupils and staff

When a school has reached a certain level on the framework it can apply for the ICT Mark which is a national accreditation which celebrates achievement in the use of ICT in working towards whole-school improvement. For more information, see http://www.naace.co.uk/ictmark.

Elements 2, 3 and 4 are of particular relevance for the classroom teacher and issues around cross-curricular teaching and learning.

Practical task

1. Arrange a meeting with a colleague from the ICT department and plan some new ways in which you could use some new ICT tools in teaching science.

   Discuss possible implications for both subject areas.

2. Look into the possibility of carrying out the self-review.

Table 5.2 Possible barriers for schools and teachers for the integration of ICT into education.

Implementing an ICT strategy in school		
Barriers	For schools	For teachers
Lack of access	Providing ICT resources including hardware and software	• Taking advantage of resources offered at school • Access to ICT resources at home
Resistance to change	Training in new pedagogical approaches	• Being open-minded towards new ways of teaching
Lack of time	Providing sufficient time: reducing the number of teacher lessons or increasing the daily lesson time	• Acquiring skills of self-organisation and time management
Lack of training	Providing training courses in dealing with the new devices, modern technologies and new pedagogical approaches	• Preparing themselves by self-training • Taking up opportunities for training offered at schools • Knowing how to access resources
Lack of technical support	Providing continued technical support	• Relying on themselves to be able to solve problems in their use of ICT • Accessing available support

Practical task

Highlight those parts of Table 5.2 that apply to you as a teacher and to your school.

Using the table above as a guide add two new columns – personal expertise/experience; areas for development/CPD.

Schools need to provide training courses for teachers to gain experience in dealing with the new devices, modern technologies and new pedagogical approaches. Technical support needs to be provided in schools. Additionally schools must provide teachers with the necessary ICT resources including hardware and software. It is important for schools to cooperate with teachers by providing sufficient time to implement new technologies in the classroom.

Teachers also need to engage with implementation. Teachers should take advantage of ICT resources offered at schools. They need to be prepared well before joining the teaching profession. Where training is absent teachers can prepare themselves by enrolling in private sessions or by self-training. They should be open-minded towards new approaches of teaching. Where support is lacking, they need to find ways to be able to solve problems involving their use of ICT in schools. Finally, teachers should acquire skills of self-organisation which will help them a great deal in conducting their classes when using ICT.

Reflective task

Make a note of every lesson in which you use any ICT over the course of a week.

Revisit the list at the end of the week and try to add some new ICT approaches you could use.

Teacher intervention which elicits, discusses, challenges and builds on learners' own ideas, describes and interprets shared experience and highlights continuities along with differences between scientific conventions and informal ideas is considered critical for pupils' ultimate (social) construction of more abstract, general and explanatory knowledge frameworks (Driver *et al.* 1994). The complex and counter-intuitive nature of scientific concepts and processes mean that opportunities for discussion, reasoning, interpretation and reflection are very important for knowledge building. Introducing technological tools and resources which pupils can use interactively potentially offers further opportunities for expressing, evaluating and revising their developing ideas as they visualise the consequences of their own learning.

For example, technologies that can be used as tools to support science learning include:

- *Multimedia simulation* which offers idealised, dynamic and visual representations of physical phenomena and experiments which would be dangerous, costly or otherwise not feasible in a school laboratory. It releases pupils from laborious manual processes, both expediting work production and enabling teachers and learners to focus on overarching or salient issues without distraction (Osborne and Hennessy 2003). Simulation use is also considered to support science learning through encouraging pupils to pose and investigate exploratory 'What if...' questions.

- *Data logging* automates the recording and handling of experimental data through the use of sensing equipment which offers immediate feedback and alleviates potentially laborious data collection and graph production. Immediate feedback from the dynamic graph display enables actions to be monitored and adjusted.

- *Interactive whiteboards* (IWBs) are a more generic tool which offers spontaneous access for a whole class to a wide range of projected Web-based and multimedia resources whose projection, manipulation and annotation features serve to facilitate visualisation of abstract knowledge.

Practical project suggestion

This project suggestion makes use of YouTube and its many educational film clips as a resource in teaching. YouTube for Schools provides schools with access to hundreds of thousands of free educational videos. See http://www.youtube.com/schools.

YouTube.com/Teachers has hundreds of playlists of videos organised by subject and class. These playlists were created by teachers for teachers, so you can spend more time teaching and less time searching.

For example, there are a number of You Tube clips that can be used in conjunction with work discussed in this book around Fibonacci (see page 83). If you enter 'Golden Ratio' and the 'Human Body' and/or 'Fibonacci's Fractals' into your web browser you will access two short and useful films.

As well as being a source of some useful science teaching material it can also be used to encourage pupils to consider developing their own short teaching films. These activities encourage the development of a range of skills as well as enhancing pupils' science knowledge.

To look at a Case Study developed by a teacher in the West Midlands go to http://www.vital.ac.uk and enter 'Hard to teach case studies' in the search box or simply type 'Using ICT on hard-to-teach topics in science' in your web browser.

Physics – a special case?

Learning physics is often considered by teachers and pupils to be a difficult pursuit. Much educational research has been directed towards the exploration of pupils' ideas and difficulties on physical concepts and processes (e.g. Duit *et al.* 1991). Research on physics and science education has often focused on the study of alternative conceptions and mental representations that pupils employ before and after instruction. Related to this is research focused on the study of the consequences of special teaching interventions aiming to transform pupils' alternative conceptions: for example, using ICT in the teaching of physics with the aim of raising interest in potential further study and employment.

Numerous ICT applications are available, aiming to stimulate pupils' active engagement and offering the opportunity to work under conditions that are extremely difficult, costly or time-consuming to be created in the classroom or the physics laboratory. The use of ICT applications has radically changed the framework under which physics teaching is being understood and implemented.

Using simulations

Among various ICT applications, computer simulations are of special importance in physics teaching and learning. Simulations offer new educational environments, which aim to enhance teachers' instructional potentialities and to facilitate pupils' active engagement. Computer simulations offer a great variety of opportunities for modelling concepts and processes. Simulations provide a bridge between pupils' prior knowledge and the learning of new physical concepts, helping pupils develop scientific understanding through an active reformulation of their misconceptions. Specifically, they are open learning environments that provide pupils with the opportunity to:

- Develop their understanding about phenomena and physical laws through a process of hypothesis-making, and ideas testing
- Isolate and manipulate parameters and therefore helping them to develop an understanding of the relationships between physical concepts, variables and phenomena
- Employ a variety of representations (pictures, animation, graphs, vectors and numerical data displays) which are helpful in understanding the underlying concepts, relationships and processes
- Express their representations and mental models about the physical world
- Investigate phenomena which are difficult to experience in a classroom or laboratory setting because they are extremely complex, technically difficult or dangerous, costly, time consuming or happen too fast.

Working in a team

One potentially important contextual factor which shapes how technology is perceived and used by teachers is the 'community of practice' (Lave and Wenger 1991) associated with their subject. This is a social framework within which the planning, support and evaluation of pupil learning takes place. Each subject community could be said to share a set of tools and resources; approaches to teaching and learning; curriculum practices; cultural values, expectations and aims. This sharing of practice and experience should encompass the introduction and integration of ICT into subject teaching. It entails developing ideas and trying them out, considering the principles and purposes that underpin activities in particular contexts and critical reflection. Subject cultures are an important influence in determining teachers' and pupils' use of ICT. There is also evidence that teachers choose ICT applications, activities and approaches to fit their own perspectives on teaching and learning (Niederhauser and Stoddart 2001).

> ## Reflective task
>
> At a departmental meeting take the lead and run an activity based on the use of ICT in the scheme of work.

In the science community outside school, the use of computer-based technologies has become a routine part of work. Indeed one of the first Internet protocols was devised by scientists at CERN, the European centre for research in particle physics, so that they could exchange data with colleagues in Italy and the Rutherford laboratory in Cambridge, UK. Today it is unthinkable that scientific research could proceed without access to online databases and email communications, the use of sophisticated monitoring equipment for data collection, powerful spreadsheets and database packages for analysing and manipulating that data and publishing software for producing papers and reports. Here we see the mismatch between pedagogic subject knowledge in science education in schools and the applied academic knowledge of the scientific community. Why then has the school science education community not been drawn into this way of using ICT? Figure 5.1 shows a

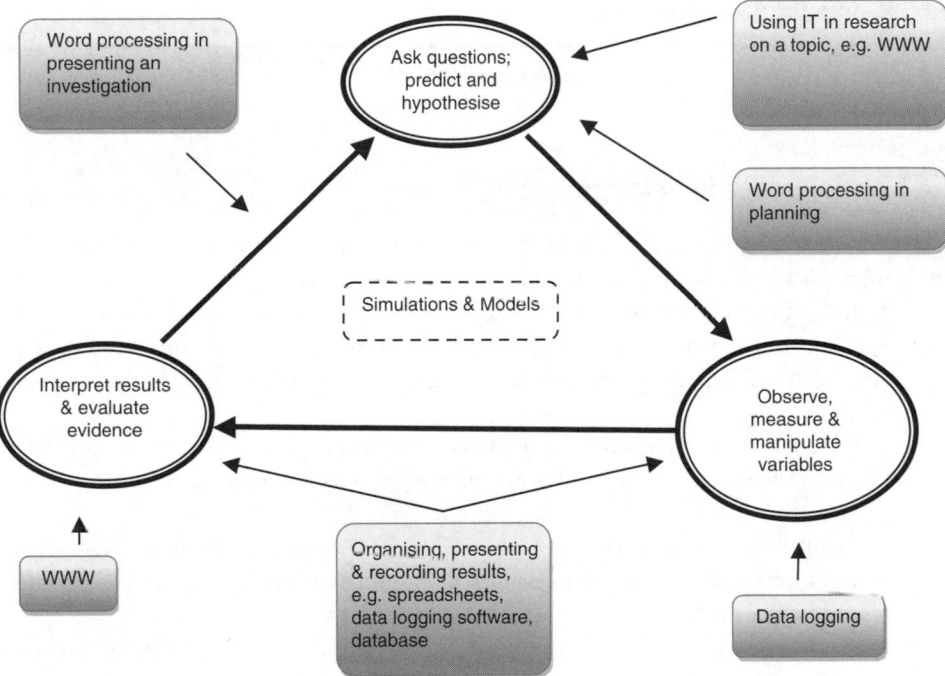

Figure 5.1 A model of the process of science that can be used with some examples of ICT.

representation of the scientific process and how ICT application may be deployed. Science in schools requires pupils to:

■ Engage in asking questions
■ Make predictions
■ Build hypotheses
■ Make observations and measurements

- Manipulate variables to inform those hypotheses
- Evaluate and interpret the results they have gained from those measurements and observations
- Feed those observations back into their original hypotheses to refine and modify their ideas.

Practical task

Annotate Figure 5.1 with some examples of lessons where these approaches could be used and indicate how you would incorporate them into your lesson plans.

ICT and literacy in science

The model in Figure 5.1 can be hard to implement in classrooms as it involves practical work that is both time-consuming and resource-intensive. However, ICT can reduce both the time and the resource constraint to enable learning. It can change the dynamic, opening up opportunities for genuine experimentation and meaningful, contextual discussion and analysis. Computer-based simulation of the practical work can address these issues.

In some specific areas there is cumulative evidence of the positive impact of ICT on learning. One such area is word processing. A systematic review concluded:

> On average, students who use computers when learning to write are not only engaged and motivated in their writing, but they produce written work that is of greater length and higher quality.

> (Goldberg *et al.* 2003: 4)

ICT is powerful in presenting or representing information in different ways. This can be through forms (texts and pictures or tables and graphs) or by enabling changes to be shown dynamically as in mathematical modelling or by helping visualisation of complex processes in science.

Observing changes in a graph when changes are made to a table of numerical information on which the graph is based on a computer or graphical calculator can develop pupils' understanding of mathematical relationships.

Computer tools can help pupils or teachers manipulate complex data sets. This then provides a context for effective discussion which in turn can help to develop understanding. Visualisation tools can help pupils to picture scientific ideas or to develop conceptual understanding.

Practical project suggestion

Simulations

There are occasions where the use of a computer simulation allows pupils to experience a situation they would otherwise not have been able to. By artificially changing factors they can observe the effects of, for example, pollution on an ecosystem or the output from a power generator when the pressure or temperature of the steam is altered.

An excellent subject for using computer simulation is that of a Nuclear Reactor. Here the pupils learn about how a plant operates but can also simulate a range of conditions that might affect that operation. The pupils have to make decisions based on what they see.

See http://www.furryelephant.com/content/radioactivity/nuclear-reactor-power-simulation/ for a simple simulation that outlines how a Nuclear Plant works. This should be viewed first as it lays the ground work for any subsequent work – see below.

http://esa21.kennesaw.edu/activities/nukeenergy/nuke.htm. This simulation allows the pupils to alter conditions and observe the consequences.

However, rather than just sit at a computer, a role play and group work activity can be planned around the simulation. For example:

Group 1 – The power station engineers

The engineers control the reactor. It is important for them to run through the programme beforehand, to familiarise themselves with the effects of changing control rods, coolant, etc.

Group 2 – The electricity generating board

A briefing session for these pupils should concentrate on estimating and predicting demand. They can use the simulation to run a range of scenarios based on demand.

Group 3 – The consumers

Consumers monitor needs based on hypothetical scenarios, e.g., weather changes, hospitals, schools, etc. and draw up a list of pros and cons concerning the use of nuclear power.

Group 4 – The environmentalists

Environmentalists monitor the performance of the other groups and draw up a list of environmental pros and cons of using nuclear power.

The activity can be concluded with a class debate.

For an example of how to use simulation in chemistry, look at a Case Study developed by a teacher in Enfiled go to http://www.vital.ac.uk and enter 'Hard to teach case studies' in the search box or simply type 'Using ICT on hard-to-teach topics in science' in your web browser.

The challenge for the teacher

ICT presents a range of tools that can be used by teachers to present and demonstrate as part of their teaching as well as something for pupils to use as part of an activity as individuals or in groups. These technological tools can be explicitly designed for use in educational context such as using an IWB projecting a calculator or they can be equipment and software also used in other contexts, such as computers with data projectors or word processors and spreadsheets. The choice of when and how to use such technologies in teaching and learning is complex but it is clear that it is *how* ICT is used that makes the difference.

Knowledge of and experience with computers is not enough to enable teachers to make the best use of ICT in the classroom. Effective use of computers within the classroom takes time even with the support of an experienced team or through collaborative learning. In addition the way in which teachers' skills, beliefs and practices are related is complex and this in turn affects the way that teachers choose to use ICT and how effective they are at using it (Higgins and Moseley, 2001).

ICT changes rapidly and new innovations offer new possibilities for teaching and learning. These not only open up new technologies to influence the existing curriculum more effectively or more efficiently but change the nature of that curriculum by altering the content of what needs to be taught, such as the area of digital literacy, instant messaging, video messaging, etc.

The potential of ICT in transforming teaching and learning

According to Osborne and Hennessy (2003), ICT offers a challenge to the teaching and learning of science and to the models of scientific practice teachers and learners might encounter.

ICT offers a range of different tools for use in school science activity:

- Tools for data capture, processing and interpreting data logging systems, databases and spreadsheets, graphing tools and modelling environments
- Multimedia software for simulation of processes and carrying out 'virtual experiments'
- Information systems

- Publishing and presentation tools
- Digital recording equipment
- Computer projection technology.

These forms of ICT can enhance both the practical and theoretical aspects of science teaching and learning. The potential contribution of technology use can be conceptualised as follows:

- Advancing and enhancing work production; offering releases from laborious manual processes and more time for thinking, discussion and interpretation
- Increasing the frequency and scope of relevant phenomena by linking school science to contemporary science and providing access to experiences not otherwise feasible
- Supporting exploration and experimentation by providing immediate, visual feedback
- Focusing attention on over-arching issues, increasing the importance of underlying abstract concepts
- Fostering self-regulated and collaborative learning
- Improving motivation and engagement.

It would be wrong to assume that the introduction of such technologies will transform science education. It is vital to acknowledge the critical role played by the teacher in creating the conditions for ICT-supported learning through selecting and evaluating appropriate technological resources and designing and structuring and sequencing a set of learning activities. Pedagogy for using ICT effectively includes:

- Ensuring that use is appropriate and 'adds value' to learning
- Building on teachers' existing practice and on pupils' prior conceptions
- Structuring activity while offering pupils some responsibility, choice and opportunities for active participation
- Prompting pupils to think about underlying concepts and relationships; creating time for discussion, reasoning, analysis and reflection
- Focusing research tasks and developing skills for finding and critically analysing information
- Linking ICT use to ongoing teaching and learning activities
- Exploiting the potential of whole class interactive teaching and encouraging pupils to share ideas and findings.

Reflective task

Look at your Key Stage 3 lessons and identify those areas/topics that present an opportunity to use ICT in your teaching. List the challenges these would present and, using the section above, devise ways of overcoming them.

ICT in the science laboratory

Teachers' motivation to use ICT can be adversely influenced by a number of constraints:

- Lack of time to gain confidence and experience with technology
- Limited access to reliable resources
- A science curriculum overloaded with content
- Assessment that requires no use of the technology
- A lack of subject-specific guidance for using ICT to support learning.

While this technology can, in principle, be employed in diverse ways to support different curriculum goals and forms of pedagogy, such constraints have often stifled teachers' use of ICT in ways which effectively exploit it interactivity. Even where technology is available it is often under-used and hindered by a set of practical constraints and teacher reservations.

Practical task

Identify a series of three to five lessons and plan to teach them using a range of ICT.

Conclusions

Teachers must continue to work towards harnessing the powerful potential of using ICT to support science learning as far as possible. Further development depends on providing them with more time, consistent access to reliable resources, encouragement and support and offering specific guidance for appropriate and effective use. Assessment frameworks may also need to change in order to evaluate – and thereby further encourage – ICT-supported learning.

As the school curriculum begins to forge links with external scientific and social communities, opportunities arise for ICT use to play a central and core role in supporting development of scientific reasoning and critical analysis skills.

Key messages

- ICT can make a difference to pupils' learning.
- More substantial gains in pupil attainment are achievable where the use of ICT is planned, structured and integrated effectively.
- Increased practice is a key feature of how ICT can help improve learning.
- Computers can motivate pupils to undertake such practice and to help ensure they are practising at an appropriate level of challenge.

- Computers can be used effectively in a range of different ways to improve teaching and learning: by individual pupils, by groups and by the teacher to focus discussion.

- ICT can help to develop pupils' thinking in a range of different ways including reasoning, understanding and creativity.

- ICT offers a wealth of possibilities to support teaching and learning.

- Effective use also depends upon the choices that a teacher makes about how to use ICT as part of their teaching.

- Technology changes rapidly and each change opens up new possibilities for teachers and pupils.

- It takes time to develop the skills necessary to use ICT effectively in teaching.

Implications

- The way equipment and resources are used by pupils and teachers is what makes a difference – providing ICT equipment will not make a difference on its own.

- Target pupils who will benefit from increased practice.

- Identify aspects of the curriculum where it is difficult to get pupils to practise and then use ICT to support this.

- Computers should be used to enhance aspects of teaching through the presentation of information in different ways and in different forms.

- Pupils should manipulate and make changes to information on computers so that they can develop understanding of the relationship between different types of information or through the process of changing that information dynamically, e.g., using data logging.

- Grouping pupils when using computers requires a deliberate choice according to the aims of the activity.

- Effective use of ICT can support the development of understanding across the curriculum.

- There is no single or simple solution to the effective use of ICT in teaching and learning.

- Teachers need support to develop both new technical ability and new pedagogical skills.

Science and design & technology, food technology and fabric technology

Professor Tim Brighouse (2006) noted that in successful schools outstanding teachers are creative about curriculum and pedagogy. While no one is advocating a return to a completely unstructured curriculum there is value for learning where subject boundaries are blurred. This is supported by *Excellence and Enjoyment* (DfES 2003) which states:

There is no requirement for subjects to be taught discretely – they can be grouped, or taught through projects – if strong enough links are created between subjects, pupils' knowledge and skills can be used across the whole curriculum.

(DfES 2003: 17)

Although targeted at the primary sector the principles ring true for Key Stage 3 as do the comments of Gardner (2004) and Barnes (2007):

Any topic of significance can, and should, be represented in a number of different ways in the mind.

(Gardner 2004: 141)

Teachers do not have to choose between *either* subject disciplines or thematic methods but should have *both*.

(Barnes 2007: 231)

Barnes (2007) favours the approach led by learning experiences and defines cross-curricular working in this way:

When the skills, knowledge and attitudes of a number of different disciplines are applied to a single experience, theme or idea, we are working in a cross-curricular way. We are looking at the experience of learning on a macro level with the curriculum as a focus.

(Barnes 2007: 8)

Importantly, carefully planned cross-curricular work can motivate pupils to engage with their learning experiences. This does not mean making tenuous, artificial links between subjects in order to fulfil a curriculum need but identifies a meaningful context that is relevant to pupils' lives and interests, e.g. making use of real situations for learning, emphasising the importance of using opportunities such a snowy day to suspend the curriculum, cross subject boundaries and allow the pupils to experience everything from the structure of snowflakes and temperature measurement, to fabrics that keep them warm, using the concept of freezing in making food items (see below), etc. It is of paramount importance that learning is enjoyable and motivating. This can be achieved when pupils are absorbed in a focused technology activity that involves working in a wider cross-curricular context. When learning has a discrete subject focus, and when subject boundaries are blurred, pupils develop a range of key skills such as communication, improving their own learning and performance, application of number, information technology, problem solving, working with others, as well as a range of thinking skills such as reasoning and evaluation. Shoemaker (1989) uses the term *integrative education* which, she argues:

[c]uts across subject-matter lines, bringing together various aspects of the curriculum into meaningful association to focus upon broad areas of study.

(Shoemaker 1989: 6)

Technology is somewhat unique in that it is often dependent on using knowledge and understanding learnt in other curriculum subjects, such as science, thus demonstrating how it can be enhanced by – *but* also contribute to – other subject areas.

Reflective task

Examine the Key Stage 3 Scheme of Work and highlight topics that you use already or could use in a cross-curricular way with the technology department.

Work with some pupils to create an exhibition of these topics.

Practical task

Invite the technology department for coffee and to view the exhibition.

Follow the visit with a meeting to discuss how you could work more closely.

Design & technology and science

Design and technology (D&T) as a distinct academic subject was introduced into the National Curriculum for schools in England and Wales in 1990. Following its introduction D&T went through a rapid rise in status over a relatively short time span. Improvements in curriculum content and delivery have led to D&T being developed from a number of subjects previously studied by less academic pupils to a more robust unified subject which for some time was compulsory for all pupils.

Implementation

- Ofsted stressed that support from senior management remains a key factor in the progress made by schools in improving standards in D&T.

- Good management of resources is also a key factor in effective delivery of D&T.

- The STEM Ambassadors Programme enables teachers to form links with practising scientists and engineers. The programme offers opportunities to make connections between the curriculum and the world of work.

Practical task

Go to http://www.diyjobdone.com/ for a range of activities based around basic DIY and home improvement skills. It includes issues around impact of building on the environment and sustainability and so links to the science curriculum.

D&T and science departments often work together on projects outside the curriculum, e.g. after schools. Check out:

- *CREST Awards* – http://www.britishscienceassociation.org/web/ccaf/CREST. CREST is a project-based awards scheme for the STEM subjects (Science, Technology, Engineering and Maths). It links the personal passions of students to curriculum-based learning.
- *The Royal Society Partnership Grants* – http://royalsociety.org/education/partnership/. This scheme helps schools to run exciting and innovative projects in partnership with a professional scientist or engineer.
- *STEM Ambassadors* – http://www.stemnet.org.uk/content/ambassadors. The STEM Ambassadors Programme enables teachers to make links from the curriculum to how STEM is practiced in the world of work, illuminating applications across a vast range of careers.

Food technology and science

There are many ways that diet and healthy lifestyle can be dealt with throughout the curriculum. Food technology and science is an obvious choice.

Practical task

Use the following headings and draw up a table of topics which could be taught in food technology and science:

Topic	Science content	Food technology content	Lesson suggestions

Work with a colleague from the food technology department to develop a series of lesson that can be taught across the two subject disciplines. Observing each other teach helps with developing the teaching approaches.

There is also an opportunity to develop school–wide activity that involves more subjects. For example, a school food day can include not only the subject areas but also other areas in the school:

- Food production – history and food technology
- Writing about food – English and library
- Food distribution – geography and technology
- What's in food – science and food technology

- Healthy eating – science, food technology, PE, school canteen
- Creating new food – D&T and food technology (see the practical task below)

Practical task

Frozen smoothies

Pupils focus on:

- Designing and making the mould
- Freezing lollies in the mould
- Designing and branding their creation.

For more information, go to https://www.ssatrust.org.uk/teachingandlearning and search for 'Frozen smoothies KS3 project'.

Another useful set of activities can be found at www.designbrief2020.com which has been developed by the Alpro foundation and consists of a Food Technology project in which pupils design a meal for 2020. The link to science can be found in that the brief centres on a plant-based diet and the pupils need to know about the biology of plants. Asda (at www.asda.com/school) has developed a free resource to assist in the teaching of food technology and can be linked to science at Key Stage 3.

Fabric technology and science

An integration of science and fabric technology will demonstrate to the pupils that there is a very important scientific underpinning to the fabric industry.

For example:

1. The pupils research the science behind a fabric such as cotton or calico and then design and make a 'bag for life'. They can design their bag on a computer. They can then research the science of dyeing before deciding if they wish to dye their bag with the understanding that the dye used must be from a natural source. This could be extended to a project that could include designing an advertising campaign using CAD.

2. The pupils research the science of insulation and heat retention before designing and making, for example, a hat. See http://digitalstorecupboard.tintisha-web.co.uk/ for a specific activity related to heat retention. It is called 'Going to Extremes' and it also involves some experiments on heat retention, ICT in that as well as designing and insulating garment, it also requires pupils to develop a short news broadcast item.

3. Instead of a specific fabric the pupils can investigate the science of colour before following the activity called 'In the Limelight' (found at http://digitalstorecupboard. tintisha-web.co.uk/) which is all about the importance of wearing the right colour clothes in specific lighting.

Practical task

Plan an interactive session with fabric technology colleagues to use scientific techniques to test some fabrics, e.g. a school uniform fabric which advertises itself as stain resistant.

Other resources that could be useful

■ *Education Quizzes* (http://www.educationquizzes.com)
This is particularly useful for D & T

■ *STEM Subject Choice and Careers* (http://digitalstorecupboard.tintisha-web.co.uk/)
This is a set of resources for Key Stage 3 pupils which have been designed to highlight the cross-curricular links between all STEM subjects but also possible careers. Of particular interest are the following units:

1. In the Limelight
2. Levitating Train
3. Adventure Incorporated
4. Car of the Future
5. Ecohouse.

Professional standards for QTS

This chapter will help meet the following standards:

Q6   Have a commitment to collaboration and co-operative working

Q7   (a) Reflect on and improve their practice, and take responsibility for identifying and meeting their developing professional needs

Q8   Have a creative and constructively critical approach towards innovation, being prepared to adapt their practice where benefits and improvements are identified

Q10   Have a knowledge and understanding of a range of teaching, learning and behaviour management strategies and know how to use and adapt them, including how to personalise learning and provide opportunities for all learners to achieve their potential

Q14   Have a secure knowledge and understanding of their subject/curriculum areas and related pedagogy to enable them to teach effectively across the age and ability range for which they are trained

Q17   Know how to use skills in literacy, numeracy and ICT to support their teaching and wider professional activities

Q23   Design opportunities for learners to develop their literacy, numeracy and ICT skills

Q24   Plan homework or other out-of-class work to sustain learners' progress and to extend and consolidate their learning

Q32   Work as a team member and identify opportunities for working with colleagues, sharing the development of effective practice with them

Q33   Ensure that colleagues working with them are appropriately involved in supporting learning and understand the roles they are expected to fulfil

Professional standards for teachers

This chapter will help meet the following standards:

C6   Have a commitment to collaboration and co-operative working where appropriate

C8   Have a creative and constructively critical approach towards innovation, being prepared to adapt their practice where benefits and improvements are identified

C15   Have a secure knowledge and understanding of their subject/curriculum areas and related pedagogy including: the contribution that their subjects/curriculum areas can make to cross-curricular learning; and recent relevant developments

C17   Know how to use skills in literacy, numeracy and ICT to support their teaching and wider professional activities

C27   Design opportunities for learners to develop their literacy, numeracy and ICT and thinking and learning skills appropriate within their phase and context

C40   Work as a team member and identify opportunities for working with colleagues, managing their work where appropriate and sharing the development of effective practice with them

Pupils' Personal, Learning and Thinking Skills (PLTS)

This chapter will help meet the following skills:

Independent enquirers	• Identify questions to answer and problems to resolve
Creative thinkers	• Generate ideas and explore possibilities • Connect their own and others' ideas and experiences in inventive ways
Reflective learners	• Evaluate experiences and learning to inform future progress • Communicate their learning in relevant ways for different audiences
Team workers	• Collaborate with others to work towards common goals • Take responsibility, showing confidence in themselves and their contribution
Self-managers	• Work towards goals, showing initiative, commitment and perseverance • Organise time and resources, prioritising actions
Effective participators	• Identify improvements that would benefit others as well as themselves

Cross-curricular practice: science and English

Key objectives

By the end of this chapter you will have:

- Identified the Key Stage 3 science curriculum areas/topics that can be used in a cross-curricular manner with English
- Discussed and planned with a colleague from the English department opportunities for working together
- Highlighted at least three science topics that can be used for developing pupil literacy

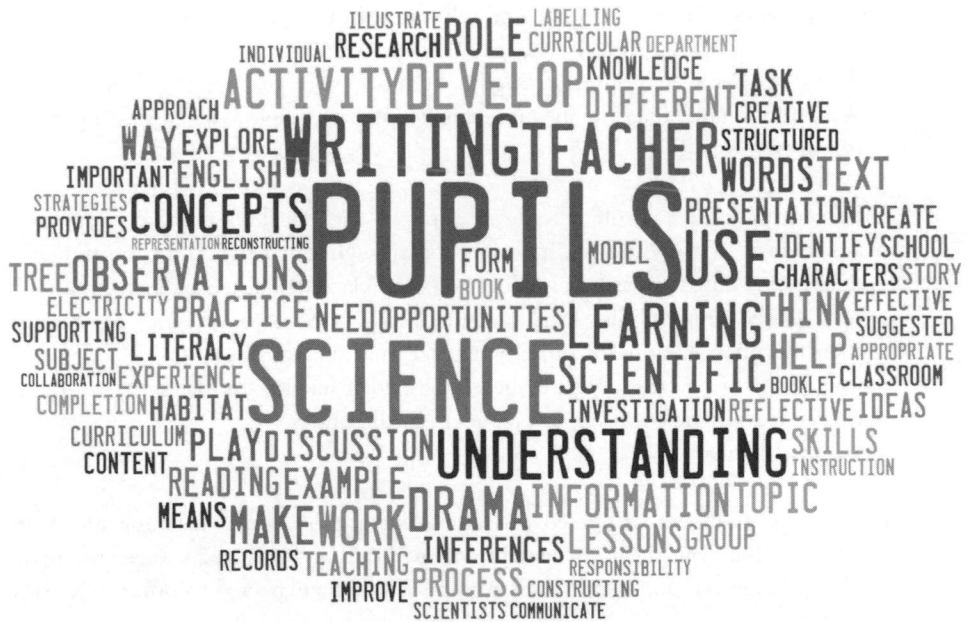

Introduction

Cross-curricular secondary teaching and learning strategies exist in many different forms and can be applied to any two or more subject disciplines. Most importantly, these strategies have proved to be effective in improving learning and the understanding of important concepts across all the subjects involved in the activity (McKinney and Hademenos 2009).

It has often been said that if someone can explain a concept to a grandparent and they understand it, then the person really understands the subject themselves.

As John Rigden (2005) stated:

We are obsessed with the quantitative to the exclusion of the qualitative. The currency of the qualitative is words and words are powerful vehicles. The currency of the quantitative is symbols and numbers, also powerful vehicles. But there is a profound difference. To discuss a concept qualitatively, students must internalize the concept so that it becomes their own. Only then can students select their own words and put nouns and verbs together into sentences that capture the subtleties, nuances and meanings.

This chapter explores the interdisciplinary relationship between science and English and offers some examples of ways to integrate the two subjects in both classroom and beyond.

Literacy and science

Pupils' low literacy skills often lead to under-achievement across the curriculum, and all teachers have a vital role to play in helping pupils to access and engage with the curriculum. When it comes to literacy, no one said it better than George Sampson (1921):

Every teacher is a teacher *of* English because every teacher is a teacher *in* English. We cannot give a lesson in any subject without helping or neglecting the English of our pupils.

The focus has to be a whole school one if pupils' literacy skills are to be improved which means teachers of every subject. It is not good enough for a teacher, for example of science, to lament declining standards in spelling and then blame the English department. There has to be a shared responsibility for literacy and at Key Stage 3 it is an opportunity for all teachers to enhance pupils' learning, whatever their subject specialism.

A number of key aims need to be established if science and English are to develop a successful working relationship to be benefit of the pupils.

Suggested aims:

- The development of agreed and consistent approaches to teaching and learning in literacy between the two departments to build an increased awareness of the skills, knowledge and understanding that pupils could be expected to bring to lessons
- To use speaking and listening to develop science learning

- To develop active reading strategies to increase pupils' ability to read for a purpose and engage with text and the learning to be gained from it

- To demonstrate the sequence for writing and modelling writing for a key text–type within science

- To make suggestions for the learning of subject–specific vocabulary.

Reflective task

Examine the Key Stage 3 science curriculum and highlight any areas/topics that can be developed for cross-curricular work with the English department.

Meet with a colleague from the English department and discuss the teaching and learning approaches you can both use for cross-curricular teaching.

Outline three topics where you will develop strategies with your English department colleague.

Scientific words

Science is rich in specialised words, many of which have an everyday meaning as well as a scientific meaning. Improving pupils' spelling and understanding of these words will improve their understanding of science.

Practical task

Consider some words that often cause difficulty – energy, cell, force, material, dissolve, tissue. These words cause problems because they have scientific and everyday meanings.

Make a list of as many words like this as you can and develop a science dictionary for your pupils so that they have a reference point if they are ever unsure about a word.

The pupils can add to this over time.

When considering the importance of words in science the main points to remember are:

- Identify words with care – match your list with the needs of the pupils.

- Explore new words together – consider their structure, word roots and scientific meaning.

Science and reading

Reading in science should require effort – the vocabulary can be highly specialised and some science books are very hard to read. Pupils will need support with ways to access some of the text they encounter. An important key is to ensure that pupils are really reading the text and Directed Activities Related to Texts (DARTs) can ensure that pupils engage with the text in a way that promotes understanding.

They are *directed* because they told why they are reading and they are *active* because they have to think and make decisions. For example take a look at Table 6.1 below.

Table 6.1 Using directed reading.

Reconstruction activities using modified text *Pupil tasks are completion-type activities with deleted or segmented text*	Analysis activities using straight text *Pupil tasks are text marking and labelling or recording*
1. *Text completion* – pupils predict deleted words (cloze), sentences or phrases 2. *Diagram completion* – pupils predict deleted labels using text and other diagrams as sources 3. *Table completion* – pupils complete deleted parts of a table using table categories and texts as sources of reference 4. *Completion activities* with disordered text – (a) predicting a logical order for a sequence; (b) classifying segments according to categories given by the teacher 5. *Prediction* – pupils predict next part(s) of text with segments	1. *Underlining* – pupils search for specific words or phrases that relate to one aspect of contents, e.g. key words 2. *Labelling* – pupils label segments of text with different aspects, e.g. labelling a scientific account with labels provided by the teacher such as prediction, evidence, conclusion 3. *Segmenting* – (a) segmenting of paragraphs or text into information units; (b) labelling of segments of text 4. *Diagrammatic representation* – constructing diagrams from text, e.g. using flow diagrams, concept maps, mind maps, labelled models 5. *Tabular representation* – pupils construct and represent information in tabular form, extracting it from a written text

Source: Adapted from Davies, F. and Green, T. 1984.

Practical task

Choose one of the DARTS listed in Table 6.1 and develop an activity.

Explain which literacy skills will be enhanced by pupils carrying out the activity.

To sum up science and reading:

- All the activities ensure information processing and selecting rather than just passive reading, copying or note taking.
- Active reading strategies ensure that pupils access text and make sense of it.
- The approaches ensure a variety of learning styles.

Science and talking

Research has shown that pupils spend about a third of their time listening in science lessons but very little time in discussion with each other or with their teacher. Pupils need opportunities to describe, explain and justify their understanding of scientific ideas and to use precise vocabulary. Speaking scientific terms aloud helps pupils to spell correctly. Pupils need opportunities to 'think aloud', to discuss and explore ideas with each other. Where talk is modelled well, it helps pupils to write – it gives them a voice into their writing.

Practical task

Consult your Key Stage 3 Scheme of Work and the National Curriculum. Where will discussion particularly aid in the development of understanding and why?

Highlight your copy or make a list.

There are many opportunities to use talk in science and discussing ideas does help pupils to develop their understanding of science. Discussion does, however, need to be organised.

Discussion can take the form of whole-class discussion, small-group discussion, talking in pairs or fours, etc.

Reflective task

How does the way talk is organised change across Years 7 to 9 to make sure pupils make progress?

How does the teaching make sure that pupils recall and use the scientific language they developed in their primary schools?

Pupil presentations

The ability to communicate ideas in a clear and interesting way is a great asset and is an opportunity for pupils to demonstrate their understanding of a topic/concept. For pupils to feel confident in presenting they need to know and understand their topic thoroughly but they also need to be well prepared in the presentation itself.

Figure 6.1 shows a checklist which is a good tool for pupils to use when they are preparing a presentation. Each task can be ticked off on completion.

Activity	Completed
What will be the basic outline or structure of the presentation?	
What information does the audience already know?	
What questions might be asked and what are the answers?	
Write a script or memory cards to help with what to say	
Who in the group will do which part of the presentation?	
Rehearsal of full presentation	
Prepare any slides and/or handouts	

Figure 6.1 Checklist for presentation.

Practical task

Devise a list of topics for the pupils to develop presentations. Divide the pupils into small groups and let them pick a topic 'from the hat' and then research and produce a presentation to be given to the class.

The presentation should last about 5 minutes.

The presentation the whole class considers to be the best could be presented at a year assembly.

Science and writing

Research shows that, on average, pupils spend about a third of their time writing in science lessons. It is important to ensure that what we ask pupils to write helps them to learn science. Writing supports learning in science when:

- The purpose is clear.
- Pupils are challenged to think and make decisions about their writing.
- The writing helps pupils to organise their thinking.
- Pupils are asked to write for a variety of purposes and audiences.
- The writing is well chosen and supports the objective of the lesson.

Reflective task

Think about how often you ask pupils to write in science at Key Stage 3. Think about the lessons for one Y7, Y8 or Y9 group over the last week.

1. What proportion of the time was devoted to writing?

2. Were all homework tasks written tasks?

3. What were the purposes of the writing?

Most of the time pupils' writing consists of reports of investigative work and notes about a particular topic. While this is important and a valuable means of developing knowledge and understanding it is by no means the only way in which pupils can explore, understand and write about their science.

Learning to write well is a long process that comes through teacher modelling, instruction, practice and feedback. Luckily the writing process can be used to improve science learning too. Below are a few writing suggestions that integrate science while helping pupils develop their informational writing skills.

Science journals

Science journals are a good place for pupils to develop informational writing skills. Daily journal prompts are one way to encourage pupils to write expansively about developing knowledge. One suggested topic could be *Trees*. This could be used as a broad theme for pupils to begin writing their journals. Figure 6.2 illustrates the prompts used by the teacher and some example entries from pupils.

Prompt	Journal entry
What do you think a tree is? How is it different from other plants?	*I think a tree is wood and leaves* *Trees are bigger than plants*
What do you think a tree is made of?	*Trees are made of wood and leaves*
What are the parts of a tree? Draw a tree	*Leaves and wood trunk* *(Later they add to this, e.g. roots)*
(After we find a tree to 'adopt') What is our tree like? What is special about our tree? How do you think our tree might change over time?	*Our tree is big* *It is special because it is ours!* *It has big leaves*
Why do you think trees are different shapes? Why do you think their leaves are different?	*Because the leaves catch the sun in different ways*
(After several weeks) How does our tree look different? How does it look the same?	*The trunk still looks the same* *It is getting leaves*
What different shapes of leaves did you find? How can we sort our leaves?	*I am putting the bigger ones together, then putting the spiky ones and then the skinny ones*
What can you tell me about a tree now? How do you think it is different from other plants?	*Trees are a kind of plant*

Figure 6.2 Science journal about trees.

In journals pupils make records of what they are doing in investigations – they organise data by creating tables and write observations based on their investigations. They record, via drawing and writing, characteristics of what they are observing. In using the journal in this way, pupils learn that making records of actual observations is something scientists often do and is a useful kind of nonfiction writing.

Beyond recording observations, pupils can use journals to write inferences based on their observations. For example, if pupils observe that woodlice prefer the damper side of a Petri dish, they could infer that the dampness is more like their natural environment – thus making meaning of their observations. Pupils will find that inferences made from early observations may change as they make more observations. This tentativeness in inferences is an intrinsic part of the nature of science, but by making the recordings in their journal pupils can track their ideas over time and note any observations that can lead to a change in inference.

Practical task

Develop a way of using journals in your lessons.

Show the pupils how journals can be useful and start the process off from the next lesson.

Run with it for a month and get feedback from the pupils about what they have written.

Observation vs inference charts

An observation vs inference chart is another tool that supports science learning while developing informational writing skills. This can also be used to introduce pupils to the difference between *observation* and *inference*. On a chart, one column is labelled 'Observation' and another 'Inference'. During a class discussion following an investigation, the teacher records the pupil observations in the Observation column and then asks the pupils to make inferences about what those observations mean in the Inferences column.

For example, after the pupils have had time to observe snails in detail, you may record their observations on the chart, e.g. 'the eyestalks move when I touch them'. In the inferences column the pupils are asked to infer the meaning behind the observation, e.g. 'They are trying to move out of my way – to keep them safe'.

After a few examples, the pupils will begin making good distinctions between observations and inferences and they can be given similar smaller charts for individual or small groups of pupils to record their observations and inferences about other investigations on their own.

Pupil-authored books

Pupil-authored books require pupils to gain simultaneous insights into a content area, research and literacy. They research and write their own book on a theme.

Project 1

So You Want to Be an Author is a project which can increase understanding in science for Key Stage 3 pupils, but also has the important objective to actively disseminate scientific knowledge to younger pupils and increase their interest in science.

The task is to work in groups of four or five and write a booklet on a randomly assigned science topic geared towards Year 6 pupils.

There will be a range of individual topics from which the booklet can be developed. These could include:

■ Electric circuits and electricity

■ Energy

■ Forces

■ Light

■ Magnetism

■ Sound

■ Temperature and heat

■ Circular motion

Once the groups are established each will be randomly assigned a topic for a five-page (ten sides) booklet. As a common feature so that the booklets form a set, each one could centre on a specific theme, character or concept. See Figure 6.3.

> *The Wonderful World of Science Adventures* of the science prodigy Maggie B and her inquisitive friend Tommy.

Figure 6.3 Sample book cover for the *So You Want to Be an Author* project.

It can be suggested that the pupils use an example for the real world to set the scene. For example, if the topic was circular motion it could be that Maggie and Tommy have been watching a merry-go-round and start to wonder about why it is going in a circle, why it might stop and what happens as the children on it jump off, etc.

So for each booklet the group must:

■ Explain the scenario

■ Define all the scientific language in easy to understand words

- Describe a simple demonstration
- Suggest a simple *Try it Yourself* activity that should include:
  - The objective of the investigation
  - The materials needed
  - The instructions
  - Explanation of the results/observation
- Include extension work
- Supply additional sources of information

The pupils should be encouraged to search for ideas and storylines, activities and projects from as many sources as possible – science books, literature, the Internet, newspapers, etc. They should be told not to copy text directly but to use their own words. Visits to museums and science activity centres could be helpful for the pupils' research.

Illustrations always improve the appearance of a book and can often help with explanations so the pupils should be encouraged to use drawings, diagrams, cartoons, etc. Everything should be in black and white, although the cover can be in colour – it makes copying easier.

The finished booklets can be displayed in the school and local public library, during open days and/or consultation events at the pupils' own school and the school of the younger pupils for whom the booklets are written. They can also be made available online through the schools' websites.

The benefits for participating students are:

- A deeper understanding of the science concepts presented in their topic
- A sense of accomplishment at seeing their work presented in a published form
- A sense of pride in strengthening school ties with local primary schools and the public library
- Opportunities for collaboration with other departments in the school
- Experiencing working to deadlines, delegating responsibility, using and developing their literacy skills to produce a publication for others.

Project 2

Another type of book that would be aimed at Key Stage 1 pupils but written by Key Stage 3 pupils is *The Science ABC Book*. Here the pupils have to create a booklet in the form of an alphabetical or counting book. Pupils will not only be practising writing and research content, they'll be learning how to gain information from nonfiction text and group it into categories. For example:

- The ABC of trees/fish/birds, etc.
- ABC for Tomorrow's World
- Counting the Animals in the Zoo

This can be a whole-class project or carried out in small groups. The pupils have to pick their own content area but the teacher assigns individual pupils a letter or number. Each pupil will research information related to that content and write an informational page related to their assigned letter or number with appropriate illustrations.

Benefits of writing activities

Incorporating various nonfiction writing activities such as those suggested above not only facilitates pupils' thinking about science content, but it also results in material/work that can help teachers assess pupil understanding.

For example, observation vs inference charts can be used to capture a picture of what the whole class understands about a given topic. If a pupil records an observation of an investigation exploring whether woodlice prefer light or dark environments as 'woodlice like the dark', the teacher will know that the pupil is confusing the observation with the inference. The teacher can then ask the pupil to describe how they know that woodlice 'like the dark'. When the pupil states that it is because woodlice tend to stay in the dark side of their environment the teacher can point out to the pupil that moving to the dark side is the observation and the inference is that they 'like the dark'.

Similarly, individual journal entries can be used to assess what individual pupils understand about a science content area. In work exploring electric circuits, pupils could be asked to respond to the prompt of 'How do you think electricity works?' several times throughout the work. Initially the pupil may respond with something like 'electricity is lightening', whereas later in the work the pupil may respond with something like 'electricity makes things work' and finally the pupil may respond with something like 'electricity works through a complete circle – a circuit'. Thus, the teacher can track the development of the pupil's idea over time, from less informed to more informed views.

> ## Practical task
>
> Write a short story about, for example, a walk through some woodland, noting the plants and animals seen. Make sure that there are species that would have relationships so that the pupils can then read the story and identify food chains and webs from the ecosystem you have described.
>
> Once they understand the process, the pupils can write similar stories for each other.

Science and drama

'Theatre' and 'theory' have a common etymological root in the ancient Greek verb *theorein* which means 'to see, to view, to behold'. The *theoria* in ancient Greece viewed dramas of everyday situations and extracted truth. This kind of knowing – attempting to draw universal generalisations based on specific observations – is also viewed as a key epistemological feature of scientific explanations. There is growing evidence that the use of drama in a carefully planned way, guided by reflective science teachers working with English specialists, may provide empowering learning environments for school pupils.

Forms of dramatic science in the classroom

Dramatic activity may vary and take many forms in the classroom. The drama may be structured in a way where pupils enact roles within the known framework of scientific theories:

- Playing electrons in a circuit to illustrate the scientific concept of electricity
- The dramatic activity may be impulsive, creating a moment, as it were; pupils have to improvise who they are and what to say.

Figure 6.4 illustrates a model of interaction regarding classroom drama. At any point along this continuum a drama can be more or less spontaneous. An intermediate form may be an improvised role play with a structural frame (e.g. role cards that describe the participating roles). Another continuous variable is the degree of teacher involvement: that is, whether it is the teacher that impels the drama or the pupils. A group of pupils who create their own model of a scientific concept are together reconstructing knowledge so as to enhance their conceptual understanding. In order to guide the pupils, it may sometimes be necessary for the teacher to provide scaffolds in complicated scientific matters. See Figure 6.4.

Dramas can also be categorised according to whether they are presentational or experiential. A *presentational drama* has a major emphasis on communicating something to others outside the drama, e.g. teachers, other pupils, parents. When a small group of pupils dramatise a scientific concept the intention is often communication with others. An *experiential drama* focuses on attempting to live through some aspect of an experience and adopting a motivation, opinion or attitude.

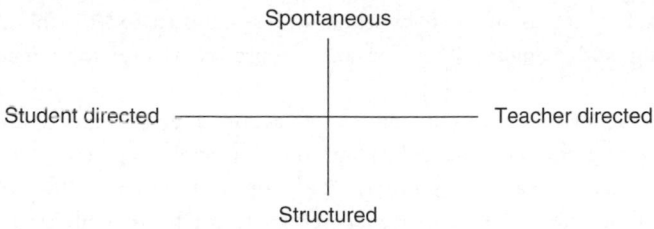

Figure 6.4 The forms of organisation in 'dramatic science' activities (source: Brown and Pleydell 1999).

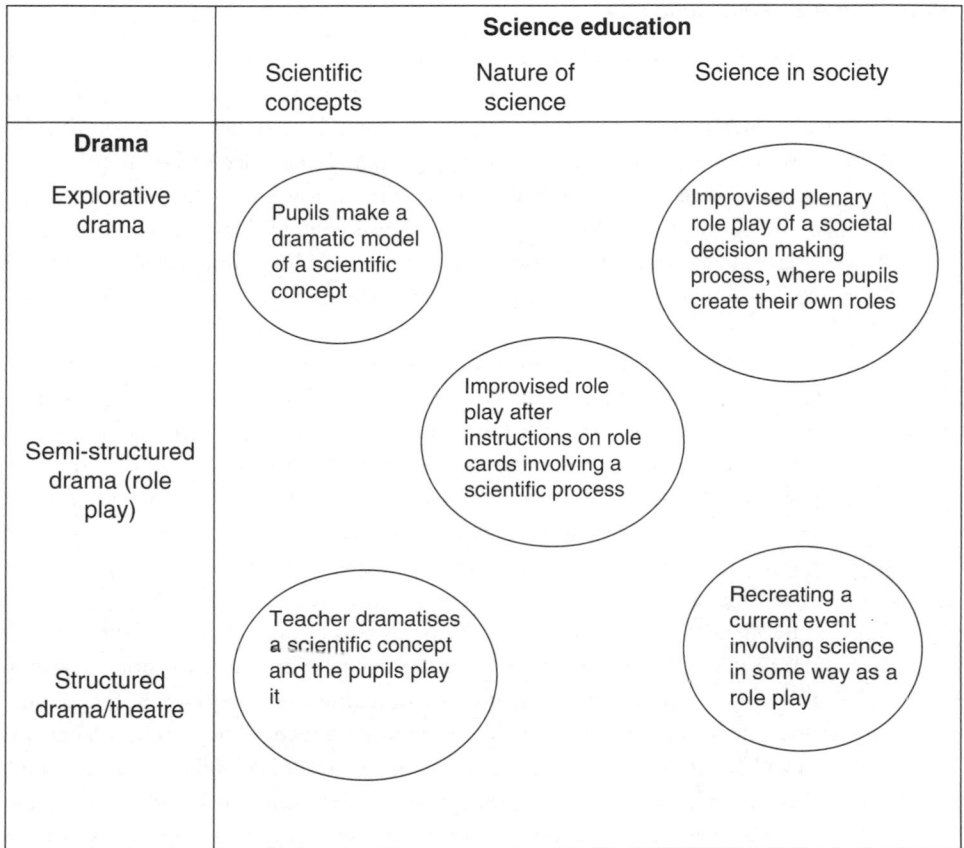

Figure 6.5 An overview of how drama may be used in science education (source: Ødegaard 2003).

Depending on which scientific issue is in focus, the teacher decides what the nature of the drama should be. In each case, however, the ideal is to optimise the pupils' degree of spontaneity and creativity, in order to encourage them to think critically and vividly about the issue in focus, and so offer possibilities for materialising their understanding. Instead of merely transmitting knowledge of science from a science textbook or from their teacher, it has to be re-worked and re-constructed by the pupils. The language (including body language) is used an interpretive system for persuading each other of their view.

The teacher's role can be an active agent directing the drama, or less active, as merely giving frames for a role play and observing passively. The invaluable role the science teacher plays is guiding the pupils in their reflection after the drama activity about how their experience relates to their own life and their relationship to science.

Figure 6.5 provides an overview of the ways in which drama can be integrated into science delivery.

Dramatising science concepts

School science has historically focused on learning scientific facts or on the products of science e.g. concepts, theories, laws, models. The dramatisation of this material can often be undertaken merely to enliven what might otherwise be a rather dull lesson, but it can, in the process, transform the teaching-learning process. The process of transferring the model or description from a text book to a three-dimensional live model requires pupils to reconceptualise their knowledge. Research identifies pupils' increased understanding and the teacher's increased ability to assess pupils' understanding immediately and informally in the course of using drama in science. For example:

1. Tvieta (1998) created a drama model of electricity that he used with pupils. This was an experiential drama structured by the teacher. The model gives pupils concrete and personal experience with the representation of voltage, current and resistance, and it helps pupils gain a better understanding of these basic concepts. The pupils play protagonists enacting electrons and batteries and their instructions on how to act and react are analogous with the protagonists' capabilities. The drama starts when the pupils enact an event, the electric current, which can be varied in different ways, according to the electrons' movement and the battery's capability. The different outcomes of these events are then discussed as consequences of the interactions of the protagonists and the context of the event. This last discussion, stepping out of role and reflecting on the different outcomes is important if the pupils are to understand the key aspects of the scientific concept. They use the language of the 'story' (electrons, current, circuit, resistance, etc.) to describe what happened and to describe what they think *might* happen in a hypothetical situation. If the pupils are able to participate in this discussion then they demonstrate to themselves and their teacher that they have understood the concept. This type of drama creates amusement, engagement and activity amongst the whole class.

2. Bailey and Watson (1998) produced a dramatic model of the complicated interplay in an ecosystem. This is an experiential and semi-structured drama. The rules of the activity are set, but the pupils will strongly influence the form and outcome. In this role play, pupils play the roles of different organisms in an ecosystem. The role of the sun provides energy in the form of a card, which is passed around the food web. When a role receives an energy card a mark is placed on it but it must be given away if someone higher in the food chain wants to eat it. By reading the

energy cards pupils can afterwards recap how energy flows through the ecosystem. During the role play the participants may stop and reflect on problems that occur, articulate them by using scientific expressions, try to solve problems aided by careful questioning by the teacher and reflect on how the activity relates to their view of nature. Even though the pupils are distanced from their roles (humans are not a part of the food web involved), once they have experienced a personal involvement in a living system, the affective domain has been brought into play and a sense of responsibility in environmental matters may well be established.

The process of designing and presenting a representation of their conception enables pupils to think about the concept in a way that is meaningful to them: they become 'owners' of the idea. During the process the teachers may gain insight into the pupils' understanding of concepts and support them, enabling instruction and assessment to occur simultaneously.

It might be argued that using creative drama to assess science places too great an emphasis on creativity, rather than scientific understanding. Yet creativity is indeed part of what is understood by science and ought to be both developed and assessed in the context of science education.

The process and nature of science

Scientific processes are centrally concerned with scientists' experimental and conceptual work both in the laboratory and elsewhere. Often the pupils' only experience of this is through pre-designed experiments which do not authentically reflect the scientific process. In particular, the important communication processes between scientists in which discussion and debate occurs is seldom mentioned. Given an insight into a set of science stories pupils will have the opportunity to understand that the nature of science is not the same as pre-designed experiments. Through stories of science and experiences in enacting scientists, pupils are offered more possibilities to gain insight into the reality of the process of scientific practice. Through stories science emerges as a human endeavour and pupils are offered an insight of the importance of creativity within the science process. For example:

1. *Role plays of an historical event either from the recent or distant past* – e.g. the Scopes 'monkey trial', the trial of Galileo, the 'great debate' following Darwin's publication. The pupils take the roles of historical characters, which show the range of ideas that were current at the time. They are introduced to the characters by a role card description, but the role playing they improvise and the fictitious context allows role play to have no defined ending. Thus this is a semi-structured drama activity, giving pupils a story as framework that acts as a scaffold while the pupils explore the historical science events. Science is portrayed as richly personal and pupils are encouraged to understand it as such by the empathy generated. In a partly improvised role play organised as a trail there is a lot of opportunity for students to engage in critical thinking. They scrutinise and challenge each other's roles and perspectives and in this way the historical science process generates empathic understanding.

2. *Pupils as scientists* – explorative drama where the pupils have significant freedom to affect the play, but where the teacher gently guides to keep the focus and tension. For example, a science-fiction drama where the pupils enact the roles of researchers from another planet that has just exploded: they wonder if they can possibly live on planet Earth. With an anthropological perspective the pupils study and describe the Earth. The pupils are free to create and fill their own expert/researcher roles. This offers several advantages as the pupils are challenged to explore science creatively. Because of the fictional setting the pupils can make real discoveries of known material, e.g. they discover the term 'blood-red' in some written material and have to make enquiries in order to verify as a scientific fact that 'earthling' blood is red. They also write a report on the findings to their Commander. Being aliens the pupils have a *need* to know. Drama strategies could readily be employed to make all this knowledge immediately *applied* knowledge and indeed to identify for the teacher the learning that has taken place.

Science as an institution in society

Classroom dramas are beneficial for focusing on the science in society dimension of science education. The real world is brought into the classroom in the context of practical action, e.g. an environmental conference. Divergent interests and ethical conflicts are essential to decision-making processes, as is also shown in all good plays and dramas. In role-play the conflicts, combined with the personal relations the pupils develop to the issue makes them able to act. Pupils explore situations that create empathy and identification: thus both thoughts and feelings are stimulated and give room for action. The cross-curricular potential in drama gives the opportunity for a style of learning that does not break down knowledge and skills into artificial units, but permits exploration of the world using whatever medium is appropriate. Pupils develop the ability to explore the world and through the practice of action-taking they potentially acquire competence to transform the world and create the future.

Another way of using theatre to put science in the context of society is exploring real events through dramatisation. Event-centred learning as an approach is an example of role play and drama in reconstructing authentic incidents. Events or circumstances for TV and newspaper reports, articles, books and popular accounts are investigated and given life again in the classroom. Occurrences are reconstructed by making, for example, an imaginary television documentary about a nuclear accident or establishing a commission of enquiry to investigate the risks, costs and benefits of constructing a nuclear power plant.

In the classroom

Very often pupils are enthusiastic about drama where teachers are not. Secondary school teachers in particular hardly ever use this instructional method in their science lessons. Over two decades ago Metcalfe *et al.* (1984) conducted an empirical investigation of the effectiveness of teaching science using drama. While there was no significant difference in factual recall between the experimental group and the control group, the experimental group pupils' ability to offer explanation and interpretation of concepts was significantly better. It was concluded that drama could help pupils to develop important insights regarding scientific concepts and promote meaningful learning.

Practical task

Examine the science curriculum at Key Stage 3 and highlight those topics that can be developed into dramas/role plays.

Work with the English department to develop one into something the pupils can perform.

Practical task

Gene Ghosts – an example of drama in science

In this activity, some pupils are challenged to look at their own understanding of biotechnology, compare it with a study of public opinion and develop it into a play. They are also challenged to use a pantomime story as a framework. What would some of the classic role figures have thought of modern technology? What do the pupils, young people of today think and why? How much do they actually know about biotechnology and what about it is relevant for them?

To begin the pupils must carry out some research:

* What do the pupils understand by 'modern biotechnology'?
* What do members of the public/their families understand by 'modern technology'?

The pupils will need to have decided which pantomime story and characters they are going to use so that they can develop appropriate dialogue based on the character but also on their research findings. For example, if they have decided on ten characters and they find in their survey that around 30% of people have negative views about biotechnology, then three of the characters could reflect this. They might decide that one has little education and unfounded opinions, one is educated but mistrusts scientists and the third is educated but has serious ethical concerns about biotechnology. The aim is to find pantomime characters to fit each character and to use these role figures as a cast of characters for developing their play.

Outcomes

In this activity the pupils have to find out more about biotechnology, develop a survey and analyse the findings, look at some well-known pantomime characters in a different way. They are forced to look at the science and the drama in a different way.

In the final play there will be evidence of the pupils' own thoughts, public opinion and completely different approach for pantomime.

The importance of integrating science and English

Pupils' experiences help them construct meaning from the facts, concepts and ideas shared in children's literature. Narrative text can enhance pupils' construction of scientific concepts:

> Science is also an ever-changing narrative as more facts and information emerge as a result of inquiry. Science as a narrative enables children to explain and interpret their experiences and clarify their own ideas within an authentic and familiar language form.
>
> (Scott 1993: 43)

In addition, writing enhances the learning of science concepts:

> Whether supporting content learning, guiding teacher instruction or furthering the development of students' literacy or science process skills – or all of the above – nonfiction writing opportunities are an essential aspect of science learning from which teachers and students benefit in many ways.
>
> (Akerson and Young 2005: 41)

Science and poetry

Robin Freedman (1999) believes 'Poems become conceptual pictures of different scientific concepts' and Calkins and Parsons (2003) suggest the strategy of encouraging pupils to try 'looking through a poet's eyes' to help them understand that poetry is a figurative language. For example, instead of saying 'The ceiling is at the top of our classroom', Calkins would teach pupils to say 'The ceiling is the sky of our classroom'. Thus the pupils begin to differentiate between *scientist's eyes* and *poet's eyes* when describing a habitat. By doing this, pupils were able to describe and illustrate a habitat using a scientist's eyes or a literal description of the habitat and organism.

Suggested approach for two lessons:

Lesson 1

1. Expose the pupils to the characteristics of a particular habitat, e.g. the seashore, by reading a book that describes all the animals in that habitat – how they live, what they eat, how they move, etc. Include in the discussion how they interact with each other and the environment. They may not be animals that the pupils have firsthand experience of but pictures and descriptions will help.

2. Ask questions such as 'What do all animals need to survive?' Pupil answers show their understanding of the idea that animals need air, water and food to survive in an environment.

3. Pupils make precise choices for their habitats and discuss the choices with other pupils.

4. Pupils apply their knowledge of an organism's needs by creating a habitat for a specific organism from the seashore habitat.

5. Next pupils use a range of sources to research information about habitats and their organisms.

6. Pupil habitats include other species that could survive in that habitat as well.

7. Finally, they draw their habitats on a poster.

Lesson 2

1. The lesson begins with the teacher's question 'What do you need to survive in your habitat?'

2. Pupils write their responses on Post-it notes.

3. Following their individual responses, the whole class then discusses the idea of a home or shelter, water and food as necessities for organisms.

4. The teacher's question 'Could a polar bear survive in your habitat?' should promote a discussion about how the needs of animals must be met for them to survive.

5. The pupils are asked to write a short poem looking through a poet's eyes about the organism they researched in lesson 1. The poem should describe the habitat and include how the organism's needs are met.

6. The pupils can also illustrate their poems.

Extension work

Imagine you are a zookeeper and you are being sent an animal for your zoo. Illustrate and/or describe what you would need to create a habitat that will allow your animal to survive. Explain why you made those choices.

This science and literacy experience provides an effective method for motivating pupils while they learn more about organisms. Throughout the lesson sequence, the pupils are engaged and are encouraged to share what they are learning with their peers. The posters and poetry created shows that the integration of English with science can enhance both subject areas.

Reflective task

Having carried out the poetry activity, assess its success from both a teacher's and pupil's point of view.

Examine the science curriculum and identify other topics that could be approached in the same way.

Teaching writing in science

Writing is a process that helps learners to think deeply about ideas and information they encounter through reading, listening, viewing and physically experiencing the world around them. Peterson explains:

[W]riting helps students make sense of the rolling, backtracking highway of thoughts running through their heads. The written words, sentences and paragraphs give thoughts some shape and form ... the very act of searching for words and then rubbing them up against each other creates space for new understandings to emerge.

(Peterson 2005: 3)

There are some parts of the science curriculum that can be unmotivating to pupils and just writing up investigations about these topics does not help develop pupil interest. By asking pupils to communicate what they have learned in their practical work in whatever genre they choose can help with motivation. They should be expected to demonstrate their understanding of the concepts within the genre they have chosen.

Practical task

Lesson about levers and pulleys:

1. To begin with introduce the pupils to the concepts through a vocabulary activity where the pupils try to define the word themselves, the class discuss all the individual definitions and then they add the accepted definition.

Word	What I think it means	What we think it means	Definition
Lever			
Fulcrum			
Load			
Effort			
Pulley			

2. This is followed by practical work demonstrating different types of levers and building a pulley system. These activities will help the pupils to develop understandings that they will draw on in their writing.
3. Next is the writing assignment. The scenario they are given is from the science fiction genre and involves a character trying to retrieve an object, e.g. a ball, from a forbidden alien city using a system of levers and pulleys to fit on a robot. A class discussion before the pupils start the assignment should cover how they are going to incorporate the science concepts into the story and some guidance from the teacher

about what s/he expects in the writing. The pupils then plan, gather information (through reading and practical investigation related to the topic) and then draft their writing. The teacher can check a first draft for the science concepts but a second draft should be read by a partner for additional feedback and editing. This can be done in small groups or as individuals.

The genre does not have to be science fiction. It can be historical, thriller, graphic novel, etc., whatever the pupils feel comfortable with.

Science opens up a universe of topics for pupils to write about. At the same time writing helps pupils to deepen their understanding and to connect science to their everyday lives, while making science more interesting.

Recommendations

- English and science teachers could co-plan and/or co-teach areas where writing projects come from science content. The content area classes could be used to help pupils gather information for their writing. A writer's workshop lesson could be used for the actual writing and writing instruction and sharing of the writing in small groups, with a partner or with the whole class.

- Elements of writing, such as developing characters in fiction writing, supporting the main point with examples and details in non-narrative writing, or making decisions about line breaks in poetry writing could be the focus of mini-lessons. Sessions could also address writing decisions such as how to determine the type of information that will be important and how to record the information so that it can be used in their writing.

- English and science teachers could collaboratively assess the writing. Figure 6.6 provides a possible model for assessment.

Whether supporting content learning, guiding teacher instruction or furthering the development of pupils' literacy or science process skills – or all of the above – nonfiction writing opportunities are an essential aspect of science learning from which teachers and pupils benefit in many ways.

Case Study 6.1: Key Stage 3 Cross-curricular project – Science Gets Fruity

Science is explored through music and physical theatre. The science of sound is brought to life by a series of cross-curricular workshops at St Saviour's and St Olave's School. Pupils are inspired by visits from a physicist, a botanist and a musician, who help them combine science and engineering. The cross-curricular day for Year 7 begins with an exploration of the physics of sound through drama. Next up the students get the chance to make music with a range of unfamiliar percussion instruments. Finally they focus on the science of plants in which they are set the challenge of making their own musical instruments out of fruit and vegetables.

See http://www.tes.co.uk/teaching-resource/KS3-Cross-Curricular-Science-Gets-Fruity-6045540/ for video footage.

Assessment criteria	Marks (out of ...)
Content:	
1. All concepts explained	
2. All concepts accurately explained	
3. A new way of looking at the concept is created that demonstrated a clear, thoughtful context	
4. The writing is easy to understand, is creative/engaging and is supported by specific details	
5. Demonstrates connections between the concepts throughout	
6. Focus is clear throughout	
7. Range of sources of information used	
Organisation:	
1. What the writer is trying to achieve is clearly identified particularly at the beginning and the end	
2. Communication throughout is effective and illustrates the genre	
Style:	
1. Uses language appropriate for the audience and genre	
2. Use of expressions and specific words together with a range of sentence types, etc	
3. The writer's voice can be clearly identified by the reader	
Conventions:	
1. Correct spelling, punctuation and grammar used effectively and consistently	
TOTAL	

Figure 6.6 Assessment proforma.

Other resources that could be useful

- *Copy Write* (www.copywrite.org.uk/)

  This website includes six lessons which introduce pupils to what it means to work in the creative writing industry. The pupils can investigate how they could copy write their science stories, poems, dramas, etc.

- *Read me* (www.readmeresources.co.uk/)

  This is a set of resources for Key Stage 3 pupils which have been designed to excite them about reading in and out of the classroom. Of particular interest for science are the lessons around writing poems, blogging, film and graphic novels, all of which can have an underpinning in science.

Professional standards for QTS

This chapter will help meet the following standards:

Q6	Have a commitment to collaboration and co-operative working
Q7	(a) Reflect on and improve their practice, and take responsibility for identifying and meeting their developing professional needs
Q8	Have a creative and constructively critical approach towards innovation, being prepared to adapt their practice where benefits and improvements are identified
Q10	Have a knowledge and understanding of a range of teaching, learning and behaviour management strategies and know how to use and adapt them, including how to personalise learning and provide opportunities for all learners to achieve their potential
Q14	Have a secure knowledge and understanding of their subject/curriculum areas and related pedagogy to enable them to teach effectively across the age and ability range for which they are trained
Q17	Know how to use skills in literacy, numeracy and ICT to support their teaching and wider professional activities
Q23	Design opportunities for learners to develop their literacy, numeracy and ICT skills
Q24	Plan homework or other out-of-class work to sustain learners' progress and to extend and consolidate their learning
Q32	Work as a team member and identify opportunities for working with colleagues, sharing the development of effective practice with them
Q33	Ensure that colleagues working with them are appropriately involved in supporting learning and understand the roles they are expected to fulfil

Professional standards for teachers

This chapter will help meet the following standards:

C6	Have a commitment to collaboration and co-operative working where appropriate
C8	Have a creative and constructively critical approach towards innovation, being prepared to adapt their practice where benefits and improvements are identified
C15	Have a secure knowledge and understanding of their subject/curriculum areas and related pedagogy including: the contribution that their subjects/curriculum areas can make to cross-curricular learning; and recent relevant developments
C17	Know how to use skills in literacy, numeracy and ICT to support their teaching and wider professional activities
C27	Design opportunities for learners to develop their literacy, numeracy and ICT and thinking and learning skills appropriate within their phase and context
C40	Work as a team member and identify opportunities for working with colleagues, managing their work where appropriate and sharing the development of effective practice with them

Pupils' Personal, Learning and Thinking Skills (PLTS)

This chapter will help meet the following skills:

Independent enquirers	• Identify questions to answer and problems to resolve
Creative thinkers	• Generate ideas and explore possibilities • Connect their own and others' ideas and experiences in inventive ways
Reflective learners	• Evaluate experiences and learning to inform future progress • Communicate their learning in relevant ways for different audiences
Team workers	• Collaborate with others to work towards common goals • Take responsibility, showing confidence in themselves and their contribution
Self-managers	• Work towards goals, showing initiative, commitment and perseverance • Organise time and resources, prioritising actions
Effective participators	• Identify improvements that would benefit others as well as themselves

Science and the humanities

Key objectives

By the end of this chapter, you will be able to:

■ Make links between your own science teaching and that undertaken within the humanities

■ Consider the place of the humanities within the science classroom

■ Use the work undertaken as part of the *Double Crossed* project to explore cross-curricular science and humanities activities

■ Reflect on various case studies of others' practices in these areas and draw lessons for your own professional development

Introduction

As has been seen throughout the course of this book so far, cross-curricular teaching and learning can be an approach that not only looks to amalgamate subjects together for the sake of greater understanding of each individual subject, but also to make meaningful connections between subjects based on disciplinary similarities. This involves a deeper understanding of each subject's specific characteristics and from the teacher's point of view, this can entail an in-depth dissection of his or her own teaching based on experience, the knowledge of one's own subject, the work undertaken by colleagues and, of course, the content prescribed by the National Curriculum. By fully understanding one's own subject specialism a greater understanding of that subject's fundamental characteristics can be reached and in turn, the potential links with other subjects can become apparent and common ground can be found. As seen in the first chapter of this book, one such way to begin this process is to complete a reflective subject audit. This chapter builds on this concept with examples of reflective audits undertaken by both science and history teachers. These examples highlight the process by which teachers, who initially describe themselves as 'opposite' in their teaching, found shared understanding.

As part of this chapter we will look in detail at the *Double Crossed* project run within the South Yorkshire region and funded by the Astra Zeneca Science Teaching Trust (AZSTT). This project sought to combine science and history to produce engaging cross-curricular classroom activities. By focusing on the *Double Crossed* project this chapter aims to:

- Introduce the rationale behind cross-curricular science/history teaching
- Explore the ways in which you can develop your own science/history classroom activity
- Improve your confidence in tackling cross-curricular teaching.

Science and history: the *Double Crossed* project

The Centre for Science Education (CSE) at Sheffield Hallam University was funded by the Astra Zeneca Science Teaching Trust to work in close collaboration with science and history teachers from two South Yorkshire secondary schools on the cross-curricular transition project, *Double Crossed*. The overall aim of the project was to explore an alternative view of Key Stage 2/3 transition within the context of cross-curricular learning in science and history. Particular focus was paid to the development of Year 7 personal, interpersonal and leadership skills, the use of historical methodology to promote thinking and reasoning skills and the use of stimulating contexts to excite young people about science. The project successfully demonstrated the benefits of cross-curricular working across science and history, but, furthermore, the creative science–history collaboration between two sets of teachers was central to this success.

> ## Reflective task
>
> Consider your own teaching in Year 7 and list the issues that you feel often arise with pupils who have just arrived from primary school.
>
> How do you normally address these issues? Are you successful? Could you do this differently?

The National Advisory Committee on Creative and Cultural Education (NACCCE) Report on Creativity (1999) encouraged all schools to relish creativity regardless of subject matter or perceived restrictions in the National Curriculum:

> Creativity is possible in all areas of human activity, including the arts, sciences, at work at play and in all other areas of daily life. All people have creative abilities and we all have them differently. When individuals find their creative strengths, it can have an enormous impact on self-esteem and on overall achievement.
>
> (NACCCE 1999: 6)

This has led to an increased acknowledgement that creativity is a fundamental aspect of learning, and the secondary curriculum attempts to provide teachers with more freedom to respond creatively to the learning needs of pupils. One such way to achieve this is through the exploration of cross-curricular dimensions.

The *Double Crossed* project aimed to smooth the transition between the Year 6 and Year 7 experiences of science by providing an innovative framework that draws upon the use of both historical contexts and the teaching and learning approaches used in history – namely the questioning of evidence and the development of sound arguments. By drawing on historical methodology, this project aimed to support science teachers to focus on the development of arguments, the questioning of evidence and the application of thinking and reasoning skills. The end result has been the development and production of two dynamic science/history resources which can be used with both Year 6 and Year 7 pupils. Each of the *Double Crossed* classroom resources aim to develop the self-confidence and personal skills of pupils by enabling them to work collaboratively on cross-curricular puzzles and challenges. The *Double Crossed* project aimed to bring together science and history to enable pupils to become conversant with techniques and processes vital to the study of science through topic based, contextualised learning. Furthermore, building upon the research of Osborne *et al.* (2004) on 'enhancing the quality of argument in science lessons' *Double Crossed* looked to secure an increased capacity for creative and independent inquiry within the school science environment.

Why history?

Historical contexts can often be used to promote a more rounded understanding of science. If applied correctly, history provides science with a context, an indispensable ingredient for the understanding of the nature of science. Furthermore, consideration of historical context is imperative to the realisation of how scientific concepts change and, in some cases, for understanding fully those concepts themselves. As we also know, history often serves as an opportunity to introduce the social and ethical issues in science, to nurture reasoning or to commemorate scientific innovation.

Practical task

Use a simple table (see below) and include all the science topics you teach at Key Stage 3 with a possible history link:

Science topic	History link

Delivering scientific topics through cross-curricular scientific–historical contexts encourages opportunities for imaginative and challenging exploration at Key Stage 3. Historical methodology can provide an extra depth through which the nature and progress of science can be explored and serves as an opportunity to introduce the social and ethical issues in science, to nurture reasoning and encourage creativity in both pupils and teachers. The focus in historical methodology on the development of arguments, the questioning of evidence and the application of thinking and reasoning skills can enrich both teaching and learning in science. The combination of history and science has proved a hugely valuable tool through which pupils can become conversant with techniques and processes vital to the study of science through topic based, contextualised learning. Figure 7.1 illustrates the science/history model.

This cross-curricular thematic classroom approach complements current government and OFSTED guidance encouraging schools to cover more than one subject at a time where possible. It links with the Key Stage 3 curriculum which outlines the need for cross-curricular dimensions and increased focus on pupils' personal skills and allows greater creativity from teachers. The Personal, Learning and Thinking Skills (PLTS) framework outlines the need for personal skills and capabilities to underpin the way learners work and

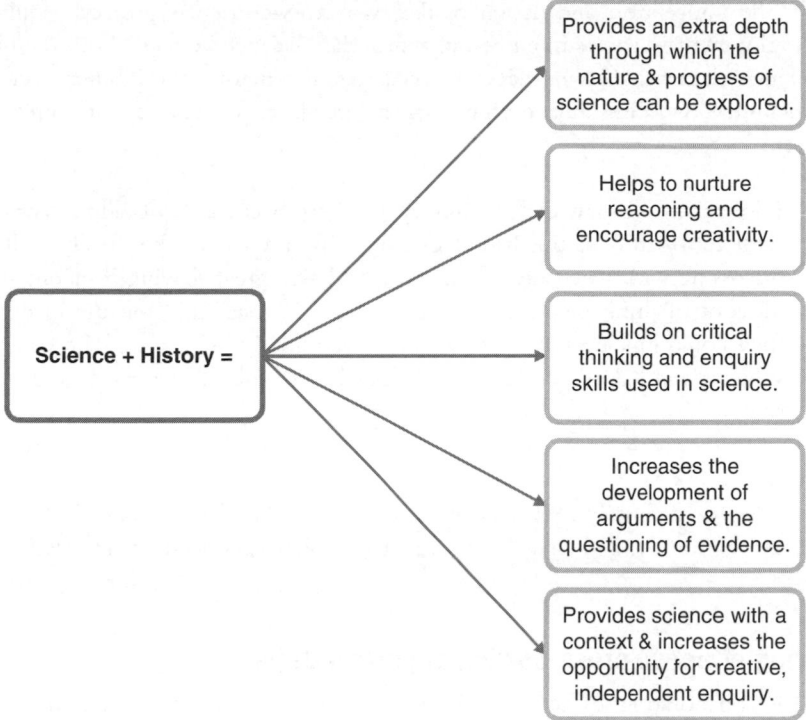

Figure 7.1 Science + history.

learn across curriculum. These skills are an integral part of all the contexts in which learning takes place in schools and are vital to the enhancement of the curriculum.

Practical task

Using a blank version of the diagram in Figure 7.1 choose a topic from your earlier table and complete the diagram with specific examples for teaching and learning. Include PLTS where appropriate.

Cross-curricular teaching partnerships

One of the key achievements of the *Double Crossed* project was the successful formation of cross-departmental science–history teacher partnerships. One partnership was formed at each of the two participating South Yorkshire schools. Throughout the project teachers received professional development inputs and a strong focus was placed on providing them with time and space away from school pressures where they could collaborate creatively on the development of their science–history activity.

The conception and design of the two cross-curricular projects required a creative developmental process to ensure an appropriate balance between both the history and the science elements. Having never worked together before, the teachers were thrown into unfamiliar working relationships which, in time, developed into proficient creative partnerships:

> I loved working with [the history teacher] because I wouldn't have ever worked with him before if this hadn't of come up and we worked really well together and discussing with [the other science teacher] was great, having someone else to bounce ideas off. I think before I'd never considered what skills you use in history and how they could link up with science and we definitely use a lot of the same skills in both subjects and I don't think even the kids had realised that they do use so many similar skills.
>
> (Science partnership teacher)

> This has definitely been a creative partnership. We have bounced ideas off each other throughout ... and have had to react to problems and issues creatively!
>
> (History partnership teacher)

Achieving effective cross-curricular partnerships

The collaboration of teachers from different departments can be initially challenging with teachers often feeling some degree of anxiety about working with seemingly divergent departments. This was the case with the teachers involved in the *Double Crossed* project:

> When we first signed up to take part I'll be honest, I was a bit anxious because I've never worked with the science department before – I've never needed to – and science is definitely well out of my comfort zone.
>
> (History partnership teacher)

These anxieties were, however, to be short lived. During training workshops the *Double Crossed* teachers were taken through a number of exercises to enable them to gain a better understanding of both the explicit and implicit parallels between history and science. The results were met with initial surprise as substantially more similarities than differences emerged (see Figure 7.2).

By working through these tasks together the teachers began to establish confident and effective working partnerships through the development of mutual understanding and shared goals. Furthermore, while the cross-departmental working was agreed to be at times challenging, feedback from all of the participating teachers indicated that a challenge such as this was integral to their professional development needs.

> Working with [the science teacher] has been great because it has challenged me – which I think all teachers need from time to time.
>
> (History partnership teacher)

Similarities	Differences
Use of hypothesis Investigation Data collection Analysis Manipulation of data Classification Evaluation Concluding to substantiate Validity Critically looking at evidence Use of empirical data	Specific topic areas Methods of collection Nature of evidence Use of experiments

Figure 7.2 Similarities and differences.

Reflective task

To start exploring cross-curricular teaching you first need to think about the subjects themselves. What do you see as the similarities and differences between the teaching and learning of science and of history? Or perhaps you are thinking of combining science with geography, or a different subject?

Complete the table below with reference to your chosen subject areas. Think about the skills, techniques, outcomes and approaches you use in your department and those used in the other subject area.

Similarities	Differences

Do any of your answers surprise you? Has this task highlighted any unexpected similarities that may allow you to exploit new cross-curricular opportunities?

Cross-departmental working partnerships can often be the key to getting the most out of cross-curricular teaching and learning. Once initial anxieties are alleviated teachers can be empowered to work together to establish projects outside of their familiar curriculum boundaries.

Practical task

To get the most out of your cross-curricular teaching you may wish to make links with another teacher within a different department at your school. Creating a cross-departmental partnership will strengthen your activity and will be a new and exciting challenge for you to undertake outside of your own department.

To get started you will need to ensure you have a member of staff in your chosen department who is willing and able to help you with your activity. Time is precious in school and we are well aware that finding a spare minute in school to sit down with a member of staff from a different department can be difficult. However, it is important that you work across the two departments to establish a new working relationship you may not have considered before. Try to make time for this as working with a member of staff from a different department is a great way to build confidence and show professional progression.

It can also be helpful (if the timetable permits) to sit in a lesson that each is teaching. It can help get a feel for subject-based teaching and learning approaches and personal teaching style.

If you have real problems finding a member of staff within a different department able to support your work it is possible to explore a cross-curricular project alone, however collaboration with a different teacher may provide more professional gratification.

Collaborative reflective task

Once you have formed your cross-departmental partnership it is worth taking five minutes together to work together on the 'similarities and differences' task (see page 152). Work together and once again consider the skills, techniques, outcomes and approaches you both use in your respective departments.

Similarities	Differences

The *Double Crossed* Resources

Each of the *Double Crossed* teacher partnerships was challenged to devise an innovative cross-curricular activity that drew on both a historical context and solid scientific teaching approaches. It was important to the project that the teachers did not produce an activity that could fall into the category 'the history of science' because this was not the purpose of the overall project. Instead the classroom activities needed to explore scientific concepts through thematic/topic based historical teaching. To get underway the teachers first needed to identify the topics that they wished to tackle. Once this initial brainstorming was complete the activities began to take shape. The first activity focused on the Ancient Egyptians, using forensic science techniques and knowledge about the human body to investigate the death of an Egyptian king. The second activity looked into the persecution of a fictitious family during the Second World War with chemical properties playing a vital role.

The two *Double Crossed* resources can be used by both Year 6 and Year 7 pupils. The project may easily be led by a science teacher, although collaboration with a history teacher would perhaps provide more professional gratification.

Double Crossed Resource one

In 'Time Raiders: Death of the Mummy' pupils take on the role of archaeologists working in small groups to examine and excavate the mummy of an Egyptian king. The aim of the excavation is to learn as much as possible about the subject and to interpret all available evidence from the tomb to determine the cause of death. Who was it? How did they live? How did they die?

Figure 7.3 Time Raiders: Death of the Mummy project introduction.

Depending on the age group involved, pupils should aim to work in teams of three or four. The context is set with an opening description – perhaps a piece of spooky music to set the scene.

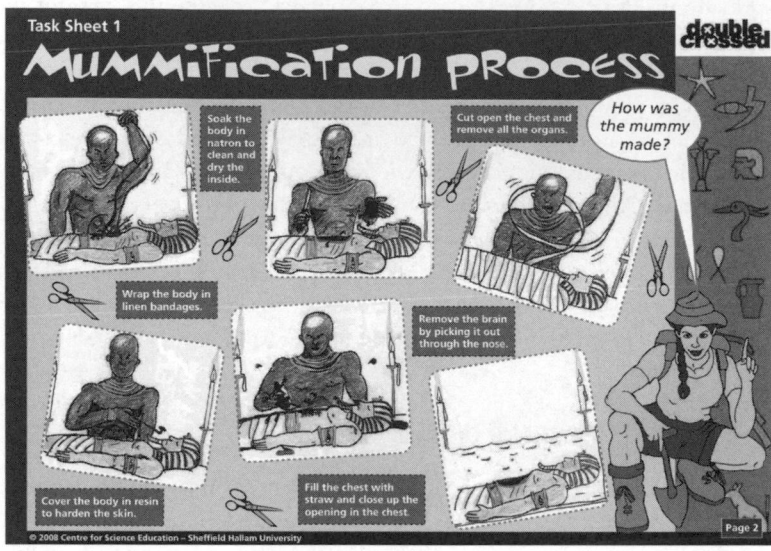

Figure 7.4 Time Raiders: Death of the Mummy task sheet 1.

The first activity asks the pupils to rearrange the pictures in Figure 7.4 to decipher the correct order of the mummification process.

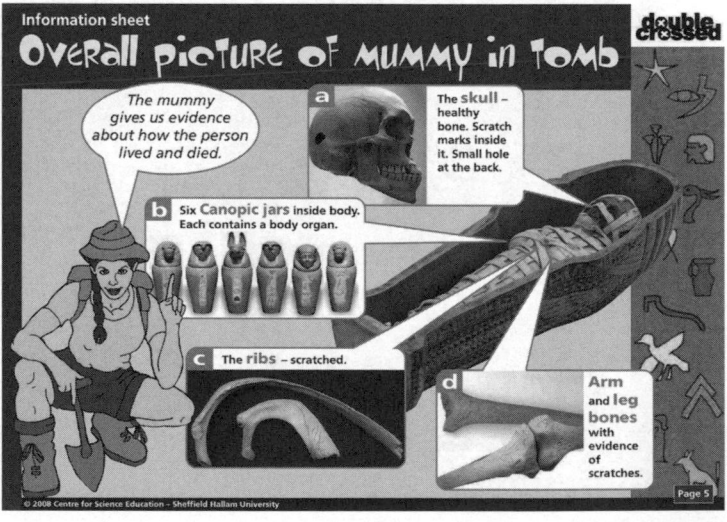

Figure 7.5 Time Raiders: Death of the Mummy information sheet.

An information sheet (Figure 7.5) highlights the medical problems and injuries found on the skeleton of the Ancient Egyptian King. This information sheet should be used as a basis for a group or whole-class discussion about the evidence shown. Possible scenarios for the marks on the skeleton and the contents of the six canopic jars should be discussed. This should be linked back to the mummification process.

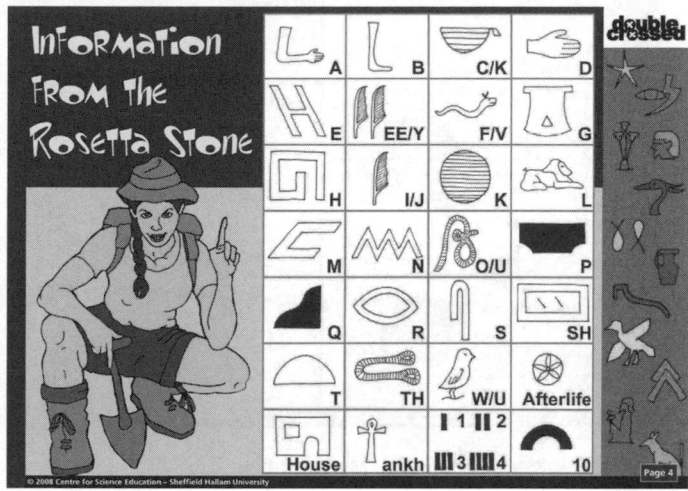

Figure 7.6 Time Raiders: Death of the Mummy information about the Rosetta Stone.

A Rosetta Stone is then provided so that the pupils can translate hieroglyphics (Figure 7.6).

Figure 7.7 Time Raiders: Death of the Mummy task sheet 3.

Using the Rosetta Stone the pupils must translate the writing on the front of six canopic jars. Each one contains a human organ belonging to the Egyptian King (Figure 7.7).

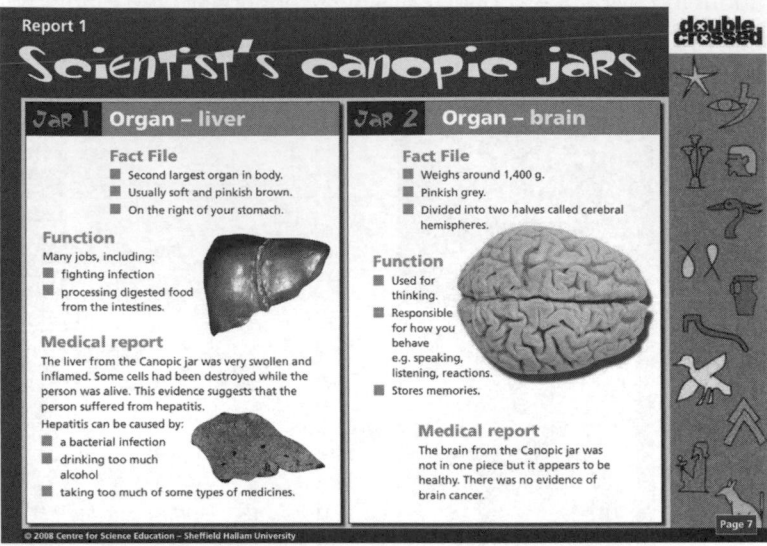

Figure 7.8 Time Raiders: Death of the Mummy report 1.

Once the pupils have translated the jars they are the given fact sheets referring to the six organs (Figure 7.8). Each one includes important information about the health of the King alongside factual, scientific information about the organ in question.

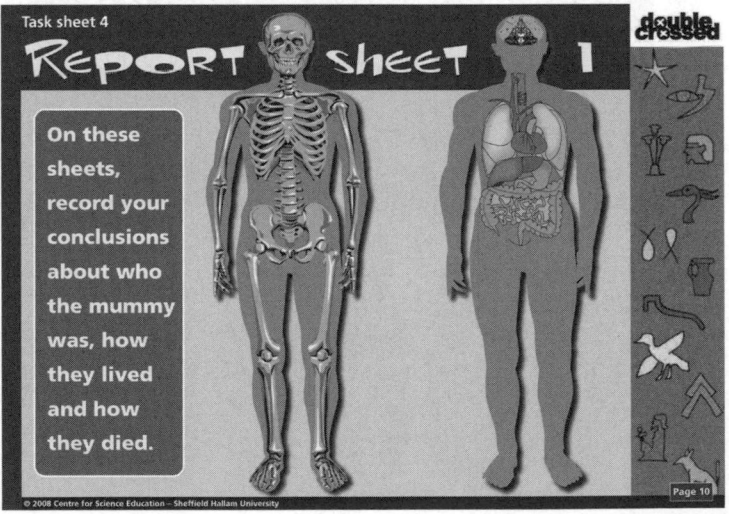

Figure 7.9 Time Raiders: Death of the Mummy task sheet 4.

Pupils are asked to gather together all of the information gathered and record their conclusions on the image of a body (Figure 7.9). They are asked to label the relevant organs and describe the symptoms the King may have been suffering from in relation to each organ.

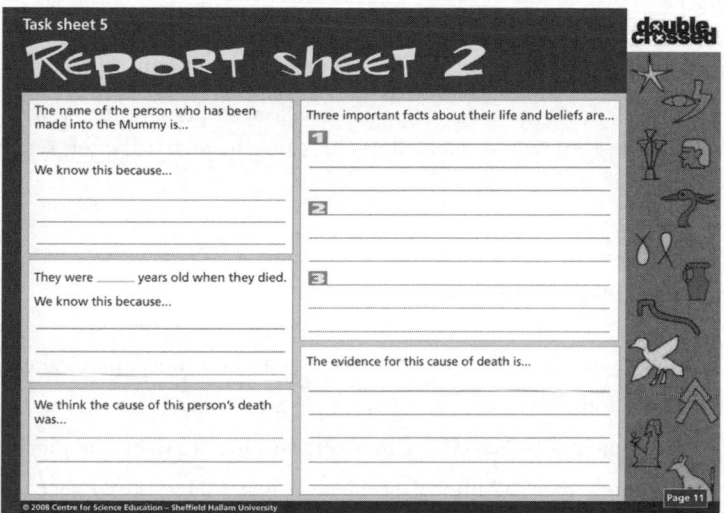

Figure 7.10 Time Raiders: Death of the Mummy report 2.

Pupils are also asked to describe their conclusions in detail on the report proforma (Figure 7.10). They are encouraged to discuss the range and types of evidence they have used. What science-based evidence and what historical evidence is available? Which evidence has most value and why? What questions are useful to ask when interpreting evidence?

Historical note

Egyptians only used three, sometimes four canopic jars which contained the stomach, intestines, lungs and liver. (For the benefit of these activities the number of jars was increased to six to provide heart, brain and kidneys. Although historically inaccurate this provides more options in the deduction process.)

Egyptian hieroglyphs are phonetic. Pupils need to know that they represent the sounds and not the spelling of the word. Occasionally hieroglyphs contain a picture of the object they were commenting on rather than a phonetic representation, e.g. a drawing of a house to represent a house.

This is only part of the 'Time Raiders' activity, to download the full resource please visit the Astra Zeneca Science Teaching Trust website at www.azteachscience.co.uk

By undertaking this cross-curricular activity the pupils are asked to think creatively when interpreting scientific and historical evidence. Working in small groups the pupils develop team working, communication and interpersonal skills culminating in the putting together of a report and presenting their findings to the rest of the class at the end of the activity. The activity also involves investigative skills and links directly to science, the human body and history.

Impact on science and history understanding and knowledge

The 'Time Raiders' activity helps to develop understanding and knowledge in both science and history while expanding the skills needed to interpret evidence and draw conclusions.

Success criteria

To be successful the pupils will:

- Compare evidence from different sources and consider their value
- Ask questions in relation to evidence such as 'Why?', 'How?' and 'What if?'
- Reach conclusions based on consideration of more than one piece of evidence
- Understand that additional evidence may have an effect on the conclusion reached.

Curriculum Links

The 'Time Raiders' activity is linked directly to both the Key Stage 2 and 3 science curriculums.

Key Stage 2 Science National Curriculum

Breadth of study statement

2a – Use appropriate scientific language ... to communicate ideas and explain the behaviour of living things, materials, phenomena and processes.

Sc1 Scientific enquiry

Ideas and evidence in science

1a – That science is about thinking creatively to explain how living and non-living things work and to establish links between causes and effects.

Investigative skills – considering evidence and evaluating

2i – Make comparisons and identify simple patterns or associations in their own observations and measurements or other data.

2j – Use observations, evidence or other data to draw conclusions.

2l – Use their scientific knowledge and understanding to explain observations, measurements or other data or conclusions.

2m – Review their work and the work of others and describe its significance and limitations.

Sc2 Live processes and living things

Humans and other animals

2b – About the need for food for activity and growth and about the importance of an adequate and varied diet for health.

2c – That the heart acts as a pump to circulate blood to vessels around the body including through the lungs.

2e – That humans and other animals have skeletons and muscles to support and protect their bodies and to help them move.

2g – About the effects on the human body of tobacco, alcohol and other drugs and how these relate to their personal health.

Key Stage 3 Science National Curriculum

Key concepts

1.4 – Collaboration

a – Sharing developments and common understanding across disciplines and boundaries.

Key processes

2.2 – Critical understanding of evidence

a – Obtain, record and analyse data from a wide range of primary and secondary sources, including ICT sources, and use their findings to provide evidence for scientific explanations.

2.3 – Communication

a – Use appropriate methods, including ICT, to communicate scientific information and contribute to presentations and discussions about scientific issues.

Range and content

3.3 – Organisms, behaviour and health

a – Life processes are supported by the organisation of cells into tissues, organs and body systems.

c – Conception, growth, development, behaviour and health can be affected by diet, drugs and disease.

Take a look at Case Study 7.1 to see how the teachers designed, developed and trialled the 'Time Raiders' activity.

The following Case Study explores the way in which the teachers at Brinsworth Comprehensive School worked together to create the 'Time Raiders' activity.

Case Study 7.1: Brinsworth Comprehensive School, Rotherham – Designing 'Time Raiders: Death of the Mummy'

The school

Brinsworth Comprehensive School is a mixed, 11–18 community school in Rotherham, South Yorkshire, with specialist Science College status. The school is hugely committed to its own development and improvement and has high expectations for its pupils.

The project

The first planning meeting took place in the middle of September at the Science Learning Centre Yorkshire and the Humber during which it was decided that the project would be based around Egyptian history as it was felt that it would lend itself well to human biology and could include some forensic activities which would get the pupils excited about science.

At the outset it was decided that along with the joint planning sessions held at the Science Learning Centre, there would be a review session held after each of the trial lessons, in which all teachers involved would discuss the lessons and how they could be improved. To help with these sessions, each lesson was filmed and part of the review would involve going over footage to pinpoint specific areas for improvement or change.

Unfortunately a few planning issues were encountered due to timetabling and staff absence. As such a couple of the sessions proved to be broken up significantly over a large number of weeks, thereby losing a degree of momentum. It was felt that when embarking on a project like this again, the teachers would ensure that it could be run over a much shorter time, thereby maintaining the interest of both the pupils and teachers alike. Despite this issue, it was felt by all participating teachers that planning lessons in this way, through peer guidance and group discussion, was a fantastic opportunity.

When the science and the history teacher involved in the project were able to meet up at school they made speedy progress in designing their activity. The forensic science angle was chosen as it allowed the historical context to be brought right up to date and it was hoped that the pupils would engage in this investigative approach. The puzzle of how the Egyptian king had died allowed for multiple answers, which it was hoped, would encourage debate within class. It would also allow the teachers to explore the concept of inconclusive evidence, which can often be experienced within many fields of science.

The activity was trialled with one Year 7 group. Both the history and science teacher were present and the lesson was team-taught. It was important to both teachers that they jointly delivered the activity to emphasise the cross-curricular nature of the work. At first a few of the pupils were confused about why they were being taught by a science *and* a history teacher during their usual science period, however, they soon adapted to the novelty and became thoroughly engaged in the investigation:

> I enjoyed finding out all the different facts because it has helped me understand how History and Science work together.
>
> (Year 7 pupil)

The pupil-led investigation allowed for a degree of creativity within the lesson and the activity itself proved very popular with the pupils involved:

> It wasn't like a normal lesson as we had to think a lot more, the teacher normally tells us things rather than us thinking for ourselves.
>
> (Year 7 pupil)

Next steps

It is hoped that the department will be able to run a similar activity in the future but will try to tackle the problems encountered over timetabling by working over a shorter period of time.

Double Crossed Resource two

In 'Vanished: A Blitz Mystery' the pupils are challenged to investigate the scene of an abandoned wartime house at the time of the Blitz. The aim of the investigation is to find out what happened to the family that used to live there by interpreting all available evidence.

Working in small groups the pupils develop team working, communication and interpersonal skills culminating in the putting together of a report and presenting of their findings to the rest of the class at the end of the activity. The activity also involves investigative skills and links directly to science, flammable liquids and Second World War history.

Figure 7.11 Vanished: A Blitz Mystery project introduction.

At the outset of the activity the teacher explains that the lesson is about thinking creatively when interpreting evidence and asking questions such as 'Why?', 'How?' and 'What if?' (Figure 7.11).

The pupils are required to solve a mystery (Figure 7.12). The residents of No. 37 have disappeared during the air raid that took place the evening before.

Figure 7.12 Vanished: A Blitz Mystery mystery.

The activity is introduced using an air-raid siren soundtrack to set the scene. A Second World War siren soundtrack can be found at www.tradebit.com/filedetail.php/1817902-air-raid-siren-sound-effect-wav

The pupils are put into groups of three or four and asked to consider what might have happened to the children's' friends.

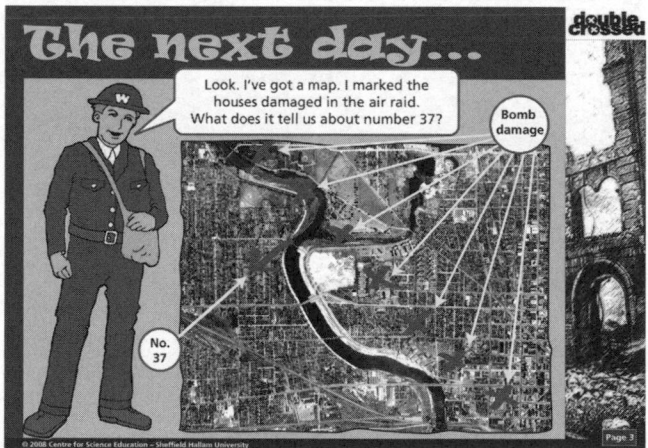

Figure 7.13 Vanished: A Blitz Mystery evidence.

Throughout the activity the pupils are given additional pieces of crucial information to allow them to build up a picture of what may have happened to the family living at No. 37 during the air raid. The first significant piece of information is a map of the bombing that took place the evening before (Figure 7.13). As can be seen by the map, the house in question was not hit by a bomb.

Figure 7.14 Vanished: A Blitz Mystery more evidence.

The second piece of evidence is a broken bottle and liquid found at the residence (Figure 7.14). The pupils are once again asked to discuss what may have caused this damage.

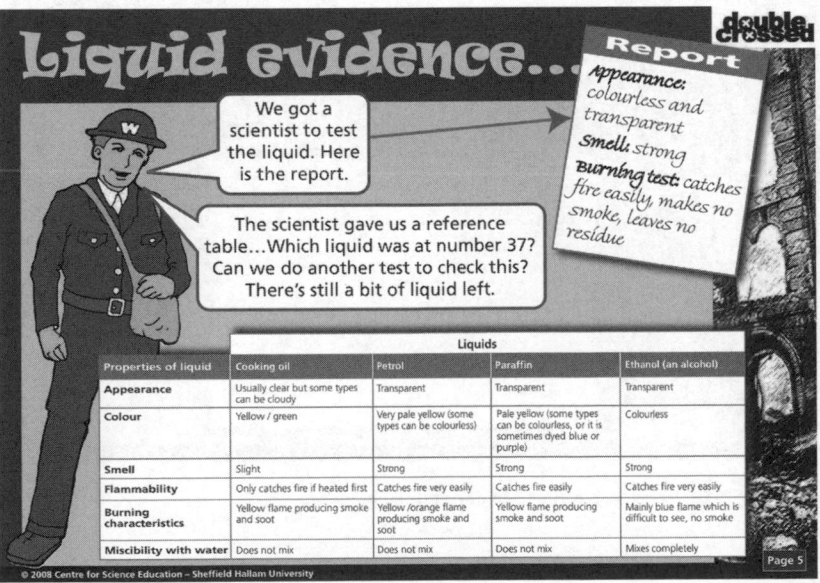

Figure 7.15 Vanished: A Blitz Mystery liquid evidence.

Using the liquid evidence sheet (Figure 7.15) the pupils are able to work out what kind of liquid was found in the bottle. This helps build up a picture of the broken bottle as a Molotov cocktail which didn't catch fire.

In relation to the evidence about the liquid used in the Molotov cocktail pupils could be involved in testing 'the liquid found at Number 37', i.e. ethanol by:

1   Igniting **a few drops** of ethanol placed on a suitable container e.g. metal lid or small foil tray. For primary aged pupils it is recommended that this is carried out as a demonstration.

2   Mixing a few drops of ethanol with water in a test tube or other suitable container to show that the ethanol is completely miscible.

Safety Note: Pupils should wear suitable eye protection and tie back long hair and avoid loose garments. When burning ethanol stand the container on sand in a larger metal tray. Ethanol is highly flammable; it burns with a blue flame which is often difficult to see. It's important to ensure that the ethanol cannot be ignited accidentally and has burnt away completely before touching the containers. Only a few drops of ethanol should be ignited. Petrol should not be used for practical work. Cooking oil should not be burnt but could be used to compare miscibility.

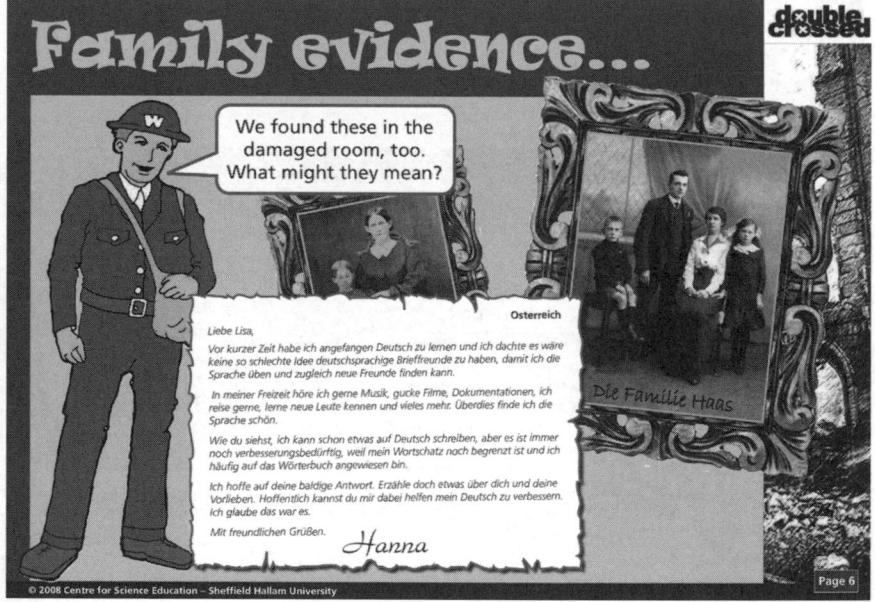

Figure 7.16 Vanished: A Blitz Mystery family evidence.

Further family evidence, as translated and read out by the teacher, suggests that the family are immigrants to Britain from Germany or Austria (Figure 7.16).

Figure 7.17 Vanished: A Blitz Mystery newspaper evidence.

The final piece of evidence is a newspaper article, which highlights an incident that took place in London, when the home of an Austrian family was attacked by suspicious Britons who mistook them for Nazis (Figure 7.17).

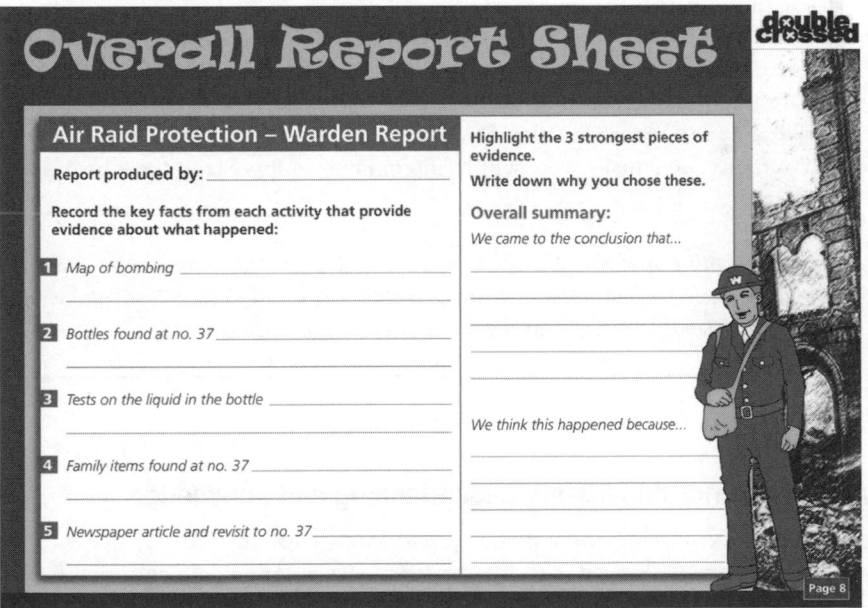

Figure 7.18 Vanished: A Blitz Mystery report.

The pupils are now asked to complete a report using all of the evidence they have gathered and make some overall conclusions about the mystery at No. 37 (Figure 7.18).

Historical note

At the start of the Battle of Britain the German Luftwaffe concentrated its efforts on destroying the British air force both in the sky and by attacking aerodromes. From September 1940, however, the Luftwaffe changed its focus to attacking British cities, a phase in the war that was to become known as the Blitz. At the start of the Blitz, London was the main target but soon other major industrially important cities were attacked including the raid on Coventry on the night of 14 November 1940 when 568 people were killed and the entire city centre was destroyed.

Many different kinds of bombs were dropped on Britain during the Blitz, including high-explosive bombs and incendiaries. Incendiaries were fire bombs which were only 9 inches long but they could burn for up to 10 minutes at very high temperatures. Although they were not used there was a constant fear of attack using poison gas bombs.

Air-raid warden posts in cities were staffed by six wardens. (Both men and women were used.) They were responsible for about 500 members of the public. During a raid the warden was expected to know the whereabouts of the people in their area. If a bomb dropped the warden was responsible for reporting the incident and helping at the scene. After raids wardens patrolled to check for damage and look for unexploded bombs.

At the outbreak of the Second World War about 80,000 potential 'enemy aliens' were identified in Britain. All Germans and Austrians over the age of 16 were called before special tribunals and categorised according to their potential security risk. During 1940 there was an outbreak of spy fever and agitation against enemy aliens although many were Jewish refugees with no Nazi sympathies. Thousands of Germans, Austrians and Italians were sent to internment camps. Many were held on the Isle of Man.

This is only part of the 'Vanished' activity, to download the full resource and accompanying 'teachers notes' (which include a translation of the letter – see Figure 7.16) please visit the Astra Zeneca Science Teaching Trust website at www.azteachscience.co.uk

Impact on science and history understanding and knowledge

This activity develops understanding and knowledge in both science and history while expanding the skills needed to interpret evidence and draw conclusions. The resource also develops team working and cooperation skills, improves communication through presentation and collaboration, and cultivates creativity and problem solving with the pupils being asked to think creatively when interpreting scientific and historical evidence.

Success criteria

To be successful the students will:

- Ask questions in relation to evidence such as 'Why?', 'How?' and 'What if?'
- Use science and history knowledge when interpreting evidence
- Reach conclusions based on consideration of more than one piece of evidence
- Understand that additional evidence may have an effect on the conclusion reached.

Science curriculum links

The 'Vanished: A Blitz Mystery' activity is linked directly to both the Key Stage 2 and 3 science curriculums.

Key Stage 2 Science National Curriculum

Breadth of study statement

2a – Use appropriate scientific language … to communicate ideas and explain the behaviour of living things, materials, phenomena and processes.

Sc1 Scientific enquiry

Ideas and evidence in science

1a – That science is about thinking creatively to explain how living and non-living things work and to establish links between causes and effects.

Investigative skills – considering evidence and evaluating

2i – Make comparisons and identify simple patterns or associations in their own observations and measurements or other data.

2j – Use observations, evidence or other data to draw conclusions.

2l – Use their scientific knowledge and understanding to explain observations, measurements or other data or conclusions.

2m – Review their work and the work of others and describe its significance and limitations.

Sc3 Materials and their properties

Grouping and classifying materials

1a – To compare everyday materials and objects on the basis of their material properties and to relate these properties to everyday uses of the materials.

New Key Stage 3 Science National Curriculum

Key concepts

1.1 – Scientific thinking

b – Critically analysing and evaluating evidence from observations and experiments.

Key processes:

2.2 – Critical understanding of evidence

a – Obtain, record and analyse data from a wide range of primary and secondary sources, including ICT sources, and use their findings to provide evidence for scientific explanations.

2.3 – Communication

a – Use appropriate methods, including ICT, to communicate scientific information and contribute to presentations and discussions about scientific issues.

Range and content:

3.1 – Energy, electricity and forces

b – Forces are interactions between objects and can affect their shape and motion

3.2 – Chemical and material behaviour

a – The particle model provides explanations for the different physical properties and behaviour of matter.

c – Elements and compounds show characteristic chemical properties and patterns in their behaviour.

Take a look at Case Study 7.2 to see how the teachers designed, developed and trialled the 'Vanished: A Blitz Mystery' Raiders activity.

The following Case Study explores the way in which the teachers at Eckington School worked together to create the 'Vanished' activity.

Case Study 7.2: Eckington School, Derbyshire – Designing 'Vanished: A Blitz Mystery'

The school

Eckington School is a mixed 11-18 community secondary school in Derbyshire with specialist Engineering status.

The project

The Eckington cross-curricular experience was quite different to that seen by Brinsworth. Early on in their involvement in the project the history teacher withdraw her involvement as a result of other commitments. This meant that the science teacher at the school was forced to press forward alone. This was, however, not a problem for the science teacher in question and highlights the flexibility of cross-curricular work of this nature.

While the circumstances at the outset of the resource design were less than ideal the science teacher in charge was quickly able to identify an historical context that interested him. With a little research into the period the teacher was able to confidently press on with his Second World War science activity. The main aim of the activity was to see the pupils undertake creative investigations that would allow them to draw conclusions, which could be shared with the rest of the class. While the activity itself was delivered and supervised by the teacher it was hoped that the activity, and the investigation would be pupil-led. It was also important to the teacher that the lesson included classroom discussion and the testing of hypotheses.

Once the activity was designed it was quickly trialled with a Year 7 class at the school. The cross-curricular nature of the lesson meant that it was well received by the pupils.

> It was the best science lesson that we've ever done. I really liked the science
> and history together, it made it make sense.
>
> (Year 7 pupil)

Next steps

Despite the initial difficulties caused by the history teacher withdrawing from the project, the activity proved highly successful. The school has also continued to work with the *Double Crossed* team at Sheffield Hallam University and have gone on to create an additional four science/history activities to be run with classes of varying levels at Key Stage 3.

Impact on teachers

By combining science with history the creative *Double Crossed* teacher-partnerships have developed dynamic and lively resources that highlight the importance of cross-curricular teaching as a method through which creativity is stimulated in both pupil and teacher. It is through creative cross-curricular teaching that pupils can begin to develop the crucial skills needed to cope with the rapidly changing world and in the case of this project, better understand scientific topics through the questioning of evidence. Working across the curriculum provided both the science and history teachers with tools to examine their discipline from different perspectives:

> Working with teachers from other departments allowed us the chance to cross-fertilize ideas and concepts. Linking the subject areas gave us the chance to look at the generic skills relevant to both, such as problem solving, teamwork, communication, interpretation, analysis and evaluation. There are huge similarities between both subjects. Also, the chance for staff to work together shows the students that education is not done to them in little packages called subjects but encompasses the world as a whole.
>
> (Science partnership teacher)

Additionally, delivering scientific topics through cross-curricular science/historical contexts encouraged opportunities for creative and independent enquiry and discursive argument within Key Stages 3. The combination of history and science has proved a hugely valuable tool through which pupils can become conversant with techniques and processes vital to the study of science through topic based, contextualised learning.

Practical task

Using the above examples as a guide work with a colleague from the history department, brainstorm some possible project ideas.

Arrange a joint science and history departmental meeting and present your thoughts to all your colleagues.

Undertaking science–history teaching

As has already been discussed in both this chapter and in the chapters preceding it, the concept of a collaborative cross-curricular, working partnership is recommended by the authors of this book. While it is of course not always feasible (because of timetable or teaching commitments) to spend any lengthy period of time with a colleague from a different subject area, even just a lunch period spent discussing the way you work within your own areas can be of incredible valuable to any teacher considering undertaking any major cross-curricular teaching. It is, however, sometimes truly impossible to find an appropriate colleague or set aside the time to work alongside another teacher within the school. This is of course, not the end of the world. Successful cross-curricular teaching can be undertaken solo if appropriate preparation is completed.

When undertaking the planning of a science–history cross-curricular activity or lesson one of the first major stumbling blocks can be the identification of a context. It can be of great importance to pinpoint this context so as to not fall into the trap of devising a *history of science* activity, which, while of immense value is not a true history/science cross-curricular endeavour similar to that seen through the *Double Crossed* project. Figure 7.19 aims to distinguish the key differences between a science–history activity and a history of science activity by illustrating two different activities.

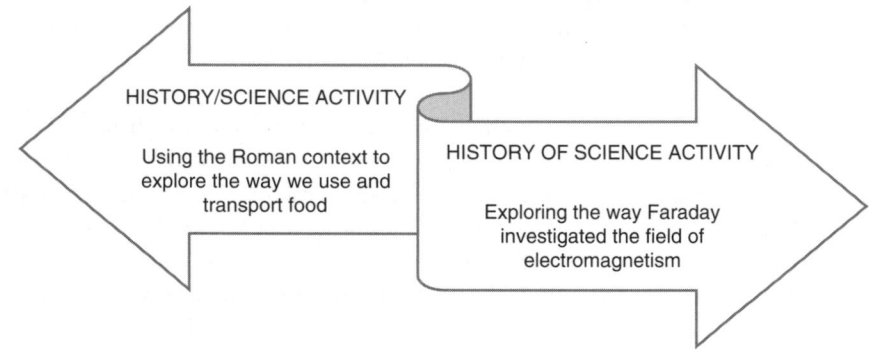

Figure 7.19 History–science and the history of science.

While the history of science activity uncovers the nature of scientific exploration and maps the field of scientific discovery, the history–science approach illustrates a contemporary (and often curriculum-based) science topic within a creative historical context.

Stimulus ideas

It can be hard to think of that initial idea that combines both science and history so Figure 7.20 provides some ideas to get you started.

For further inspiration take a look at the Key Stage 3 National Curriculum for both history *and* science to help you with your ideas. However, if you are looking to complete an activity during an off time-table session then you may want to move away from the topic areas prescribed by the National Curriculum and think more widely.

The Ancient Egyptians: why not combine the history of the pyramids with engineering and physics to explore forces and the way the pyramids were constructed?	The History of Alcatraz: how about exploring the prison and some of its famous inmates using the reactivity of metals as a context...why are prison bars made of a certain metal?	World War 1: why not set a data analysis activity based on the civilian death toll suffered during World War 1. The figures can be analysed, inputted into graphs, and interpeted
The Cold War: exploring espionage and spies while setting cryptography and code breaking puzzles	Sir Walter Raleigh: Explore the history of Sir Walter Raleigh and his relationship with Queen Elizabeth I. Look at the claim he introduced the potato and then conducting an experiment that explores how potatoes can produce energy	The History of the Football World Cup: how about looking at the way the World Cup has grown and spread, the political and social implications of the competition, and the science behind football materials and techniques
World War 1 Trenches: looking at life in the trenches and the way soldiers on both sides were able to hear each other at certain points and under certain conditions (such as when the wind was low). This leads into an exploration of sound waves.	1906 San Francisco Earthquake: why not look at the social implications at the time, as well as the earth science behind the quake?	The 'flu epidemic of 1918

Figure 7.20 Ideas for science–history lessons.

Reflective task

Your ideas

Now it's time to start work on your own ideas. Use a mind-map to brainstorm some potential topic areas or general themes.

My Ideas

Figure 7.21 Brainstorm for new lesson ideas.

Possible extensions

Once you have designed, developed and trialed your activity you may be looking for further professional challenges and for a way to extend your cross-curricular work. Two possible options are:

- Transition – To adapt and develop your activity for use with Year 6 pupils as a transition exercise
- New subjects – To introduce another subject area.

Transition

Transition from primary school to secondary school can often be an unsettling time for pupils. The creation of new friendships, exploration of new curriculum structures and new teaching and support staff pose great demands on even the most confident individuals. Cross-curricular lessons and resources can lend themselves well as potential transition activities to be used with Year 6 children during the final weeks of primary school or with Year 7 pupils during their first few days at secondary school. As a Key Stage 3 activity that combines both history and science it may be possible to adapt your cross-curricular activity to be used for this purpose.

Introducing new subject areas

The follow-on project to *Double Crossed* was *Triple Crossed* which introduced citizenship as an additional subject combining it with the original subjects of science and history. The *Double Crossed* project demonstrated that the bringing together of history and science is a hugely valuable tool through which pupils can become conversant with techniques and processes vital to the study of science. Adopting the skills relevant to citizenship education created a unique arena in which pupils explored contentious, ethical and controversial issues in science within a recognisable and familiar methodological context regularly practised within citizenship lessons. That is to say, the *Triple Crossed* project encouraged engagement in discussion and debate and increased the ethical decision making skills and values relevant to the nature of both scientific and historical enquiry. By using citizenship in conjunction with science and history, pupils can increase their ability to recognise bias, evaluate arguments, weigh up evidence and look for alternative viewpoints, all of which serves to increase their skills in both the study of science and of history. Figure 7.22 illustrates the science–history–citizenship model.

Citizenship was the chosen subject of the *Triple Crossed* project, however there are numerous other subjects that can be combined with science and history to enhance an activity, such as technology, art, English, mathematics or modern foreign languages. To do this the first step should always be to approach a member of staff in the relevant department to gain specialised input and support. This will also mean that you are now forming a small team of teachers within school that will all be developing and enhancing their cross-curricular skills.

As was the case with the Double Crossed *project,* Triple Crossed *was also run by the Center for Science Education at Sheffeild Hallam University and funded by the Astra Zeneca Science Teaching Trust.*

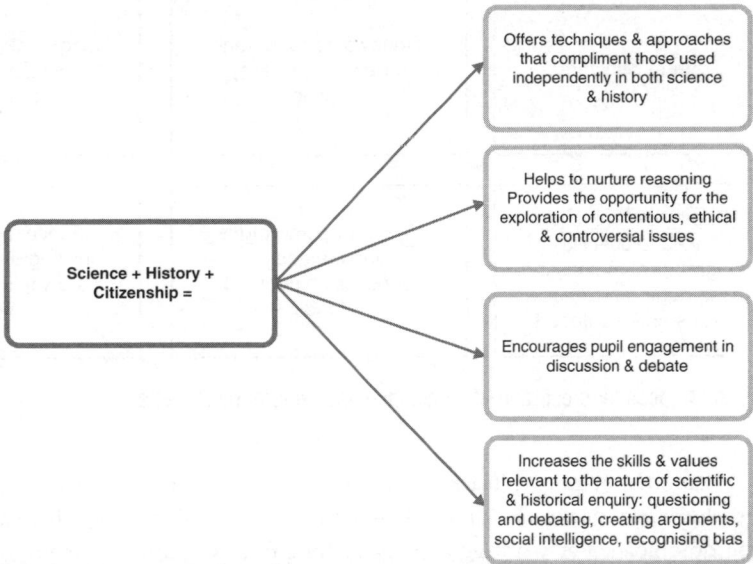

Figure 7.22 Science + history + citizenship.

Science and geography

Science and geography are perhaps, in some ways, a more obvious match than the teaching of science with history. The overlap between the subjects within the arena of environmental and earth sciences allows for extensive cross-curricular activity. Section 3.4 (The Environment, Earth and Universe) of the Key Stage 3 Science National Curriculum Programme of Study refers directly to geological and environmental phenomenon such as the rock cycle processes, rock formation, weathering, human activity and natural processes that can lead to changes in the environment (QCA 2007b: 3).

The changing nature of the world we live in requires today's educators to ensure they are preparing young people for the future. Issues such as climate change, fuel shortages, the distribution of food globally and natural disasters mean young people today need to be resilient and flexible towards their changing environment. Teachers play a crucial role in this process and their responsibility seems somehow greater than ever in the face of such uncertain times. Knowledge and understanding of environmental issues are known to directly impact upon environmentally responsible attitudes and behaviour (Bamberg and Möser 2007). Figure 7.23 illustrates possible starting points for global and local cross-curricular science–geography projects.

Stimulus ideas

For further inspiration on the cross-curricular applications of geography and science, the Royal Geographical Society has produced some exciting Key Stage 3 resources focusing on geographical flashpoints such as Swine Flu, the Sichuan earthquake and a flooding of London. They describe flashpoints as being 'major world events which may impact on

Natural disasters	Renewable (and non-renewable) energy supplies	Geographical mapping of diseases and pandemics across the globe
Plants and animals linked to specific geopgraphical regions e.g. the rainforests, the oceans and the desert	World food shortages and the use of genetically modified foods	A local activity, e.g. building developments, brown vs green field sites

Figure 7.23 Ideas for cross-curricular science and geography projects.

a large number of people/places'. Flashpoints are used to demonstrate ways in which geographers and scientists can work together to find solutions. The various resources can be downloaded at www.geographyteachingtoday.org.uk/ks3-resources/resource/the-geography-of-science.

It is important, however, that the exploration of environmental matters is not done solely on a global level. Work undertaken to explore local environmental issues is equally as important. School-based investigations often have a greater impact on attitudes and behaviour in regards to environmental responsibility (Uitto *et al.* 2001: 181). Some possible *local* topic areas are illustrated in Figure 7.24.

Stimulus ideas: local

Measuring the school's (or homes') energy consumption with a view to reducing the energy used or exploring more renewable energy sources	Recycling and the ways waste can be (re)used

Exploring the local region. What kind of terrain surrounds the school? Is it urban or rural? Is the area famous for any natural resources such as water or rocks? Does the local area include any major energy plants?

Figure 7.24 Local science–geography topic areas.

By making the lesson relevant to the immediate surroundings it can have a lasting impact on pupils' understanding and engagement in the topic.

Science and RE

Cross-curricular teaching of science and religious education is seen by some as being an often difficult and ethically volatile combination. This is in part due to the nature of science and religion's 'big questions' such as 'Who are we?', 'How was the earth created?' and 'When do you become a person?' Indeed in many countries the topic of evolution is skimmed through quickly or avoided entirely due to the apparent tensions between science and religion. While the topic is not without its difficulties, education writers such as Seals believe that it is crucial to embrace religious points-of-views within the science classroom to ensure each individual pupil has a 'voice' (Seals 2010: 252), be it secular or religious. One way in which he has previously tackled this issue is by exploring the history of scientists and by discussing with his pupils the lengthy list of creationist scientists:

Physics:	Newton, Faraday, Maxwell, Kelvin
Chemistry:	Boyle, Dalton, Ramsay
Biology:	Ray, Linnaeus, Mendel, Pasteur, Virchow, Agassiz
Geology:	Steno, Woodward, Brewster, Buckland, Cuvier
Astronomy:	Copernicus, Galileo, Kepler, Herschel, Maunder
Mathematics:	Pascal, Leibnitz, Euler

(Seals 2010: 252)

By exploring the concept of 'religious scientists' he hoped to reduce the perceived conflict between science and religion. But how easily can these two worldviews sit together?

In 1932, Sigmund Freud discussed the idea of a *Weltanshauung* (worldview) associated with both religion and science. In his lecture 'On the Question of a *Weltanshauung*' (Freud 1965) he defined a *Weltanshauung* as 'an an intellectual construction which solves all the problems of our existence uniformly on the basis of one overriding hypothesis, which, accordingly, leaves no question unanswered and in which everything that interests us finds its fixed place' (as quoted from Glennan 2009: 798). While he perceived the religious *Weltanschauung* to offer people a sense of security with its spiritual *answers* Freud saw the scientific viewpoint as somewhat different.

> The *Weltanschauung* of science already departs noticeably from our definition. It is true that it too assumes the uniformity of the explanation of the universe; but it does so only as a programme, the fulfillment of which is relegated to the future. ... It asserts that there are no sources of knowledge of the universe other than the intellectual working-over of carefully scrutinized observations ... and alongside of it no knowledge derived from revelation, intuition or divination.

(Freud 1965: 158–159)

So if the worldviews of both science and religion are so different, how well can they be paired? Nord's exploration of the relationship between science and religion leads him to define four different viewpoints based upon the two subjects' tensions and bonds:

1. Religion trumps science
2. Science trumps religion

3. Independence
4. Integration

(Nord 1999: 30)

His first grouping is that of 'Religion trumps science'. This refers to the notion of religion as the possessor of the ultimate truth about nature. In contrast, his second category of 'Science trumps religion' means that only science can provide consistent and trustworthy knowledge, particularly in the face of conflict with religious argument. By this thinking if something has not been proven by science it does not exist. The third grouping identified by Nord is that of 'Independence'. This position is led by the belief that science and religion are so incomparable that they cannot create conflict as they hold nothing in common. Each field possesses its own methods, approaches and theories – so much so that this is often defined as the 'two-worlds' approach. As such, they can only seek to provide *truth* within their own separate fields. This third position is the one most often seen within science education in the USA since the mid 1980s:

> Religion and science are separate and mutually exclusive realms of human thought whose presentation in the same context leads to a misunderstanding of both scientific theory and religious belief.
>
> (National Academy of Science 1984: 4)

The final position is that of 'Integration'. While science and religion are no doubt different they are still able to clash *and* strengthen each other as they both focus on the same world. As such, to gain a full picture of the world one must draw upon both fields.

These four groupings go some way to help us to understand the tensions between science and religion, but what direct impact do they have upon science education, and particularly cross-curricular, science and religious education teaching? While the first two positions have difficult and somewhat positivistic approaches to the debate, it is the third position that potentially creates the most problems for the science teacher. If science and religion are completely separate, does that therefore undermine and challenge any attempts to explore cross-curricular teaching between these two subjects? Some would argue yes – the differing theories and ideologies of these two areas damage any well-meaning attempt to unite them within the classroom and as such each should be taught separately by teachers with expertise in the *very* different branches of learning and therefore they should not meet. This, however, is contradictory to the nature of cross-curricular teaching and may lead to greater moral and spiritual confusion among young people. The separatist nature of this approach may see pupils being taught seemingly contradictory concepts at the same time, within the two school departments:

> It is no good teaching about evolution … in a science lesson at 9am then, at 10am, in a religious education lesson, instructing pupils not to believe it.
>
> (Harris 2010: 1)

For this reason, cross-departmental communication becomes crucial and cross-curricular teachings can be immensely powerful. Equally, if Nord's fourth grouping is to be believed, there is an indisputable need for both science and religion to be taught in conjunction and, in turn, the debate between the two can be embraced as a means through which to make further discoveries about our world. But it is the question of how this issue is tackled that is more tricky.

While in some countries a separation between religion and the state imposes legal restrictions on what can be taught (e.g. France, Turkey, USA) for other countries, 'the provincial reason for science educators dealing with the interface between science and religion is to help students ... to better learn science' (Reiss 2010: 97). That is not to say that the teaching of religion within the science classroom should be undertaken without serious thought to such matters as expertise and/or potential religious indoctrination or offence. As such the advice or involvement of a specialist religious education teacher is always recommended before undertaking any cross-curricular science/religion work about which you feel uncertain. However, to support any work you may wish to undertake resources can be found online. For example, the BBC Learning Zone has some useful video footage from Christian Professor Alister McGrath with accompanying classroom activities at www.bbc.co.uk/learningzone/clips/religion-and-science/451.html.

Reflective task

It may not be something you have considered before, but take some time to examine your own views on science and religion. If you embark on teaching it, pupils will ask you for your opinion.

Science and RE *through citizenship*

Within the science classroom the cross-curricular teaching of science and religion can often be tackled from a citizenship perspective. With many of the joint issues associated with religion and science being ethical in nature the opportunity for classroom discussion and debate becomes obvious. In Key Stage 3 Citizenship, pupils are expected to 'take an interest in topical and controversial issues and to engage in discussion and debate' (QCA 2007c: 27) and through this curriculum programme pupils should be able to 'engage with and reflect on different ideas, opinions, beliefs and values when exploring topical and controversial issues and problems' (QCA 2007c: 30).

While it is to some degree indisputable that science teachers should be exploring ethical and moral dimensions to their science teaching, it can be sometimes difficult to begin tackling the moral and ethical issues related with religion. Reiss (2008) suggests that one way to investigate this issue is to explore the nature of both science and religion from a very personal perspective. In his teaching of undergraduate trainee science teachers Reiss asks each student to express the relationship between Religious Knowledge (RK) and Scientific Knowledge (SK) by drawing a picture or diagram that represents their attitude. Figure 7.25 illustrates one hypothetical response to this activity.

The two separate spheres show that this student believes that both scientific and religious knowledge have worth, but that they are very separate, with no overlap, and that the scientific knowledge, being larger, is of more value. This student clearly fits into Nord's (1999) third category on the relationship between science and religion. In contrast

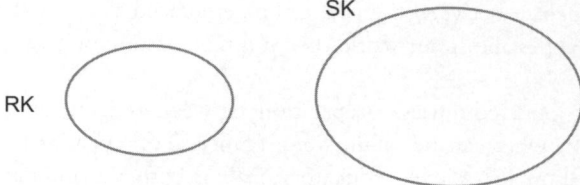

Figure 7.25 Hypothetical representation of how someone may view the relationship between scientific and religious knowledge – Example 1 (source: Reiss 2008: 175).

Figure 7.26 highlights the hypothetical response given by a student whose worldview is predominantly religious.

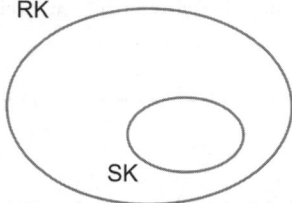

Figure 7.26 Hypothetical representation of how someone may view the relationship between scientific and religious knowledge – Example 2 (source: Reiss 2008: 175).

Reflective task

Draw your own diagram or picture that you feel represents the relationship between scientific knowledge and religious knowledge. Perhaps you too have separated the two subjects or perhaps you see them as interdependent. Your diagram will help you to gather your own thoughts before planning any lessons.

The moral and ethical issues surrounding science and religion may be caricatured by the extreme and opposing arguments published by radical creationists (often perceived to be based in the USA) and work such as that undertaken by the scientist Richard Dawkins (2008). The two camps at their extremes can be divided into the viewpoints 'religion undermines science' and 'science proves religion incorrect'. There is, however, room for a middle ground. For example, issues relating to the history of medicine can be used to explore modern-day medicine. The high-tech nature of today's hospitals seems dependent on science with very little place for religion. But is this true? Why do hospitals still include chapels for both patients and families? What part (if any) can religion play in a patient's recovery? What part does spirituality play in modern medicine? These all stand alone as great debate questions for pupils without having to enter into some of the more difficult issues such as when is a human being no longer a collection of cells and how was the world created – both of which have religious implications.

Practical task

This task will involve you working with at least one member of staff from the religious education department.

Working with your colleague(s), discuss the following questions:

- Within your own classrooms how do you both tackle the teaching of contentious and controversial issues? How do you explore morals and ethics? Is there any overlap in your techniques or approaches?

- What subject areas do you both perceive to be contentious and/or controversial? Is there any overlap in your identified topic areas?

Drawing upon these two discussions think about any ways in which you could support each other's teaching. Are there any skills or techniques that you could offer your colleague? Are there any techniques or skills that you feel you would benefit from exploring further with your colleague?

The purpose of this discussion is not necessarily that you identify a shared topic or subject area and design a lesson plan around the area (although this is of course of immense value); it is instead to share knowledge and understanding of each other's methods. This should have a lasting impact on your teaching of contentious or religious topics within the science classroom.

Conclusion

Science and the humanities can provide an exciting forum for teacher and pupil creativity. The *Double Crossed* project demonstrates ways in which teachers from different school departments can work together to create dynamic classroom activities that can be used during a lesson, an afternoon or a thematic/collapsed timetable day. This model can be applied to any cross-departmental collaboration for the purposes of a meaningful, context-rich resource. Both history and geography provide numerous exciting topic avenues to explore in conjunction with science. Religious education, however, is a more difficult topic. While there may be significant arguments for exploring religion through science, it can be a difficult and contentious issue, and one which should always be approached with caution.

Professional standards for QTS

This chapter will help meet the following standards:

Q6	Have a commitment to collaboration and co-operative working
Q7	(a) Reflect on and improve their practice, and take responsibility for identifying and meeting their developing professional needs
Q8	Have a creative and constructively critical approach towards innovation, being prepared to adapt their practice where benefits and improvements are identified
Q10	Have a knowledge and understanding of a range of teaching, learning and behaviour management strategies and know how to use and adapt them, including how to personalise learning and provide opportunities for all learners to achieve their potential
Q14	Have a secure knowledge and understanding of their subject/curriculum areas and related pedagogy to enable them to teach effectively across the age and ability range for which they are trained
Q17	Know how to use skills in literacy, numeracy and ICT to support their teaching and wider professional activities
Q23	Design opportunities for learners to develop their literacy, numeracy and ICT skills
Q24	Plan homework or other out-of-class work to sustain learners' progress and to extend and consolidate their learning
Q32	Work as a team member and identify opportunities for working with colleagues, sharing the development of effective practice with them
Q33	Ensure that colleagues working with them are appropriately involved in supporting learning and understand the roles they are expected to fulfil

Professional standards for teachers

This chapter will help meet the following standards:

C6	Have a commitment to collaboration and co-operative working where appropriate
C8	Have a creative and constructively critical approach towards innovation, being prepared to adapt their practice where benefits and improvements are identified
C15	Have a secure knowledge and understanding of their subject/curriculum areas and related pedagogy including: the contribution that their subjects/curriculum areas can make to cross-curricular learning; and recent relevant developments
C17	Know how to use skills in literacy, numeracy and ICT to support their teaching and wider professional activities
C27	Design opportunities for learners to develop their literacy, numeracy and ICT and thinking and learning skills appropriate within their phase and context
C40	Work as a team member and identify opportunities for working with colleagues, managing their work where appropriate and sharing the development of effective practice with them

Pupils' Personal, Learning and Thinking Skills (PLTS)

This chapter will help meet the following skills:

Independent enquirers	• Identify questions to answer and problems to resolve
Creative thinkers	• Generate ideas and explore possibilities • Connect their own and others' ideas and experiences in inventive ways
Reflective learners	• Evaluate experiences and learning to inform future progress • Communicate their learning in relevant ways for different audiences
Team workers	• Collaborate with others to work towards common goals • Take responsibility, showing confidence in themselves and their contribution

Science and the arts

Key objectives

By the end of this chapter you will have:

- Explored the debate surrounding science and the arts
- Identified the Key Stage 3 science curriculum areas/topics that can be used in a cross-curricular manner with the arts.

Introduction

Study the science of art and the art of science.

(Leonardo da Vinci)

The work of Leonardo da Vinci epitomises the image of Renaissance culture as a hotbed of cross-curricular artistic and scientific exploration. This can be a somewhat misleading image because, in reality, many of da Vinci's contemporaries lacked his versatility and resourcefulness. However, the period does boast a great awareness of mathematics, geometry and optical instruments within the realm of artistic expression. Let us use da Vinci as an example by exploring his famous work, the Vitruvian Man (see Figure 8.1).

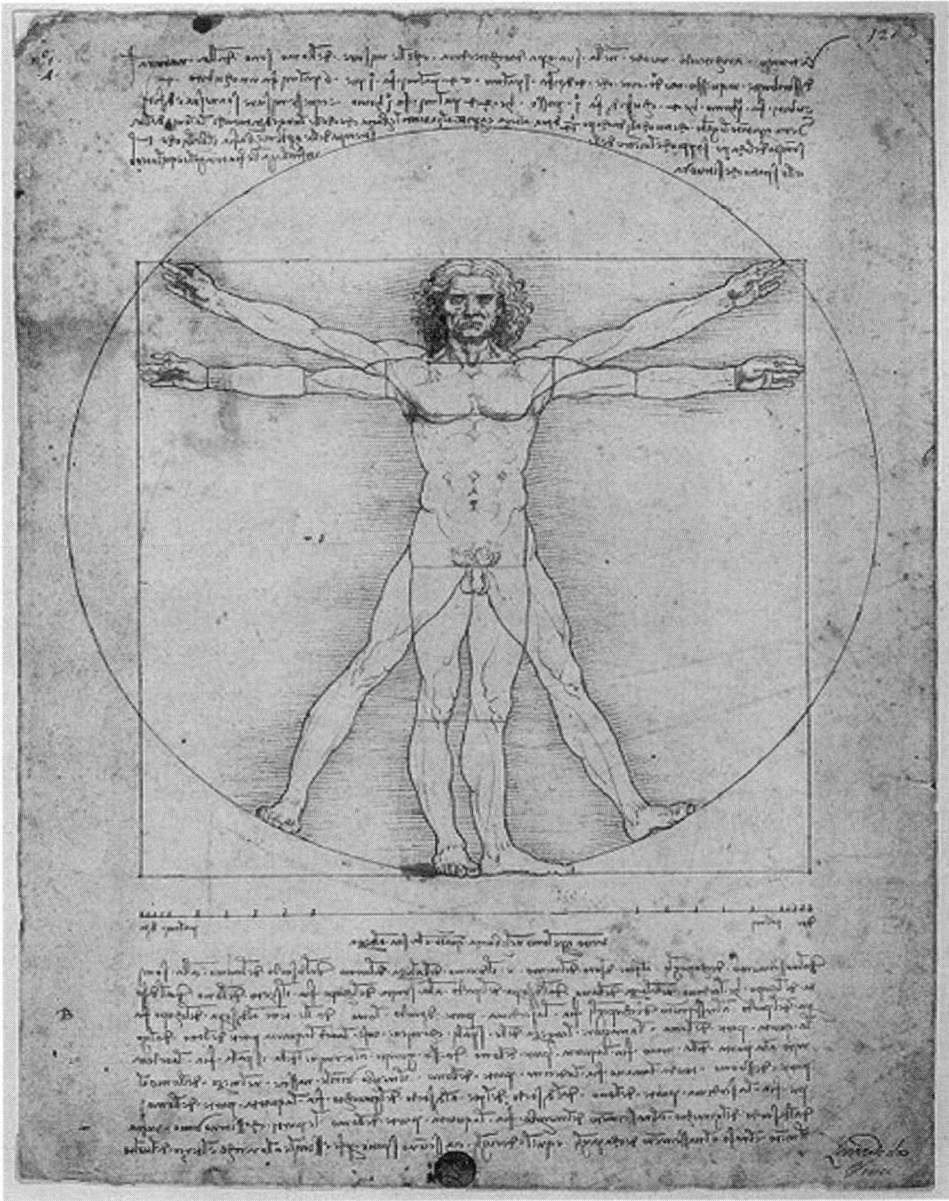

Figure 8.1 The Vitruvian Man.

The Vitruvian Man (sometimes known as the Canon of Proportions) uses proportional relationships to study the (male) human body. The text that accompanied the image stated relative measurements such as the palm being the width of four fingers, the length of the hand being one-tenth of a man's height and the distance from the bottom of the chin to the nose is one-third of the length of the head. While it is true that the concept of universal proportions is erroneous, the Vitruvian Man brings to light the ideas of average proportions. To bring things right up to date, this concept of human proportions is featured in a fascinating cross-curricular mathematics activity developed by the National Centre for Excellence in the Teaching of Mathematics (see www.ncetm.org.uk/public/files/615718/NCETM_Newsletter_12+(2).pdf). The resource uses Roald Dahl's *The BFG* as its context. Pupils are given a large cut-out of a hand (made by enlarging a photocopy of a hand) and asked, using large pieces of sugar paper, to recreate their giant correctly in proportion to the hand they were given. The problem-solving activity explores average proportions and can be directly linked back to da Vinci's work created more than 500 years ago.

The Two Cultures

One of the most influential debates surrounding science and the arts surfaced over fifty years ago when the trained scientist and author C. P. Snow delivered his Reed Lecture in Cambridge entitled 'The Two Cultures' (1959). The thrust of his argument was that a communication breakdown between the two disciplines was harming education and social development. In response to this crisis Snow proposed the notion of practitioners from the two disciplines coming together for the benefit of human knowledge and progress.

One of Snow's main arguments was that scientific progress, as a mechanism for solving many global issues, was being hindered by the predominance of politicians and educationalists with backgrounds in literacy and the classics … and not science. For some this issue still resonates. The mathematician Marcus du Sautoy feels that this concern now extends beyond politicians into the British media as well:

> I think it tends to be politicians and the media, which tend to be run by humanities graduates, where I think we've still got a fight on … we've got big scientific challenges ahead and we have to open up the debate.
>
> (du Sautoy, speaking on the BBC Today Programme (2009))

For du Sautoy the divide between science and the arts in the education system continues to perpetuate this problem with an increased fluidity between the subjects offering one possible solution. Whether the 'Two Cultures' debate continues to be of any major significance or not, it seems clear that public engagement in science has increased over the last few years. The popularity of TV personalities such as the physicist Professor Brian Cox and the geneticist Professor Lord Robert Winston goes some way to illustrate the increased public interest in science. Society has also changed since the late 1950s when Snow delivered his seminal lecture. The world has seen extraordinary levels of scientific and technological development. Contemporary topics such as climate change, energy consumption, genetics and communication technology mean science is very rarely out of the news in one way or another – the same thing can not be said of contemporary art which relatively speaking receives very little attention in the common press. But have the scientific advancements of the past half-century brought the two subjects closer together or in fact, contributed to a wider chasm between the arts and science?

Practical task

The 'Two Cultures' debate is interesting and could perhaps form the basis of a classroom activity to introduce a cross-curricular science and arts-based activity.

Snow's argument was heavily criticised by the literary critic F. R. Leavis. Ask the pupils to research the two arguments and reenact the famous debate in class.

Science and Art

An article in the *Guardian* on the Natural History Museum's 'Darwin's Canopy' commission (Jones 2008) pours scorn on the work undertaken by contemporary artists and the way they took up the challenge. The project involved proposals for a new ceiling at the Natural History Museum in celebration of Charles Darwin and his work. While the writer credits artists such as Rachel Whiteread for her relief of animal and human footprints used to represent the early human footprints found in mud pools and caves, he is highly critical of some other well-established artists involved whose work he describes as having 'run a mile' from the challenge. In conclusion he puts forward a strikingly bleak picture of the interchange between science and art:

> [T]he exhibition is a dismal insight into the total lack of interest in science displayed by most contemporary British artists. I guess Art still isn't an A-level you can combine with biology or physics.
>
> (Jones 2008)

This somewhat gloomy outlook cannot, however, be applied to all science–art initiatives. The Wellcome Trust is an independently funded research charity whose work focuses on the biomedical sciences. As a means through which to explore the ethical and social dynamics of its work the Trust set up an arts funding scheme. Arts Awards are offered to practitioners of science and the arts to 'support imaginative and experimental arts projects that investigate biomedical science'. The project uses art to examine the social, cultural and ethical implications of science and encourages creative thinking and collaborative practice between the two disciplines. Previous projects have included drama, dance, music and fine art and have explored issues ranging from identity to infectious diseases. The Wellcome Trust arts programme aims to engage the general public in scientific debates using art as its medium. It embraces the notion of cross-curricular art and science as a way of exploring often-complex scientific and contentious topics through creativity and expression. This approach to science and art can be replicated in the school classroom. Synthesising art and science offers a platform through which pupils can explore science alongside their own creativity. It loosens science up to become open to personal expression: while fundamental scientific *facts* must remain, the way in which these facts are expressed or presented becomes a matter of personal expression. If an activity seeks to harness the creativity of the pupils through an artistic interpretation of a specific scientific phenomenon, experiment or process then the quest for creativity must be at the core of the activity. This can often mean science teachers are required to move out of their comfort zones and explore their subject matter through pupils' personal expression. This is for some a scary prospect but in many ways, art allows science to let its hair down a little and celebrates its intricate beauty and wonder. Despite the notion of science with its hard facts on one side and art with its fickle creativity on the other, the two disciplines are not unfamiliar bedfellows.

Practical and reflective task

How could you use the science you teach at Key Stage 3 in a way that requires input from the arts?

Think through some possible topics (for ideas visit the Wellcome Trust website at http://www.wellcome.ac.uk/Funding/Public-engagement/ Funded-projects/Awards-made/All-awards-made/WTX035067.htm).

Then meet a colleague from the art department and discuss possible collaboration.

Science has a great tradition of influencing and inspiring the art world. From the precise work of Leonardo da Vinci to the modern geometric paintings and sculptures of Peter Randall-Page, artists have long been fascinated by science. Damien Hirst's *The Physical Impossibility of Death in the Mind of Someone Living* (1991) was a shark suspended in formaldehyde in a vitrine. *Away from the Flock* – a sheep in a tank of formaldehyde – followed three years later. Both exhibitions seemed to resonate with the clinical world of science. In 1997 the word BioArt was coined by a new breed of artists who decided their artistic medium of choice was to be living tissue, DNA and cells. A recent exhibition at Dublin's Science gallery entitled *Visceral: The Living Art Experiment* (2011) claimed to showcase art that works at the frontier between fine art and biotechnology. The exhibition was created to provoke discussion about the nature of the living (and non-living) and what constitutes life itself. It included the work of Kathy High, whose piece entitled *Blood Wars* consisted of a Petri dish that contained the white blood cells from two different people. After a few hours of combat on the dish, one set of the cells will have destroyed the other. The winning group of white blood cells will then go on to fight a new competitor. Equally, in 2001 Marc Quinn showcased his Genomic Portrait of Nobel Prizewinning geneticist Sir John Sulston. The work used the subject's sperm to extract segments of his DNA as its medium. Some may argue that this is art using science as a way to shock and not inspire, but others would argue that these, sometimes uncomfortable, creations are intended to stimulate debate about our relationship with science itself.

Despite the seeming rise in popularity of what some call SciArt, is it really possible to integrate science and art? At the core of this problem are the conflicting epistemological backgrounds of the two subject areas. For many in science the discipline is about exploring truths that exist independently of the scientist's mind and are out there waiting to be discovered. By way of contrast, in art knowledge and truth are subjective and changing. It is a construction of the human mind and can bend and shift in relation to prevailing ideology and culture. The traditional characteristics of the two disciplines present a difficult position from which to approach cross-curricular teaching. However, all is not lost. Knowledge of science through art and an understanding of art through science can deepen and enrich our understanding of the world we live in:

> These are two quite different forms of knowledge, not reconcilable, but mutually curious to each other and as individuals we can accommodate both simultaneously. A better understanding of and respect for art as a reflection of what it feels like to live in the world should affect our reinterpretation of science. A knowledge of science, its rational discourse, metaphors, images, technologies and politics, can invigorate our reinterpretation of art.
>
> (Ede 2005: 180)

The traditional neo-realist thinking of many working in science is also shifting. The idea of science being the study of something tangible and 'out there' is being questioned by some who believe that science requires the subjective human mind to connect theories, findings and data. The physicist Erwin Schrödinger described the aim of science in this way:

> The task is not to see what has never been seen before, but to think what has never been thought before about what you see every day.
>
> (Schrödinger in Arends and Thackara 2003: 10)

This alternative way of thinking about science presents new opportunities in science to explore this 'methodology gap'.

Reflective task

Think about the Ede quote above. As a science teacher how do you engage with art in your classroom? Make a list of any lessons you can think of that touch upon art.

Science and art in the classroom

An interconnected dialogue between art and science can produce thought-provoking learning opportunities. While the epistemological debate above highlights the differences between art and science, the inherent similarities allow collaboration – if sensitively explored.

The two disciplines both maintain a search for answers despite their apparent disparity of what is meant by truth. Art can offer visually stimulating representations of the work undertaken in science which allow a wider audience to understand complex concepts. In the school classroom art can help pupils to:

- Embed learning
- Interpret a specific phenomenon, event or process
- Explore contentious or controversial issues in science
- Express themselves creatively
- Record data, findings or learning
- Develop (both generic and specific) skills.

Art can be an effective field through which young learners can become engaged with science and a method through which debate can be encouraged. But while the concept of cross-curricular science and art may provide an excellent opportunity for creative learning, it is important that any curriculum integration is undertaken with sensitivity to both/all subjects involved. With this in mind it is critical that the science teacher undertaking a science/art project has a sympathetic understanding of the work carried out by the school art department so as to not undermine the philosophy and theory behind the subject. Activities insensitive to the cross-curricular balance can result in the science teacher effectively reducing the subject to its lowest common denominator – e.g. drawing and painting. To explore science and art together with the sensitivity required it is helpful to briefly touch upon the purpose of art as drawn from the Key Stage 3 National Curriculum.

As defined by the National Curriculum at Key Stage 3, art and design sees 'pupils explore visual, tactile and other sensory experiences to communicate ideas and meanings' (QCA 2007d: 17). Equally learners are required to explore and experiment with ideas while taking risks and learning from their own mistakes. As such, the work carried out within the school art department goes beyond a superficial interaction with artistic materials such as paint, pencil and paper. The subject boasts deeper theoretical purposes and curriculum requirements and any cross-curricular activity completed alongside science must recognise and respect these.

Reflective task

Explore the National Curriculum for Art and Design at http://curriculum.qcda.gov.uk/key-stages-3-and-4/subjects/key-stage-3/art-and-design/index.aspx.

What areas of the curriculum cross over with science? Look at curriculum opportunities, key concepts, key process, range and content.

Visual science

To begin to explore cross-curricular science and art we first need to identify a meaningful starting point. In the case of art and design one of the first things to consider is what is visual in science. One example might be the colours of various chemicals before, after and during a chemical reaction; another might be the geometric shapes present in nature.

Reflective task

Thinking about the science you teach, what are the visual aspects of your work? List any areas of your curriculum that can be defined as visual. What do you ask your pupils to look at? Do any of the areas you have identified offer opportunities for artistic expression?

One visual area of science that is a great starting point for a science–art collaboration is the use of microscopes. Figure 8.2 is a wheat seed magnified under a microscope. This is just one example of the visual nature of plant and cell biology. Most plants and cells can appear eye-catching under a microscope and can be the basis for a classroom project that integrates art with science.

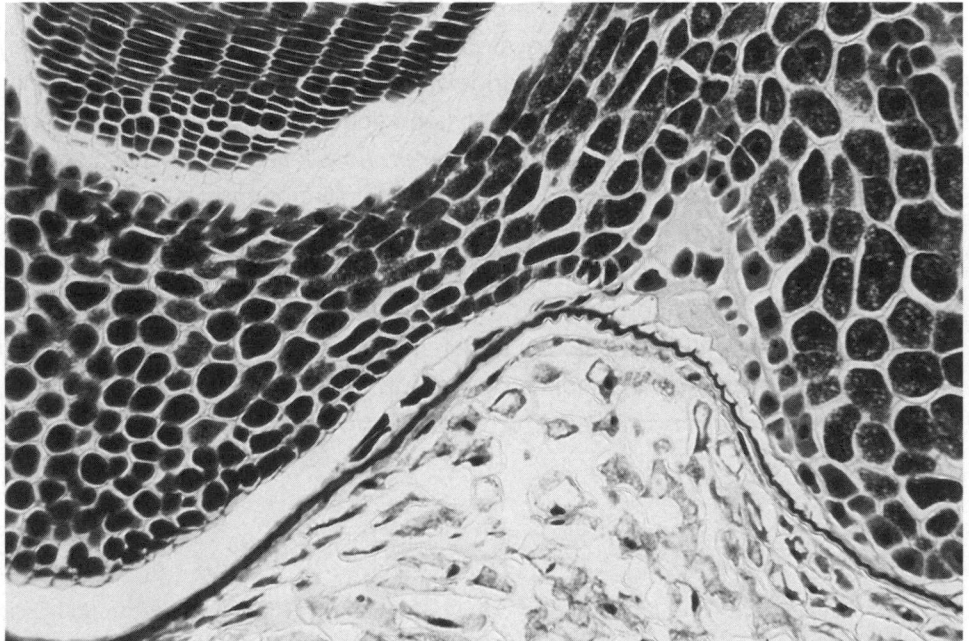

Figure 8.2 Magnified wheat seed.

Practical task

Science under the microscope

To explore further the concept of art under the microscope while at the same time teaching cell biology, one activity would be to magnify the cells of an onion. Pupils must carefully remove the thin, transparent membrane from the inner surface of an onion. This must then be placed onto a slide, covered with a drop of water and a cover glass. The slide can be observed through the microscope and both low power and high power magnification. Pupils can then answer questions on what they have observed, these may include for example:

1. What is the general shape of the cells?

2. Is the membrane made up of one or many cells?

3. Do the cells have a cell wall?

The pupils can then produce a sketch of the onion cell under the microscope. This can then form a piece of artwork produced in the science lab – an exciting concept for many pupils. While it is important that the images produced represent a solid scientific understanding of the cell biology being explored, the need for creativity allows a freedom of expression that may not be familiar to the usual diagram drawings completed in the science classroom. The images should represent a sense of what the pupils are seeing down the microscopes and not necessarily an exact replication of the image. Cross-curricular science and art is about pushing boundaries and exploring a new sense of creativity in science. This may require teachers to step out of their familiar comfort zones into a more exploratory way of science delivery. It is about understanding the fundamental science involved but finding new and exciting ways of expressing this knowledge. From the point of view of the learner this can be a very personal expression of understanding that can be shared *with* and supported *by* their immediate peer group.

Science and colours

The sensation of colour and the way we engage with it is an interesting strand of scientific exploration. It is also of fundamental importance to the work of most artists. This is an exciting common ground on which the two subjects can engage in cross–curricular activities. Such interaction, however, is based upon an illusion, because colour does not (in a literal sense) exist. Colour is a product of light and as such the sky is blue because the atmosphere scatters sunlight. Light with shorter wavelengths (blue, purple, violet) is scattered more in the atmosphere, so the sky appears blue; this is the same reason that sunsets and sunrises appear red and orange: at sunset/sunrise, the sun's light hits the atmosphere at a low angle, increasing the distance that the light must travel through the atmosphere. Thus, more colours are 'scattered out', even the blue-end of the spectrum, leaving red and orange colours.

There is little doubt that scientists and artists can have different relationships with colour. For scientists colour can be used in a flame test to identify the metal ions present in a sample material or to measure the temperature of a star. Used in this way colour can provide a formula against which flames or stars can be compared to produce accurate assumptions. For the artist, colour does not need to be static. It can be manipulated at whim to produce something beautiful, or shocking, or thought provoking. Take for example the way Vincent van Gogh engaged with colour:

Instead of trying to reproduce exactly what I see before me, I make more arbitrary use of colour to express myself more forcefully ... To express the love of two lovers by the marriage of two complementary colours ... To express the thought of a brow by the radiance of a light tone against a dark background. To express hope by some star. Someone's passion by the radiance of the setting sun.

(Vincent van Gogh 1888)

With this in mind, how can we begin to explore colours in the school science classroom? Let us begin by thinking about the primary colours.

The primary colours of pigment are called absorptive colours. They are red, blue and yellow and when mixed produce orange or green or purple. When all three are mixed you get brown.

The primary colours of light when mixed produce white light. The light from the sun contains all the colours which we can see if we use a prism to split it. The primary colours are red, blue and green. These are the colours seen in the 'triangles' that produce the pictures on a TV. We also see them used in spotlights for stages because their combination is white. The secondary colours of light when mixed are cyan, magenta and yellow. The primary colours of light are called additive colours, whereas the paint colours are called subtractive colours.

Practical task

A quick classroom activity concerning colours would be to create a rainbow using refraction. This can be done with few materials and can be very meaningful to pupils. One way to undertaken this activity can be found at http://micro.magnet.fsu.edu/optics/activities/students/prisms.html.

Creating the colour spectrum in the classroom can open a discussion on the psychology of colour, colour in nature and the way we engage with colour in art and design. It can also provide an opportunity to explore the work of Isaac Newton who discovered that pure white light, such as sunlight, is made up of the visible colours. He made this discovery while confined to his home during the Great Plague. To alleviate the boredom he punched holes in his curtains to consider the way light behaves when passed through a prism. He discovered that by using a second prism each colour is monochromatic – made up of a single, unique wavelength – and cannot be separated further to produce other colours. His work illustrated that light can be combined to produce other colours – for example, blue and yellow light can be combined to produce green light. This concept of mixing colours to create new colours is an important aspect of the work of an artist. The three primary colours in art (red, yellow and blue) are mixed to create other secondary colour combinations (see Table 8.1).

Table 8.1 Primary and secondary colours.

Primary colour		Primary colour		Secondary colour
Yellow	+	Blue	=	Green
Blue	+	Red	=	Purple
Red	+	Yellow	=	Orange

The colour wheel below (Figure 8.3) positions the secondary colours in between the primary colours. The colour wheel is used to identify complimentary colours. The colours positioned opposite to each other are thought to visually work well together.

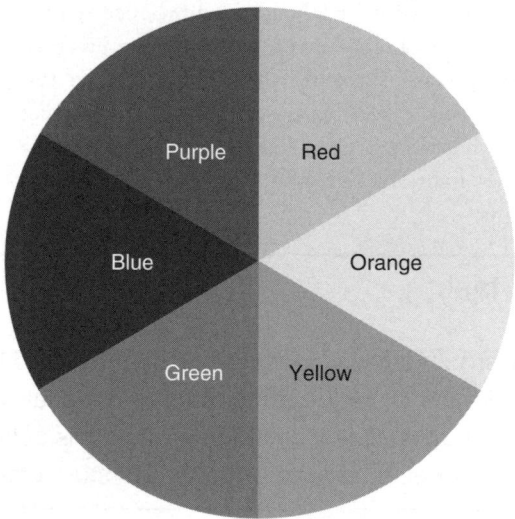

Figure 8.3 The colour wheel.

Practical task

An engaging classroom activity is to ask pupils to complete a colour survey. They should ask twenty or thirty people at random 'What is your favourite colour?' They can produce a bar chart to represent their findings. Most interestingly, the pupils must then begin to think about why people choose the answers they do and explore our relationship with colour.

To be able to explore this further we need to look further into the psychology of colours.

Psychology of colours

Different colours can impact on mood, attitude and even behaviour in human beings. We have deep-set cultural and personal connections with colours that are created through experience and association. Red is often associated with heat and fire. This is a product of traditions, customs, societal beliefs and life experiences but is accentuated further by industry and targeted advertising. For example, in the energy industry companies often use red in their logos or for advertising campaigns to emphasise warmth and heat. This association is true of many colours and is not a new phenomenon. Historically, religious artists reflect emotions or moods in their work: green in a stained glass window denotes hope and blue expresses contemplative faith. Meanings may have changed over time but the concept remains. Figure 8.4 shows seven colours and the emotions commonly associated with them.

Figure 8.4 Common emotion–colour associations.

In an experiment completed by the neuroscientist Beau Lotto and his team (2005), 150 people of different ages, backgrounds, gender and race were asked about colours in relation to different emotions. Nearly every adult participant assigned yellow to happiness, blue to sadness and red to anger. This psychological association with colours can often prove more powerful than the visual encounter itself. For example, the colour blue is associated with tranquillity and as such has been proven to calm the mind, while red can have the opposite affect and can actually physically raise the blood pressure. This is known as chormodynamics: we interact with colour in this way all of the time – from the clothes we choose to wear when we get up in the morning to the way that we decorate our homes. Colour and the combination of certain colours can create both pleasant *and* unpleasant reactions.

The psychology of colours is of great importance to the design industry. Whether it is to sell a product, or advertise on a website, or in interior design to decorate a home, the way we react to colours can be hugely influential. For example, it has been proven that people will gamble more if they sit under a red light: as a result red neon is common throughout Las Vegas.

Practical task

An interesting introduction to the psychology of colours can be explored through interior design. Using the cross-section of a house (see Figure 8.5) pupils are asked to colour in the walls of each room. Very little information is provided at the beginning of the activity. Each pupil must separately complete the diagram as they would paint it if it were their own house. It is very important that a full range of coloured crayons (or pens) is available to each pupil – their choice cannot be forced by a shortage of colour options. The results of this activity often see a degree of predictability with many pupils choosing blue or green for the bathroom and pink, purple or blue for the bedroom. What can be more interesting than the predictability of the activity is to explore further the reasoning for choosing the colours. This can draw out emotive feelings in regards to colours that may be as a result of cultural thinking or experience.

Figure 8.5 Cross-section of a house.

Do we all see the same colours?

Do we all see the same colours differently? This question has puzzled scientists for many years. The link between colour recognition and language seems to provide some answers to this problem.

Various studies have been conducted to explore the human brain's reaction to colour. In one such study (Franklin *et al.* 2008) adults and infants were asked to focus on a briefly flashing target that appeared against a background of a similar colour. This requires the participant to distinguish between the two colours quickly. The subject's visual field was examined in relation to the task. The infants were more successful at the task when the target appeared in their left visual field – this is connected to the pre-linguistic right hemisphere of the brain. Adults on the other hand were more successful with targets in their right visual field – which is linked to the left hemisphere of the brain where language processing takes place. This seems to go some way to highlight the fundamental connection between colour recognition and language. To illustrate this point further we can look to the Russian words *siniy* and *goluboy* which mean dark blue and light blue. For Russians the distinction between these two colours is as clear as our English speaking distinction between, for example, yellow and red. So while an English speaker may describe the dark blue as 'navy blue' to us it is still blue while for the Russians their language and culture differentiates them as two completely different colours. This does not mean that the colour itself is seen differently, but as a result of language, Russians are able to differentiate the two blues as easily as we could differentiate yellow from red.

Practical task

A quick activity that explores the brain and colour is the 'Say the colour not the word game'. In this activity the participant must name the colour written on the screen not the word. For example, the word orange might be written but the font colour is green so the participant must name green not orange. Individual pupils can complete the game against the clock at www. purposegames.com/game/say-the-colour-not-the-word-quiz and the results can be used to produce a class leader-board in terms of both accuracy of answers and speed. The exercise demonstrates that the brain is divided into the left and the right hemisphere. The left hemisphere is responsible for logical reasoning and conscious thought – so the things you are consciously aware of. The right hemisphere, in contrast, is used for creativity and abstract thought – this can mean the things you know without really having to think about them. People tend to use one or the other sides of the brain at any given time so when you try to use both hemispheres at the same time it can get quite confusing. In the case of this activity the left side of the brain is being used to read the words while the right side of the brain is undertaking the more abstract task of recognising colours.

Optical illusions

Optical illusions can help learners to understand the role the brain plays in sight. With around 40% of the brain dedicated to vision it is a critical part of the process of sight. Without the brain we would not be able to make sense of everything we see, pick up an object in front of us or retain information such as how to read. The brain is always learning when it comes to things it has never seen before. Look at Figure 8.6 for example. What do you see? Not many people see it straight away because it can take a while for the brain to process the image but once your brain has learnt to see it properly you will never struggle to identify the image again – even if you wait ten years your brain will allow you to recognise it immediately.

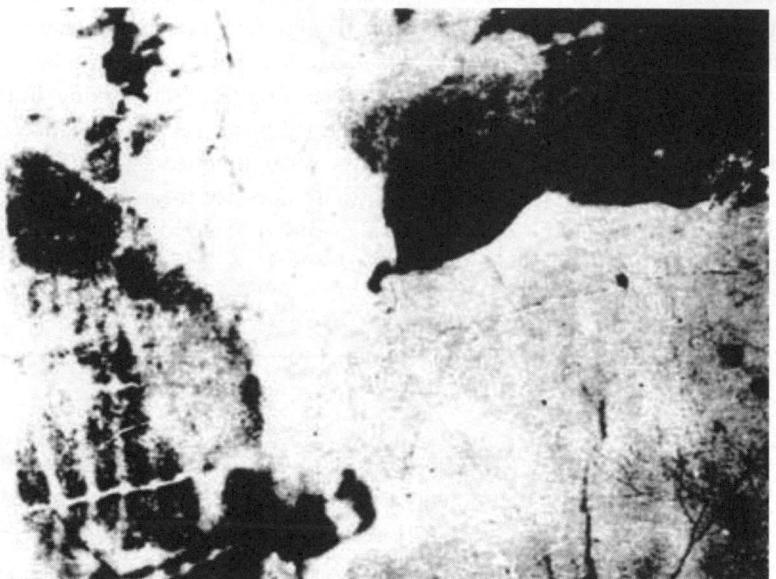

Figure 8.6 Optical Illusion 1.

This illustrates the amazing capacity of our brain to work in coordination with our eyes, but there are ways to play tricks on your brain known as optical illusions. Scientists, and in particular neuroscientists, are still incredibly interested in the way our brain reacts to optical illusions as they may provide further insight into the way our brains function. The logic being – to be able to understand how we can see correctly we must understand how we can sometimes see incorrectly. The illusion in Figure 8.7 shows what appears to be a convexed shape protruding from the page. This is of course a trick of the eye (or, more accurately, brain) – the lines on the grid are actually perfectly straight.

Another example is the unreal geometric object in Figure 8.8. At first glance it appears to be a cube, however closer inspection reveals that the shape is in fact impossible.

Figure 8.7 Optical Illusion 2.

Figure 8.8 Optical Illusion 3.

The study of optical illusions is a fascinating field of science that explores the way that, as humans, we use the brain in conjunction with sight. Illusions allow scientists to explore the way the brain retains information and looks for familiar patterns, and as such, does not look at the worlds *as it is* but instead in terms of the past and previous experiences. This is the search for useful patterns that link to previous, relevant behaviour to prompt and guide current behaviour.

Optical illusions have also influenced the world of art and design. Op Art (or Optical Art) is a style of abstract art that draws inspiration from optical illusions. Artists such as Bridget Riley, Victor Vasarely and Josef Albers have all contributed to this field of fine art. Much like the traditional optical illusions shown here the pieces are created by the careful positioning of patterns, lines and colour. Riley produced some of the field's most famous pieces including *Movement in Squares* (1961), which tricks the brain into thinking that the squares on the page are visibly shifting. Some of her work is so intense that exposure can actually cause the eyes to hurt. If the work of Bridget Riley can be compared to the type of optical illusion seen in Figure 8.7 then the illusion in Figure 8.8 is reminiscent of the artwork produced by the artist M. C. Escher. Escher experimented with mathematics, shapes, tessellation and perspective to produce beguiling works which, much like optical illusions, trick and confuse the brain. In one of his most famous works, *Relativity* (1953), Escher depicted a series of interrelated staircases that at first glance appear to follow a logical structure, but on second look appear to inexplicably cross-cross each other and produce an impossible maze of gravity–defying stairways.

Practical task

One exciting way to explore optical illusions in the classroom is to get pupils to create their own illusions. To do this, pupils must follow instructions carefully. First they must draw horizontal, wavy lines across a piece of A4 paper (in landscape). The lines must not be too close together or too bumpy. They must then draw a small circle somewhere on the page, off-centre. This circle should be approximately the size of a 10 pence piece. They should then continue drawing concentric circles to the edge of the paper. This should create a grid. Now for the fun bit … beginning at the outside edge and working inwards, every other square should be lightly marked with a pencil. This is just providing a guide before permanent colour is added. Once this is completed colour can begin to be added carefully inside every square that has been marked with pencil. The final result will be a psychedelic, colourful optical illusion (Figure 8.9).

Figure 8.9 Example of a pupil's optical illusion.

The mathematics of science and art

A mathematician, like a painter or poet, is a maker of patterns. If his patterns are more permanent than theirs, it is because they are made with ideas.

(G. H. Hardy)

The mathematician G. H. Hardy once described his interest in mathematics only as a creative art. This suggests that one approach to the application of science through art can be through the examination of mathematics as a bridging subject. Geometry and tessellation are two areas of mathematics that can work effectively with both science and art. Take a look at Chapter 6 of Robert Ward-Penny's cross-curricular mathematics book (2011) for more ideas relating to geometry and mathematics.

Practical task

Inspired by Mondrian

The lesson should begin with a brief look at the work of Piet Mondrian and his painting style. His work focused on vertical and horizontal grid lines as the basis for geometrically inspired artwork. For a good background to the Mondrian take a look at: www.pietmondrian.org.

During the lesson pupils can recreate a Mondrian-style piece of art while learning important mathematical terms such as vertical, horizontal, perpendicular, parallel, converge, diverge, diagonal, perimeter, area. Pupils can do this by drawing lines vertically and horizontally across a piece of paper with different lines in parallel and perpendicular to each other. The lines can be drawn in pencil and then made permanent with a thick black marker pen in the style reminiscent to that of Mondrian. Poster paints in red, yellow and blue can be used to decorate the squares and rectangles created by the pupil's lines.

Fibonacci

Following on from the geometric patterning we can now turn again to Fibonacci (for more on the mathematics of Fibonacci please see Chapter 4) and the concept of beauty in mathematics. The Fibonacci sequence (1, 1, 2, 3, 5, 8, 13, 21, 34, 55 …) shows that each number is the sum of the two preceding numbers. It is a sequence that is seen and used in many different areas of mathematics and science. The sequence is an example of a recursive sequence. Using the Fibonacci sequence pupils can create a Fibonacci spiral. This introduces the concept of the Golden Rectangle as a means by which to begin an understanding of the way the sequence impacts upon aesthetics.

The shape in Figure 8.10 uses the Fibonacci sequence to form a rectangle. Starting with a 1x1 square, each following square is a multiple of the next number in the sequence, e.g. 1x1, 2x2, 3x3, 5x5, 8x8 and 13x13. Use the template in Chapter 4 to draw this shape. The rectangle produced by the pattern is known as the Golden Rectangle.

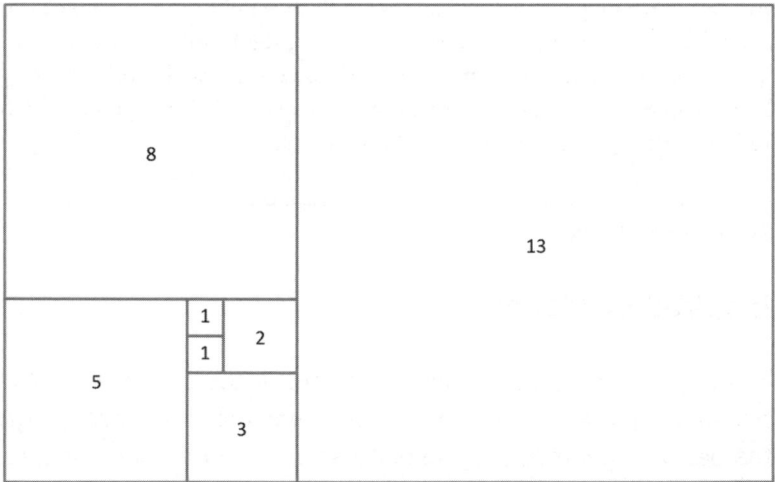

Figure 8.10 A Fibonacci template.

Once you have drawn the Golden Rectangle, it can be used to create the Fibonacci spiral (Figure 8.11). To do this you must draw arcs (quarter circles) in each of the squares that make up the Golden Rectangle. Starting at the first 1x1 square you drew first, work outwards with the arcs meeting at the opposite corners of the squares. Figure 8.11 illustrates how the image should look. The Fibonacci sequence defines the curvature of naturally occurring spirals, such as snail shells and even the pattern of seeds in flowering plants. The curl of the chameleon's tails in Figure 8.12 demonstrates the Fibonacci curve in nature.

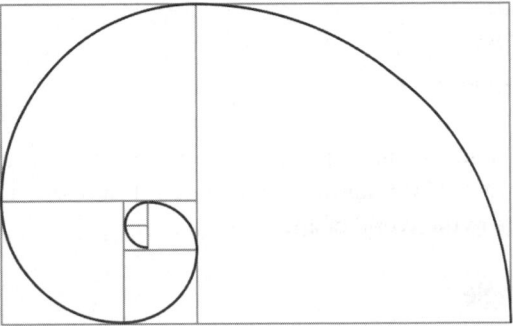

Figure 8.11 A Fibonacci spiral.

Figure 8.12 A chameleon's tail curled up.

As we have seen, by adding together the sequential numbers we can create the Fibonacci sequence, which can in turn be used to produce a Golden Rectangle. But what if, instead of adding the two numbers in the sequence, we divide them? For example, 8÷5, or 13÷8 and so on:

$1 \div 1 = 1$

$2 \div 1 = 2$

$3 \div 2 = 1.5$

$5 \div 3 = 1.6666$

$8 \div 5 = 1.6$

$13 \div 8 = 1.625$

$21 \div 13 = 1.61538\ldots$

$34 \div 21 = 1.61904\ldots$

As we work through the sequence the ratio seems to be settling down to a particular value – around 1.62. This is known as the Golden Ratio ($\phi = 1.618$), which, as we will see, is very important to the world of art.

The Golden Rectangle

Fibonacci is important in art as his calculations are linked with what we find aesthetically pleasing. For example, take a look at the rectangles in Figure 8.13. Which one do you find most pleasing?

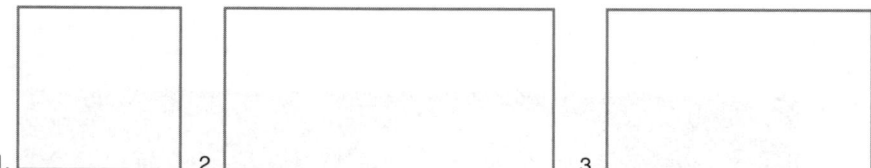

Figure 8.13 Three rectangles.

If you chose the first shape you may be the type of person who likes symmetry and order. Unfortunately for the second rectangle not many people like its proportions and as such do not choose it. Most people tend to find the third shape most appealing and you may be interested to learn that it is all down to the Golden Ratio. This third shape is a Golden Rectangle!

The ratios of each rectangle (length to width):

Rectangle 1   1:1

Rectangle 2   2:1

Rectangle 3   1.618:1   **The Golden Ratio!**

The Golden Rectangle is created when the length and the width of the rectangle are in the Golden Ratio – the length is approximately 1.618 times the width. See Figure 8.14a.

If a square is placed within the Golden Rectangle, the shape that remains is also a Golden Rectangle. So using Figure 8.14b we can see that ABCD forms a Golden Rectangle, as does ABEF.

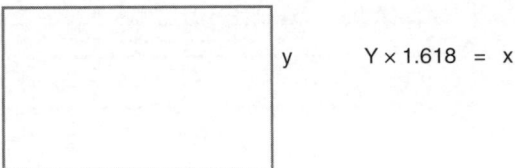

Figure 8.14a The Golden Rectangle.

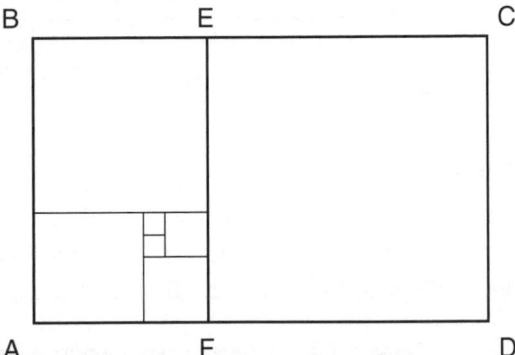

Figure 8.14b The Golden Rectangle.

Similarly to the workings of the Golden Rectangle we can see the Golden Ratio at work in the Golden Section (Figure 8.15a).

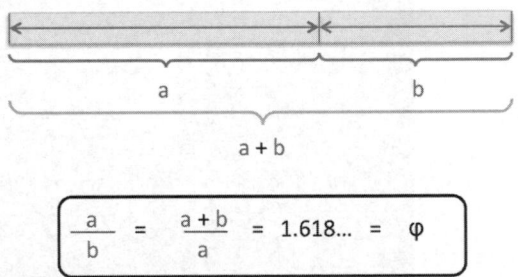

Figure 8.15a The Golden Section.

This is a little more complicated so could be used as a piece of extension work or is suitable for Key Stage 4 and above.

The line is divided into two parts, *a* (the longer section) and *b* (the shorter section). We want the ratio of the shorter section (*b*) to the longer section (*a*) to be the same as the ratio of the longer section to the whole line (*a+b*). In other words, as *b* is to *a*, so is *a* to *a+b*. If you divide the line so that the longest section is about 1.618 times the shortest section, you've divided it in the Golden Section. Take a look at the worked example in Figure 8.15b.

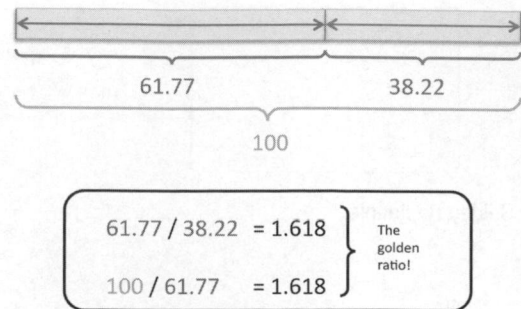

Figure 8.15b The Golden Section.

The Golden Ratio and art

So how does the Golden Ratio relate to the world of art? Take a look at the image of Paris's Notre Dame Cathedral in Figure 8.16. Using the Golden Section we can see how Fibonacci's Golden Ratio is used throughout the architecture.

Figure 8.16 Notre Dame Cathedral, Paris.

The CN Tower in Toronto (Figure 8.17) also uses the Golden Ratio. Standing at 553.33 metres tall, the tower's main observation deck is at 342 metres from the ground. So the ratio of the tower's height to the height of the observation deck is 1:1.618! Once again we see the Golden Ratio at work.

Figure 8.17 The CN Tower, Toronto.

Architects use the Golden Ratio in building design because the proportions are pleasing to the eye. Equally, as the Golden Ratio can be found regularly in nature it is a way of artistically connecting the structure of buildings to the natural world. As in architecture, the Golden Ratio can be found in art. For example, take a look at Leonardo da Vinci's *Mona Lisa* (Figure 8.18). The image appears to draw heavily on the Fibonacci's Golden Rectangle with her body and facial features placed carefully in relation to the Golden Ratio.

Figure 8.18 *The Mona Lisa* by Leonardo da Vinci.

Practical task

Using the Golden Ratio in artwork

Ask your pupils to draw a Golden Section on a piece of blank paper. They may place it anywhere on the sheet and it may be any overall length as long as it is calculated accurately and uses the Golden Ratio of 1:1.618. This can be calculated using the equations earlier in this chapter.

Make sure they draw the line in pencil so it can be removed later.

They must then use this line to create a piece of artwork. You may wish to set a theme for the class such as animals, transport, buildings etc. or alternatively you can leave it broad allowing them the freedom to design anything they feel. Equally, you may wish them to produce an abstract piece of work – take a look at an artist such as Mondrian for inspiration.

The main focus of the piece must be based around the Golden Section although for the more able pupils they may be encouraged to introduce additional Golden Sections which can be used to draw further shapes or objects.

Science and music

Music can be a highly personal experience appreciated by many people who may not necessarily consider themselves lovers of the arts. We can surround ourselves in music in a way that some perceive to be impossible with fine art and design. We can be (figuratively) *lost in music* and the effect of certain harmonies or compositions can produce physical reactions – for example shivers or goosebumps. Scans have shown that listening to music can increase activity of nearly every part of the brain (Ball 2010). All of this despite the fact that music appears to have no evolutionary benefits to humans:

> Neither the enjoyment nor the capacity of producing musical notes are faculties of the least direct use to man in reference to his ordinary habits of life.
>
> (Darwin 1871)

Even without any claims to evolutionary significance the human production of music can be traced back to early civilisation when people made rhythms using bones, wood and skins. The relationship between science and music can boast a notable history. The diatonic scale still used as the basis for most Western music today has Pythagoras to thank for the calculations he made in Ancient Greece. The study of science and music today is predominantly interested in the reasons why we interact with music as we do, how we go about creating music and what it is. Current research into the integrated discipline includes topics such as acoustics, software development, pitch, tone, memory, emotion and perceptions.

A solid cross-curricular science–music endeavour may begin with an exploration of sound and how we hear. This can include some time spent learning about the ear, airwaves, pitch, vibration and so on. A discussion on how the ear works can be linked to why speakers on a stereo system vibrate. This can be demonstrated with the use of dominoes. The dominoes represent air molecules, which vibrate against each other, each one putting pressure on the next until the vibrations reach the ear and the brain recognises it as sound. This can form a solid introduction and basis for a more context driven exploration of music and sound.

Another interesting starting point for cross-curricular work of this kind can include an exploration of frequency and hearing. It is well known that different animals are able to hear sounds at different frequencies (Figure 8.19 illustrates this). However, it is also interesting to explore the notion of different humans being able to hear different frequencies. The Mosquito alarm is a social deterrent that can generally only be heard by people below twenty-five years of age. The alarm has met with some controversy but it has been implemented in some urban areas to deter loitering by young people and combat anti-social behaviour. While some advocates claim the Mosquito can protect businesses and individuals from crime, the alarm's critics argue that it represents a basic infringement of human rights by discriminating against all young people regardless of behaviour. This can form the basis of an interesting classroom debate that brings in issues relating to citizenship, the law and ethics. The introduction to this activity can include the playing of the Mosquito alarm in the classroom. You will find a version of the alarm at http://theoatmeal.com/quizzes/sound/.

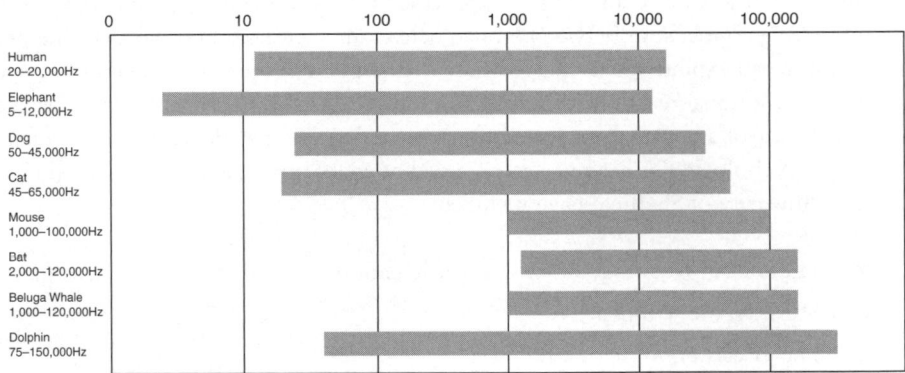

Figure 8.19 Different frequencies heard by animals.

Musical expression

The creation of music and rhythm has been recorded throughout history and across a vast number of different cultures. We engage with music all of the time through our daily life. Music can be heard via TV, radio, shops, public transport – the list goes on – but if we want to identify a rhythm closer to home we need look no further than our own human bodies with our breathing, blood flow and pulse.

The past decade has seen significant advances in scientific research relating to human engagement with music. This has involved some highly technical studies using brain-mapping technology. It has even seen the way we dance to music broken down into a scientific process undertaken in the brain. This begs the question – should we be looking in such a *scientific* way at what is an expressive, and often very personal art form?

This question is also central to any cross-curricular science art work undertaken. While the arts can add a rich and engaging depth to science, this should be pursued with a degree of caution. As with any cross-curricular activity the work must be sympathetic to all subjects involved. In the case of art, the focus is on expression, meaning and personality:

> The aim of art is to represent not the outward appearance of things, but their inward significance.
>
> (Aristotle)

It is crucial that this emphasis on personal expression is prized along with all of the other differences evident in the purposes and aims of both science and the arts. As we have seen already, that is not to say that the arts and science lack common ground. They both seek to inspire a sense of wonder and harness creativity – be that through musical compositions or mathematic hypotheses. Once again, it is important to emphasis this need for academic compassion and understanding when undertaking cross-curricular ventures.

Music and psychology

One area of interest within the sphere of music and science is the psychology of music. Much like the work explored in the previous section on colour, psychology can draw out interesting connections between human behaviour, emotions and the arts. The psychology of music can explore a wide range of different aspects of musical behaviour, engagement in music, emotional reactions to music, musical performance and musical preferences. It is a broad area of study that explores cognitive understanding, developmental education and social psychology. For example, recent psychology of music research projects undertaken by the University of Sheffield have included:

- The social psychology of musical participation
- Music in the workplace
- The effects of music on driving
- The physiology of emotional responses to music
- Key-mood associations
- Perception of sound source and location in music recordings
- Pleasure and boredom responses to a musical cadenza
- Personality and musical preference
- Expression in musical performance
- The role of the body in musical performance
- Sight reading in performance

- Teacher/pupil relationships in music lessons
- The social and therapeutic functions of singing
- Perceptual and semiotic approaches to musical meaning.

How we respond to music can be an interesting classroom activity that draws upon the concepts of human psychology and music therapy. Certain music seems to provoke a similar reaction in a large number of people: a good example of this is Barber's *Adagio for Strings*. The composition recently made the top five in a BBC Radio Four poll of the *saddest* pieces of music of all time. The arrangement was famously featured in a highly emotive scene of the Oliver Stone classic movie *Platoon*, but do we find this piece so sad because we subconsciously (or indeed consciously) connect it to an emotional event in a film, or is the music inherently sad?

The online science and music website Exploratorium (www.exploratorium.edu/music/) explores this issue of sadness in music and explains that it can often be linked to use of the minor key. The website also includes sound bites to listen to the music played in both a major and minor key to compare the difference between the two. In the case of Barber's composition, whether as a result of, or indeed in spite of, its inclusion on TV and film, the music is firmly connected with the feeling of loss and sadness. So much so it was performed at the Last Night of Proms in 2001 in memory of the lives lost in the September 11 attacks on New York.

Practical task

Exploring the link between music and emotions can be an engaging and interesting classroom activity. Table 8.2 lists eight example pieces of music that can be used in the classroom to discuss the psychology of music – this is not an exhaustive list but a starting point using a variety of contemporary and classical pieces. As each piece (or excerpts from each piece) is played to the pupils they should consider how the music is making them feel. They may wish to close their eyes for this. Each pupil should identify one emotion that they are feeling in direct response to the piece: for example fear, anger, happiness, joy and sadness. The teacher may also wish to ask the pupils to think of a colour they would associate with this music. As seen in the section on science and colour, cultural and psychological connections between colours and emotions may mean their choices of colours during this activity tell an interesting story about the emotion they felt while the music was being played. This task should be completed individually but answers can be discussed as a group. Were the pupils feeling similar emotions during each piece? If so, how could this be possible? Can they think of any other music that they immediately associate with a specific emotion?

Table 8.2 Examples of music to consider.

Music	Web link
Samuel Barber, *Adagio for Strings*	http://www.youtube.com/watch?v=1dPDO3Tfab0
Sigur Rós, *Hoppipolla*	http://www.youtube.com/watch?v=hnAwPeqrdAk
Bach, *Toccata and Fugue in D minor*	http://www.youtube.com/watch?v=IVJD3dL4diY
Snow Patrol, *Crack the Shutters*	http://www.youtube.com/ watch?v=GhK81hZj4L4&ob=av2e
Holst, *The Planets, Mars, The Bringer of War*	http://www.youtube.com/watch?v=L0bcRCCg01I
Kate Bush, *This Woman's Work*	http://www.youtube.com/watch?v=iEHqPCA_IzQ
The Strokes, *Under Cover of Darkness*	http://www.youtube.com/watch?v=OwxcQvB_vcQ
Bob Marley, *Three Little Birds* (instrumental)	http://www.youtube.com/watch?v=t22I8P0otj4& feature=related

One of the main discussions that can take place after the initial activity is complete is that of clever musical placement within TV and film. Many movies and TV shows use certain music to influence the emotions of their viewers. Is this because certain songs produce certain emotions, or alternatively do we feel a certain way when we listen to some music because it has been used on TV, in films or in advertising in certain contexts? For example Kate Bush's song *This Woman's Work* is often used in the background of very upsetting scenes on charity appeal shows such as Comic Relief. This can result in many people associating the work with a feeling of sadness. Does this mean that the song itself is not sad, but it is fact deemed sad because of its association? This is, in some ways, a *chicken or egg* debate. It may be hard for some pupils to disassociate the emotions they connect with a piece of music from its appearance in a film or TV show, however, there may be students in the group who have never seen the film or show in question and therefore have not been influenced by its placement on screen. In this case more discussion is required – why does the pupil who has not seen the film associate the arrangement with the same emotion as the pupil who has seen the film? Equally, a pupil may not have heard a song before but the piece itself still produces an emotional response.

Practical task

Follow-on task

A meaningful follow-on project sees pupils select one piece of music that they enjoy or wish to explore further. They must then conduct a small research study by asking around ten or twenty other school pupils how the music makes them feel. The music must be played to the participating pupils in full and their responses must be recorded. This can be conducted on a Likert scale from positive to negative. See Figure 8.20.

How does the music make you feel? (please circle one)

negative   1   2   3   4   5   6   7   8   9   10   positive

Figure 8.20 Likert scale.

Once all pupils have completed their research the results can be compiled as a whole class. This will allow the class to map each song across a spectrum from positive to negative in comparison to other pieces of music. Each pupil should produce a graph of their findings that can be shared with the class. Graphical representations of the group's findings can be drawn up alone or as a whole class. The activity itself draws upon sound research skills and focuses on pupil-led investigations.

Practical task

Another possible activity is to explore world music. This activity focuses more on the social sciences as well as psychology and human behaviour, so it may be a useful activity through which aspects of citizenship can be introduced into the science classroom. The activity begins with the teacher playing different types of world music to the class (see Table 8.3 for examples of global music). The pupils are then asked to discuss what colours they feel fit with the music, what emotions they associate with the piece and what dancing/movement they think corresponds with it. This can produce a group or whole class discussion. The pupils must then try to locate the origin of the music on a world map. While this activity does not emphasise any major scientific learning, as a short follow-on activity it can explore some aspects of music recognition and music psychology.

Table 8.3 World music to consider.

Country of origin	Music
Indian	http://www.youtube.com/watch?v=QUeMuFa0VSM&feature=related
South African	http://www.youtube.com/watch?v=gVLu16IU4il
China	http://www.youtube.com/watch?v=xJl7I2f1Atc
Irish	http://www.youtube.com/watch?v=IjmpKk4F30s
Cuban	http://www.youtube.com/watch?v=Z4e7VcnWCT0&feature=related
Hawaiian	http://www.youtube.com/watch?v=Nqj_mtdpV-o

Science and drama

Much like the rise in fine art and design projects that are exploring the world of science, drama is no longer hesitant in tackling, often complex, scientific concepts. The nature versus nurture debate was portrayed in the Caryl Churchill play *A Number* while Yasmina Reza's drama *Life x3* explored the notion of parallel universes. Drama can be an exciting way to explore science in the classroom. The teaching can be spontaneous and unpredictable and if approached appropriately the process can embed learning and support cognitive understanding. Drama can assist the development of skills such as team working and communication while at the same time building confidence. As with the other arts–based disciplines explored in this chapter drama can provide a highly creative framework on which teaching can be delivered.

Drama gives pupils the opportunity to inject their personality into the science they are exploring. Dramatic activity may vary and take many forms in the classroom. The drama may be structured in a way where pupils enact roles within the known framework of scientific theories:

- *Dramatisation of a scientific process or theory* – e.g. playing electrons in a circuit to illustrate the scientific concept of electricity

- *Role-plays of an historical event either from the recent or distant past* – e.g. the trial of Galileo or the 'great debate' following Darwin's publication

- *Pupils as scientists* – explorative drama where the pupils have significant freedom to affect the play, but where the teacher gently guides them to keep the focus and tension. For example, a science-fiction drama where the pupils enact the roles of researchers from another planet that has just exploded: they wonder if they can possibly live on planet Earth. With an anthropological perspective the pupils study and describe the Earth.

A more detailed exploration of science and drama can be found in Chapter 6.

Science and dance

In the world of professional dance science has been explored by choreographers such as Mark Baldwin and David Bintley. While Baldwin has tackled the work of both Einstein and Darwin through contemporary dance, Bintley has used abstract ballet to explore the theory of relativity. For Bintley science and ballet share a need for order and discipline and therefore make happy bedfellows. The connection between movement and the brain offers an interesting starting point for a classroom project that combines the two disciplines.

It was previously thought that only humans responded to music through rhythmic movement. While dancing animals such as bears and elephants had traditionally been seen in circus acts, their movement was thought to be a response to intensive (often highly cruel) training. However, an interesting and somewhat amusing video of a bird dancing to the pop act, The Backstreet Boys, implies animals and birds can in fact independently engage with music through a form of dance. (See http://www.youtube.com/watch?v=N7IZmRnAo6s.) What can this tell us about music, movement and the brain?

The issue of rhythm and mathematics is also an exciting angle through which science and dance can be investigated. Mathematical sequencing can be learnt through dance, as can some aspects of geometry. Many dance moves can be described using scientific and mathematic terminology such as symmetry, patterns and shapes. Pupils given a specific mathematic sequence can be set the task of choreographing a dance routine that fits with their assigned sequence:

> When students act out mathematical concepts with steps, movements, and gestures, the concepts become real to them. Weaving dance into mathematics instruction is viewed as a way of integrating the arts into the mainstream curriculum and, at the same time, making mathematics more interesting and extending the attention span of students.
>
> (Burg and Lüttringhaus 2006: 2)

It is also true that to interpret a concept or story in dance you must first fully understand that concept. As such, if pupils are asked to create a dance (or indeed short dramatisation) based around a specific scientific process, concept or event they must first undertake thorough research to ensure their piece is accurate. This process can provide a meaningful context and cement learning in students.

Conclusion

The cross-curricular collaboration of science and the arts embodies the creative nature of integrated teaching. Not only does the teacher require a creative approach in planning (and often delivering) an activity, but the activity itself fosters pupil creativity.

Professional standards for QTS

This chapter will help meet the following standards:

Q6	Have a commitment to collaboration and co-operative working
Q7	(a) Reflect on and improve their practice, and take responsibility for identifying and meeting their developing professional needs
Q8	Have a creative and constructively critical approach towards innovation, being prepared to adapt their practice where benefits and improvements are identified
Q10	Have a knowledge and understanding of a range of teaching, learning and behaviour management strategies and know how to use and adapt them, including how to personalise learning and provide opportunities for all learners to achieve their potential
Q14	Have a secure knowledge and understanding of their subject/curriculum areas and related pedagogy to enable them to teach effectively across the age and ability range for which they are trained
Q17	Know how to use skills in literacy, numeracy and ICT to support their teaching and wider professional activities
Q23	Design opportunities for learners to develop their literacy, numeracy and ICT skills
Q24	Plan homework or other out-of-class work to sustain learners' progress and to extend and consolidate their learning
Q32	Work as a team member and identify opportunities for working with colleagues, sharing the development of effective practice with them
Q33	Ensure that colleagues working with them are appropriately involved in supporting learning and understand the roles they are expected to fulfil

Professional standards for teachers

This chapter will help meet the following standards:

C6	Have a commitment to collaboration and co-operative working where appropriate
C8	Have a creative and constructively critical approach towards innovation, being prepared to adapt their practice where benefits and improvements are identified
C15	Have a secure knowledge and understanding of their subject/curriculum areas and related pedagogy including: the contribution that their subjects/curriculum areas can make to cross-curricular learning; and recent relevant developments
C17	Know how to use skills in literacy, numeracy and ICT to support their teaching and wider professional activities
C27	Design opportunities for learners to develop their literacy, numeracy and ICT and thinking and learning skills appropriate within their phase and context
C40	Work as a team member and identify opportunities for working with colleagues, managing their work where appropriate and sharing the development of effective practice with them

Pupils' Personal, Learning and Thinking Skills (PLTS)

This chapter will help meet the following skills:

Independent enquirers	• Identify questions to answer and problems to resolve
Creative thinkers	• Generate ideas and explore possibilities • Connect their own and others' ideas and experiences in inventive ways
Reflective learners	• Evaluate experiences and learning to inform future progress • Communicate their learning in relevant ways for different audiences
Team workers	• Collaborate with others to work towards common goals • Take responsibility, showing confidence in themselves and their contribution

9

The assessment of cross-curricular teaching in science

Key objectives

By the end of this chapter you will have:

■ Explored the nature of assessment in relation to cross-curricular teaching and learning

■ Examined the Key Stage 3 science curriculum and identified potential assessment possibilities

■ Identified areas for cross-curricular and skills development and assessment.

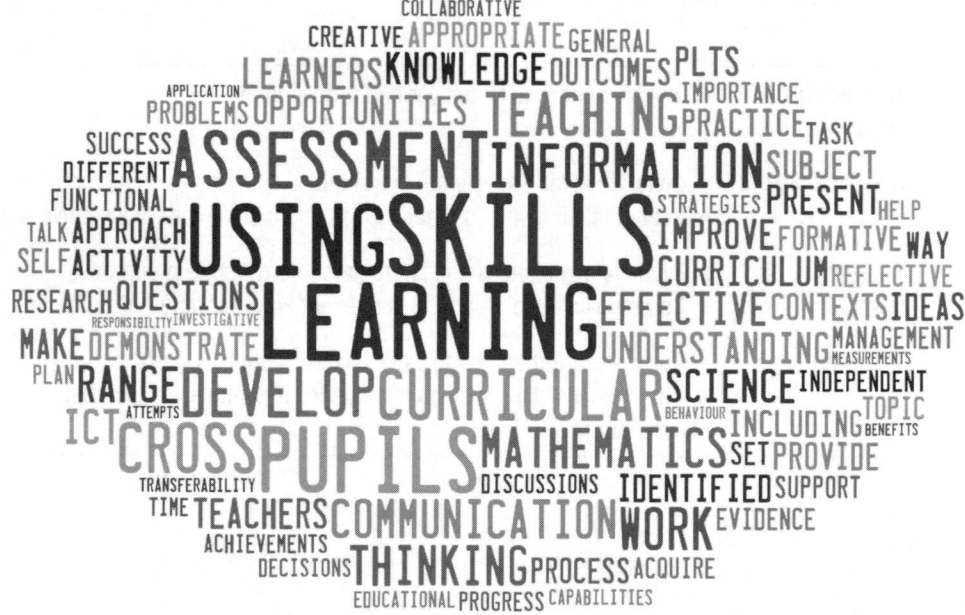

Introduction

It is now agreed that the acquisition of knowledge is not of sole importance for learners. Apart from knowledge, learners should acquire general skills (e.g. Pressley and McCormick 1995). The necessity to teach general skills has also received increasing attention among educational policy makers. The thought behind this is that in a society, which undergoes continuous change, it is important that pupils are capable of functioning properly by means of general skills, in the sense that they will acquire new knowledge by themselves and solve problems independently. Pupils who do not only acquire knowledge at school, but also learn these types of skill will profit from this in their further school careers and later lives. Using cross-curricular teaching and learning and skills development can improve the general quality of education, strengthening general knowledge and skills adapted to technological developments can help pupils in their future decision-making about their further educational career and beyond.

The challenge to develop cross-curricular skills started in the early 1990s when it was recognised that there was more to teaching and learning than just subject knowledge and understanding. At that time two key questions emerged. What kinds of skills are needed for young adults to live as responsible citizens? To what extent do pupils already possess these skills (Trier 1991)? Two of the cross-curricular skills that were identified were problem-solving and communication. These are now two of the six Personal Learning and Thinking Skills (PLTS) recognised by teachers in schools: teaching these skills is part of the National Curriculum and teachers are required to address them in their daily work with pupils. By using these skills pupils can focus on *knowing how* as well as *knowing what* – learning how to learn.

By working in a cross-curricular way teachers and pupils can experience a collaborative approach wholly different from having lessons confined to particular curriculum subject areas. This then raises some important issues for successful implementation and assessment in the classroom.

Cross-curricular functional skills

The importance of cross-curricular skills is that of transferability. By teaching and assessing cross-curricular activities teachers can see how pupils perform and if required take the necessary action to develop achievement further. By assessing across a number of subjects a better picture emerges of pupils' achievements. The functional skills common to all cross-curricular activity are those of Communication, Using Mathematics and Using ICT.

Communication across the science curriculum

Communication is central to the entire school curriculum and pupils should be able to communicate in order to express themselves socially, emotionally and physically. They should also develop as individuals, engage with others and contribute as members of society. Therefore, pupils should be given the opportunity to engage with and demonstrate the skill of communication and to transfer their knowledge about communication concepts and skills to real-life meaningful contexts across the curriculum.

The modes of communication include talking and listening, and reading and writing. However, effective communication can also include non-verbal forms, wider literacy and the use of multimedia and ICT technologies which may combine a range of different ways. Pupils should, therefore, be encouraged to become effective communicators by using a range of techniques, forms and media to convey information and ideas creatively and appropriately (see Table 9.1) – many of which can be formally and informally assessed using both formative and summative techniques.

Table 9.1 Communication skills.

Skill	Pupils should be enabled to:
Talking and listening	• Listen to and take part in discussions, explanations, role plays and presentations • Contribute comments, ask questions and respond to others' points of view • Communicate information, ideas, opinions, feelings and other thoughts using an expanding vocabulary • Structure their talk and speak clearly so that ideas can be understood by others • Adapt ways of speaking to audience and situation • Use non-verbal methods to express ideas and engage the listener
Reading	• Read a range of texts for information, ideas and enjoyment • Use a range of strategies to read with increasing independence • Find, select and use information from a range of sources • Understand and explore ideas, events and features in texts • Use evidence from texts to explain opinions ('Texts' can be in written, spoken, visual or symbolic forms.)
Writing	• Talk about, plan and edit work • Communicate information, meaning, feelings, imagination and other ideas in a clear and organised way • Develop and express and present ideas in a variety of forms and formats, using traditional and digital resources, for different audiences and purposes • Write with increasing accuracy and proficiency

Practical task

Take a topic from the Year 7 Scheme of Work for science and add a section that includes the skill of communication. Indicate how you would teach and assess this topic.

Incorporate as much cross-curricular teaching and learning as you can.

Using mathematics across the science curriculum

This is the skill of applying mathematical concepts, processes and understanding appropriately in a variety of contexts. Ideally these should be in relevant real life situations that require a mathematical dimension.

Pupils are likely to acquire and consolidate their mathematical knowledge, concepts and skills within the area of mathematics but they should also be given opportunities to transfer their understanding, as appropriate, to other contexts in the curriculum. Pupils can demonstrate their mathematical knowledge, understanding and skills in a variety of ways to communicate, manage information, think critically, solve problems and make decisions.

Across the curriculum, pupils should be enabled to:

- Choose the appropriate materials, equipment and mathematics to use in a particular situation
- Use mathematical knowledge and concepts accurately
- Work systematically and check their work
- Use mathematics to solve problems and make decisions
- Develop methods and strategies, including mental mathematics
- Explore ideas, make and test predictions and think creatively
- Identify and collect information
- Read, interpret, organise and present information in mathematical formats
- Use mathematical understanding and language to ask and answer questions, talk about and discuss ideas and explain ways of working
- Develop financial capability
- Use ICT to solve problems and/or present their work.

Practical task

Take a topic from the Year 8 Scheme of Work for science and add a section that includes the use of mathematics. Indicate how you would teach and assess this topic.

Incorporate as much cross-curricular teaching and learning as you can.

Using ICT across the science curriculum

Using ICT provides powerful tools and contexts to support meaningful learning and has the potential to transform and enrich pupils' experiences and environments across the curriculum. The creative use of ICT can empower learners to become independent, self-motivated and flexible, helping in turn to develop self-esteem and positive attitudes to learning, with which to realise their full potential. It also provides opportunities to collaborate within and beyond the classroom to pose questions, take risks and respond positively to 'What if' questions.

To help develop skills in researching, handling and communicating information pupils should have opportunities, using ICT, to engage in genuine research and purposeful tasks set in meaningful contexts (see Table 9.2). They should be encouraged to re-work information, present and exchange ideas and translate their thinking into creative products and productions which show an awareness of audience and purpose.

Table 9.2 ICT skills.

Skill	Pupils should be enabled to:
Explore	• Access and manage data and information • Research, select, process and interpret information • Investigate, make predictions and solve problems through interaction with digital tools • Understand how to keep safe and display acceptable online behaviour
Express	• Create, develop, present and publish ideas and information using a range of digital media • Create information and multimedia products using a range of assets
Exchange	• Communicate using a range of contemporary methods and tools • Share, collaborate, exchange and develop ideas digitally
Evaluate	• Talk about, review and make improvements to work, reflecting on the process and outcome • Consider the sources and resources used
Exhibit	• Manage and present their stored work • Showcase their learning across the curriculum

Practical task

Take a topic from the Year 9 Scheme of Work for science and add a section that includes the use of ICT. Indicate how you would teach and assess this topic.

Incorporate as much cross-curricular teaching and learning as you can.

Assessment for learning (AfL)

AfL is an approach that can support effective learning and teaching. AfL focuses on the learning process rather than the end product. It attempts not to prove learning but rather to improve it, i.e. it is formative assessment. It is a way of taking stock of learning during the process and it can help inform teachers of how learning is progressing. Cross–curricular teaching and learning is an ideal assessment tool for AfL. In AfL:

- There is a high emphasis on *transferable* learning.
- Assessment becomes a much more transparent process because it is based on critical information that is shared with the learner.
- Learners are able to take responsibility for their own learning and for aspects of their assessment.

AfL is not an extra that is 'bolted on'. It integrates with existing classroom practice and involves the key actions set out in Table 9.3.

Table 9.3 AfL criteria.

Sharing learning intentions	A learning intention describes what teachers want pupils to know, understand or be able to do by the end of an activity: It tells pupils what their learning is going to be. It helps teachers and pupils to focus on the learning rather than the activity, e.g. • *We are learning to …* • *We are learning this because …*
Sharing and negotiating success criteria	Success criteria are statements that help pupils recognise success in their learning: Pupils may be involved in deciding these. They summarise the processes or characteristics needed for success, and they link to the learning intention, i.e. they spell out the steps needed to achieve the learning intention and offer guidance on how to be successful.
Giving feedback to pupils	Quality feedback is essential for effective teaching and learning: Feedback motivates pupils by building self-esteem and to be truly formative it informs the next steps in the learning process, e.g. • Identify two occasions where the pupil has achieved success. • Identify an aspect of a pupil's work that can be immediately improved. • Give the pupil with a strategy on how to improve. • Give the pupil time to improve.
Effective questioning	Effective questioning is about asking questions in a way that elicits maximum feedback from pupils: This can then be used to evaluate, plan and extend learning, e.g. • Ask better questions – ask 'open' questions where there is no single correct answer. • Ask questions better – give pupils time to think. This can make a significant difference to the question's effectiveness.

Table 9.3 (*Continued*).

Self and peer assessment	Pupil reflection promotes independent learning, communication and support in the classroom:
	Teachers can develop pupil reflection in the classroom by using peer and self-assessment and self-evaluation.

Adapted from Black and William (2006)

Reflective task

How can AfL be used in cross-curricular work?

Examine one of the cross-curricular areas that have been discussed in this book and outline those aspect of AfL that could be employed in your teaching strategies.

Personal Learning and Thinking Skills (PLTS)

Is thinking a skill? In other words can it be improved in the same way as, say, whistling? White (2002) argues that understanding thinking as an activity means that it is something at which pupils can improve. That is, the activity can get better with practice and it is precisely this reason why thinking is sometimes characterised as a skill.

In contrast to this Johnson (2001) draws attention to the dangers associated with the attempts to teach thinking as a set of skills or simple rules to be followed. Attempts may lead to specific-subject knowledge being viewed not only as mere material on which to practise such skills, but worse still as a source of great inconvenience or waste of pupils' time. Specific subject knowledge, as pointed out by Johnson (2001), is far more important than proponents of general thinking skills care to admit. That is, what counts as good thinking is determined largely by the subject matter and as such one cannot separate thinking from the context within which it is applied. And to have knowledge of subject matter is to acquire certain ways of saying or doing things.

A key justification for seeking to include thinking skills within the school curriculum is the belief in the potential economic advantage of having such skills. In their provision of a broad survey of the development of generic skills in England from 1977 to 2002, Hayward and Fernandez (2004) concluded that despite an evident demand for generic skills in the English economy, education and training policy, planned to motivate the supply of such skills, have failed to deliver the desired results. They argue that not only have policy developments to teach such skills suffered implementation failure, the attempts have resulted in long prescriptive lists of skills with little educational merit, which had the unintended effect of limiting rather than expanding opportunities for learners. Furthermore, such skills have failed to deliver on their transferability, the supposed key feature of generic skills.

Higgins *et al.* (2005) on the other hand presented a comprehensive research review for evidence to support the efficacy of thinking skills across subject areas. One of the main reasons for the research was to quantify the impact of thinking skill interventions in order to test the conclusions of the mainly descriptive reviews in Britain as presented by Higgins *et al.* (2004), McGuinness (1999) and Wilson (2000). The research report concluded that the impact of thinking skills may vary according to subject. The implication of the findings by Higgins *et al.* (2005) was as follows:

> Whilst thinking skills programmes and approaches have a positive impact on pupils' attainment, such impact is not always consistent. The evidence from this review suggests that there is a need to select interventions carefully and to be prepared to persist with an intervention, as it may not always provide improvement on curricular measures in the short-term. Research also indicates that the causes of improvement in pupil learning are complex and a more general emphasis on making aspects of teaching and learning explicit in classrooms (particularly in terms of making reasoning explicit) may have similar benefits to those obtained through a particular programme of intervention. Further research across a wider range of subjects and age groups would be particularly useful, as would comparative research to evaluate the relative benefits of different thinking skills programmes and approaches, as well as a comparison of such approaches with other educational interventions.
>
> (Higgins *et al.* 2005: 45–46)

The framework for PLTS emphasises the importance of acquiring and improving skills that enable young people to cope with change and to learn effectively. These skills, together with the functional skills of English, mathematics and ICT, play a crucial role in preparing learners for successful learning, work and life.

For each group of skills, a focus statement sums up the range of skills and gives a set of outcome statements that indicate the skills, behaviours and personal qualities associated with each group.

However, PLTS are not qualifications in their own right. The groups of skills are interconnected and learners are likely to encounter skills from several groups in any one learning experience. For example, independent enquirers set goals for their research with clear success criteria (acting as a reflective learner) and organise their time and resources effectively to achieve these (acting as a self-manager). To develop these independent learning skills, learners need to apply skills from all six groups in a wide range of contexts.

The framework comprises six groups of skills that, together with the functional skills of English, mathematics and ICT, are essential to success in learning, life and work.

The framework captures the essential skills of:

- Independent learners
- Creative thinkers
- Reflective learners
- Team workers
- Self-managers
- Effective participators.

Each group of skills is distinctive and coherent but the groups are interconnected and pupils will encounter the skills from several groups in any one learning experience but they can be identified particularly when cross-curricular learning is happening.

Each strand is broken down into further detail (see http://curriculum.qcda.gov.uk/uploads/PLTS_framework_tcm8-1811.pdf) and these can facilitate lesson planning and provide criteria against which pupils' performances can be assessed and reported.

Many of the skills are not new but a single approach would make the development of PLTS and cross-curricular teaching and learning more structured and more explicit and encourage application across a range of context and provide a common language that pupils and teachers can use to talk about their work.

There are a number of strategies that promote cross-curricular assessment and PLTS development, e.g. setting open-ended tasks, effective questioning, using thinking frames and diagrams, reflecting and talking about thinking and learning, providing meaningful opportunities for collaborative learning, etc. Note that many of these types of activities also support the principles of AfL.

The shift in teaching and learning and its assessment is to focus on opportunities in cross-curricular links with science where a specific thinking and/or learning skill can be used to deepen understanding of a particular topic or concept or context in science. The context used provides opportunities for the development and practice of the thinking and/or learning skill. This can lead to lessons where there is a parallel development of subject knowledge and understanding as well as the development of, for example, a way of thinking.

Practical task

1. Look across a series of topics for Year 7 and identify where the most appropriate contexts are for the development of specific skills and cross-curricular links.

2. Identify the specific skills best developed through science and devise contexts for teaching and learning

Topic	Cross-curricular link	Specific activity	Approach	PLTS

Learning outcomes

Learning outcomes state what the skills are that pupils should be able to demonstrate throughout Key Stage 3 in each subject. These are similar across each area of learning and promote the combination of the cross-curricular skills of communication, using mathematics and using ICT. The learning outcomes also promote the combination of thinking skills and personal learning.

As with all subjects, it is statutory for teachers to provide opportunities for pupils to acquire and develop the cross-curricular skills and PLTS in science. Pupils should also be given opportunities to demonstrate their skills and application of knowledge and understanding of science to meet the learning outcomes.

Evidence of the application of skills, knowledge and understanding for a learning outcome can be demonstrated at any point in the learning process. Learning outcomes can be based on process or product. They may be evidenced by teacher, pupil or peer assessment of a range of pupils' work and performance, including work generated using ICT. The nature of feedback on learning outcomes can be qualitative, quantitative, verbal or written to suit the purpose of the assessment. Learning outcomes can be demonstrated through formal and informal assessment, formative and/or summative assessment.

Evidence of learning outcomes can be:

- Recorded informally, i.e. primarily for feedback to pupils and for teacher reference
- Recorded formally, i.e. in line with departmental and internal whole school assessment policy requirements
- Used to inform reporting requirements, e.g. in relation to pupil profile requirements.

Skills and learning outcomes

The relationship between the learning outcomes for science and the cross-curricular skills and PLTS is set out in Table 9.4.

Table 9.5 highlights one possible way of relating cross-curricular teaching and learning, functional skills and science.

Table 9.4 Learning outcomes and cross-curricular skills/PLTS.

Learning outcome	Cross-curricular skills/PLTS
Demonstrate a range of practical skills in undertaking experiments, including the safe use of scientific equipment and appropriate mathematical calculations	Using mathematics
Use investigative skills to explore scientific issues, solve problems and make informed decisions	Thinking, problem solving, decision making
Research and manage information effectively including using mathematics and using ICT where applicable	Managing information, communication, using mathematics, using ICT
Show deeper scientific understanding by thinking critically and flexibly, solving problems and making informed decisions, demonstrating using mathematics and using ICT where appropriate	Thinking, problem solving, decision making, using mathematics, using ICT
Demonstrate creativity and initiative when developing ideas and following them through	Being creative
Work effectively with others	Working with others
Demonstrate self-management by working systematically, persisting with tasks, evaluating and improving own performance	Self-management
Communicate effectively in oral, visual, written, mathematical and ICT formats, showing clear awareness of audience and purpose	Communication, using mathematics, using ICT

Adapted from *Cross-curricular dimensions: A planning guide for schools* (QCA 2009)

Table 9.5 Cross-curricular functional skills in science.

Cross-curricular skill	Communication	Using mathematics	Using ICT
Purpose	To provide opportunities for pupils to acquire, develop and demonstrate the cross-curricular skill of Communication	To provide opportunities for pupils to acquire, develop and demonstrate the cross-curricular skill of Using mathematics	To provide opportunities for pupils to acquire, develop and demonstrate the cross-curricular skill of Using ICT
Examples of processes	Discussion, presentation, demonstration, asking questions, reading text for information, using evidence from text to explain opinion, communicate information in a clear and organised way, present ideas in a variety of formats for different audiences and purposes, etc.	Use mathematical knowledge and concepts, use mathematics to solve problems and make decisions, mental mathematics, make and test predictions, data handling, using statistics, developing financial capability, etc.	Explore information using electronic tools, create, develop, present and publish ideas using a range of digital media, communicate electronically, etc.
Examples of contexts in science	• Discuss and explain their opinions and views on science-related issues • Debate and argue both sides of an issue before reaching their own conclusion • Talk about their work in science, using correct scientific terminology, as appropriate • Write reports on practical work	• Measurement. Choose appropriate units and apparatus to record accurate measurements. Convert between different metric units, e.g. metres to cm • Handling data. Use mean/average where appropriate. Understand how repeating measurements and taking an average improves/confirms the accuracy of an investigation • Constructing and interpreting graphs • Constructing and reading information from tables • Using formulae	• Creating multimedia presentations which allow pupils to become their own directors/editors/artists/musicians/camera operators/researchers/script writers/actors • A PowerPoint presentation with sets of images on a science-related topic • Record large sets of information/data using data logging equipment • Organise and present data (e.g. graphs, tables, charts databases) in order to search and sort data in answer to an enquiry question • Use a spreadsheet to process data recorded in science investigative work • Use electronic methods to communicate and share information.

Adapted from *Functional Skills Support Programme: Developing functioning skills in science* (DCSF 2010)

Practical task

Choose a cross-curricular science topic and by adding a column to Table 9.5 outline how you would assess the pupils' work.

Which learning outcomes do you see as the most challenging? How do you think these could be overcome?

Connecting the learning

The curriculum should be able to accommodate links across subjects. Many natural links exist as has been demonstrated in earlier chapters although they are often under-exploited. When these links are identified and planned for they have the potential to make learning more meaningful, informed and purposeful. Opportunities to connect learning range from small and informal to whole school and formally planned. Skills assessment, be they PLTS and/or functional skills, can be ideal catalyst for this cross-curricular development.

Learners are more likely to understand the importance of PLTS and be able to apply them effectively if they are made explicit as part of the teaching and learning process, and they lend themselves to assessment of cross-curricular activity. Figure 9.1 shows the links between PLTS, functional skills, cross-curricular activities and assessment. It illustrates a possible way in which skills and assessment can be embedded in the PLTS agenda and all can be enveloped by cross-curricular teaching and learning.

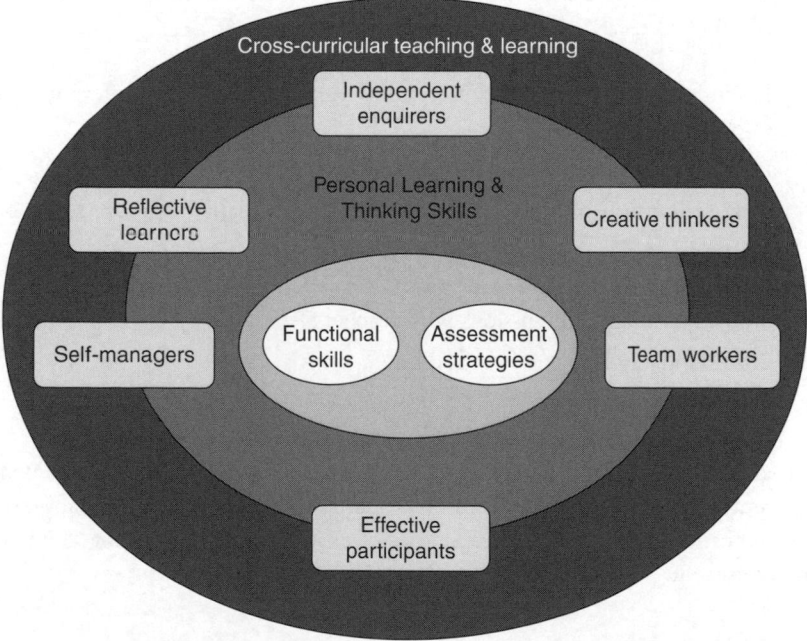

Figure 9.1 PLTS, functional skills, cross-curricular activities and assessment.

Practical task

Develop a learning grid for pupils to use that allows them to demonstrate their progress in PLTS and also includes functional skills development.

They will need to be able to present any cross-curricular links alongside the subject knowledge and skills development

Assessing Pupils' Progress (APP)

Assessing Pupils' Progress (APP) is a national approach to assessment that puts the pupil at the heart of the assessment process. APP builds a more well-rounded individual profile of pupils' achievements that highlights strengths and areas for improvement. The information APP provides helps teachers to tailor their planning and teaching and can support productive discussions between teachers, pupils and parents. By working in a cross-curricular manner a clearer picture emerges for each pupil.

The APP approach is straightforward. In line with their school's assessment policy and practice, teachers periodically review collections of pupils' work and build a profile of their achievements. Through their day-to-day interactions, observations and ongoing assessment teachers see evidence of what pupils understand and can do. APP is most effective when it draws on a broad range of evidence that shows what pupils can do independently. It has an obvious link to both skills development and cross-curricular assessment. Assessment evidence could include:

- Extended or shorter focused pieces of writing in a variety of different forms for a range of purposes
- Information from different curriculum areas
- Text annotation or visual organisers such as thought mapping, storyboards or time-lines
- Oral work such as pupil presentations to the class, contributions to class discussions, drama activities or discussions with teachers
- Observing pupils' behaviour and interactions
- Pupils' self-assessment.

When a teacher has enough evidence about what a pupil is able to do independently and in different contexts, a periodic assessment can take place. Regular collaborative assessment and discussion is another important way of ensuring that assessment standards are reliable and consistent.

Conclusion

Educational assessment sets out to determine how well pupils are learning and should form an integral part of the pursuit to improve education for all. It not only provides feedback for pupils but also informs teachers and parents together with policy makers and the general public about the effectiveness of that education. If there are clear links across the curriculum in subject teaching then it goes without saying that those links should continue into assessment. The collaboration that teachers develop when teaching in a cross-curricular manner should also become an assessment collaboration. This type of collaboration and its associated discussion by teachers can only enhance the whole assessment process by ensuring reliability and consistency. That way a clearer 'all round' picture of a pupil's progress in knowledge and understanding and skill development will emerge. This can only be beneficial, to not only the individual pupil, but to the teachers especially when reporting to parents. The development and assessment of cross-curricular transferable skills will enhance all pupils' learning and prepare them more fully for further study and/ or employment.

Reflective task

Examine the Key Stage 3 curriculum and analyse how you teach the topics. Consider how you could develop your approaches to incorporate all this chapter's suggestions for assessment.

Prepare a short presentation or paper for your colleagues to outline your suggested cross-curricular assessment developments.

Other resources that could be useful

- The Personal Capabilities Programme encourages opportunities for children to develop a range of generic personal skills and capabilities, such as teamwork, self-management, creativity, communication, problem solving, tenacity and a positive self image.
  http://www.personalcapabilities.co.uk/about_personal_capabilities

Professional standards for QTS

This chapter will help meet the following standards:

Q6	Have a commitment to collaboration and co-operative working
Q7	• Reflect on and improve their practice, and take responsibility for identifying and meeting their developing professional needs
Q8	Have a creative and constructively critical approach towards innovation, being prepared to adapt their practice where benefits and improvements are identified
Q10	Have a knowledge and understanding of a range of teaching, learning and behaviour management strategies and know how to use and adapt them, including how to personalise learning and provide opportunities for all learners to achieve their potential
Q12	Know a range of approaches to assessment, including the importance of formative assessment
Q14	Have a secure knowledge and understanding of their subject/curriculum areas and related pedagogy to enable them to teach effectively across the age and ability range for which they are trained
Q17	Know how to use skills in literacy, numeracy and ICT to support their teaching and wider professional activities
Q26	• Make effective use of a range of assessment, monitoring and recording strategies • Assess the learning needs of those they teach in order to set challenging learning objectives
Q27	Provide timely, accurate and constructive feedback on learners' attainment, progress and areas for development
Q28	Support and guide learners to reflect on their learning, identify the progress they have made and identify their emerging learning needs
Q32	Work as a team member and identify opportunities for working with colleagues, sharing the development of effective practice with them
Q33	Ensure that colleagues working with them are appropriately involved in supporting learning and understand the roles they are expected to fulfil

Professional standards for teachers

This chapter will help meet the following standards:

C6	Have a commitment to collaboration and co-operative working where appropriate
C8	Have a creative and constructively critical approach towards innovation, being prepared to adapt their practice where benefits and improvements are identified
C12	Know a range of approaches to assessment, including the importance of formative assessment
C17	Know how to use skills in literacy, numeracy and ICT to support their teaching and wider professional activities
C26	Plan for progression across the age and ability range they teach, designing effective learning sequences within lessons and across series of lessons informed by secure subject/curriculum knowledge
C27	Design opportunities for learners to develop their literacy, numeracy and ICT and thinking and learning skills appropriate within their phase and context
C31	Make effective use of an appropriate range of observation, assessment, monitoring and recording strategies as a basis for setting challenging learning objectives and monitoring learners' progress and levels of attainment
C33	Support and guide learners so that they can reflect on their learning, identify the progress they have made, set positive targets for improvement and become success-ful independent learners
C34	Use assessment as part of their thinking to diagnose learners' needs, set realistic and challenging targets for improvement and plan future teaching.

10

Conclusion: the future for cross-curricular science

Key objectives

By the end of this chapter you will have:

- Explored the current situation in science education and what the future holds for cross-curricular work

- Considered your own classroom practice and the potential for cross-curricular activity in your teaching

- Reflected on the way in which cross-curricular teaching and learning can inform your own practice

Introduction

The aim of this book has been to explore the ways in which science teaching can be enhanced and strengthened by cross-curricular work. It has sought to do so through an examination of the theory and philosophy behind integrated delivery. This theory has been interspersed with school-based case studies, reflective tasks and practical activities. While the activities have formed a practical base on which teachers may wish to develop their own teaching, the theory has provided the framework. To explore practice without first unearthing theory is like trying to wallpaper a wall without paste – theory is the glue that holds educational practice together. Having worked through the book it is now time to turn to personal reflection and look to the future.

This final chapter explores the current situation in science education and the potential future importance of cross-curricular teaching and learning. In our rapidly changing world of scientific advances in medicine, technology and engineering, how can science education meet the needs of our young people? What impact do these advances have on young people's attitudes to science? And how can the new frontier of the digital age inspire them?

In addition, this final chapter will focus on personal reflection and the ways in which you may wish to pursue cross-curricular delivery. As with many aspects of teaching such as classroom management or lesson development, cross-curricular teaching can be a highly personal matter and as such, this concluding chapter aims to support a particularised approach by exploring individual preferences.

What does the future hold for science education?

2011 saw a significant rise in the number of pupils taking single science at GCSE. Physics saw the greatest rise, up 16.4% on 2010; chemistry was not far behind at 16.2%; and biology experienced a 14.2% increase. This news followed the announcement that A-level entries for physics had risen by 19.6% since 2005, with chemistry rising by 19.4% during the same period. This paints an optimistic picture of the current state of science education in both England and Wales, but what has influenced the growing interest in science? For Ziggy Liaquat, the managing director of the exam awarding body Edexcel, such enthusiasm is, in part, a response to the new love affair popular media is having with science. Physicist Professor Brian Cox has become a well-loved TV personality whose programmes refrain from dumbing-down their science content. Cox's 'Wonder's of the Universe' series was so well received it became the first BBC factual series to reach the top of the iTunes chart. Liaquat describes the impact this has had on the entries for science based A-levels as 'The Brian Cox effect' (Vasagar 2011). Could it be that science is becoming trendy?

In the United States, science has found a new champion in the form of platinum selling musician Wil.i.am from the pop band the Black Eyed Peas. In an article he wrote for the *Huffington Post*, the singer described science as 'rock n roll' and technology as 'recession proof'. In partnership with the entrepreneur and inventor Dean Kamen the artist has created and self-funded a TV documentary exploring education, science and technology. Using high-profile guests such as Justin Bieber, Britney Spears, Bono and Justin Timberlake the documentary follows young students competing in the 20th Annual FIRST

(For Inspiration and Recognition of Science and Technology) Robotics Championship. Wil.i.am's motivation for the endorsement for science education is a response to the economic issues facing the US and the need for more young people to be exploring careers in science – a barrier to which can be the negative public perception of scientists and engineers:

> I'm writing this on my laptop and you're probably reading it on your phone or tablet, and none of the stuff we are actually buying 'regardless' of a recession is made in America. Technology is recession proof and most kids are not dreaming of being programmers, scientists or engineers. The ones that are, do not get the spotlight or attention. Instead, they are looked at as geeks or uncool, when in actuality technology is the only thing that is cool today. iPhones, Android devices, Facebook, Twitter (all tech), all exciting.
>
> (Wil.i.am 2011)

The increased public enthusiasm for science has coincided with the global financial downturn. For some commentators this has also influenced young people's educational decisions. The uncertainty of the UK job market has meant many students have been encouraged to make more informed choices about the subjects they pursue in relation to employability. In terms of the increases in the number of pupils undertaking science at A-level Liaquat feels that this will have been a decisive factor:

> When these students would have made their choices, it would have been at the very beginning of the global economic downturn, when businesses were crying out for students and young people to have skills in science, engineering and maths.
>
> (Liaquat as featured in Vasagar 2011)

The popularisation of science coupled with the global economic downturn has without a doubt influenced some people's attitude to science, but unfortunately it is not all good news. The top ten most popular A-level subjects shows physics at the very bottom (see Table 10.1), and industry leaders in the UK still remain worried about a science skills gap 'with over 40% of companies saying they are having difficulty recruiting people with science, technology, engineering and maths skills' (Vasagar 2011). And despite the rise in numbers completing science subjects at A-level the numbers are still low in relation to demand.

In addition to this there is a significant social divide in relation to the uptake of science: pupils from private and grammar schools are twice as likely to take A-levels in physics and chemistry as those from state schools (Shepherd 2011). There is also a UK divide with almost twice as many young people studying science in Scotland compared to the rest of the UK. The Royal Society's State of the Nation report (2010) found that 49.7% of pupils aged 16–19 chose to study Higher science in 2009. In contrast only 27.7% of pupils took the equivalent A-level in science in England; in Wales it was even worse at 26.6%. This is a somewhat bleak picture that saw nearly 500 schools and colleges in England not enter a single candidate for A-level physics during the same year. Despite the rise in science A-level applicants there is obviously still a serious problem in terms of young people's engagement in science. And this has implications for classroom practice.

Table 10.1 2011 A-level entries in order of popularity.

1	English
2	Mathematics
3	Biology
4	Psychology
5	History
6	Chemistry
7	Art & Design
8	General Studies
9	Media Studies
10	Physics

Source: Vasagar 2011.

Simon (2003) draws on extensive research to identify three main factors influencing students' attitudes. These are:

- Effective teaching
- Perceived difficulty
- Gender.

To overcome these issues Simon suggests a move away from the 'How much?' questions and a move towards the 'How?' and 'Why?'. For this teachers need to provide exciting and engaging context in which science learning can take place:

> Teachers need to be enthusiastic and knowledgeable about their subject, setting it in well-chosen contexts and running well-ordered and stimulating science lessons. The tendency for prescriptive national curricula to constrain science teaching, at the expense of interest and depth of involvement, has implications for the promotion of students' positive attitudes towards science beyond the experience of school.
>
> (Simon 2003: 115)

One way to provide creative contexts for delivery is of course through cross-curricular teaching and learning. Whether the influence of music on the brain or the mummification of an Ancient Egyptian pharaoh, these exciting integrated contexts can be used to implement a cross-curricular approach to teaching which encourages creativity, challenges thinking and supports the sharing of ideas. As has been explored throughout this book, there are many benefits to cross-curricular teaching and learning as a strategy. It teaches knowledge using an integration of content and skills simultaneously from several subject disciplines to teach one particular academic subject area – in this case, science. This is a highly motivational style of teaching as the pupils experience a sense of cohesiveness across different subjects taught within the same lessons. Pupils begin to view a definite relationship between the different subjects. When pupils are taught in this way, they can use it as building blocks to add to their knowledge base, consolidating the connections and reinforcing learning from other topic areas. This inter-collaborative teaching establishes a level of thinking that can support young people to recognise connections and question evidence – both of which are invaluable skills for active, mature citizens. Cross-curricular teaching can help to give science a place in the real world and pupils can begin to see its relevance to themselves and everything else they are learning in school.

Can cross-curricular teaching really help?

Cross-curricular teaching and learning is a strategy which calls for teachers to develop different teaching skills, work with colleagues from different departments and begin to use their imagination when planning lessons. The trick is to bring the various branches of learning under one umbrella, while keeping the pupils from feeling lost or uncomfortable. Increased emphasis is given to the field of learning while taking maximum advantage of diverse subject disciplines. With the elimination of isolated, separate subject teaching, pupils can begin to enjoy and come up with fresh ideas themselves. The curriculum is thus enriched.

Benefits of cross-curricular teaching

There are a number of benefits of cross-curricular teaching, including:

- Since inter-disciplinary teaching consists of a conscious attempt to call upon the knowledge, values and principles of more than one subject, it reinforces them all. Pupils gain greater depth of understanding of all that is covered within each such lesson. Their horizons are widened, while their educational base becomes broader and stronger.

- Breaking down the dividing barrier, pupils begin treating the entire learning process as one large experience and not broken up into isolated periods of fixed time.

- Cognitive learning changes as pupils interact, collaborate and co-operate in small groups. This cross-curricular teaching and learning practice lends increased viability, authenticity, contextualisation and relevance to what pupils take in.

- Pupils are offered a vaster scope to select topics that they want to learn in accordance with their capabilities, needs and interest. This aspect is a catalyst for learners who put in greater efforts to achieve more at school.

- The teachers too tend to become more cooperative, just as the pupils do.

Issues for schools to address

There are issues for individual teachers, departments and whole schools to address when they consider cross-curricular teaching and learning.

Interdepartmental cooperation

This will probably start on a small scale with just a couple of teachers meeting and planning one topic to *try out*. The important thing is that those involved really want it to be a success. It might even start as part of extra-curricular activity such as an after-school club. A stumbling block can be the issue of 'time' – time for meeting, time for planning, etc. If this is viewed as an element of professional development it might be possible to get some agreement for a small amount of planning time. Otherwise it will have to be arranged during breaks, lunchtime and/or after school. Having developed one topic for teaching, the teachers concerned should arrange a dissemination session with respective departments with a view to rolling the approach out across more topics and, ultimately more departments. It is not something that can happen overnight but the benefits of even just one topic taught this way will be apparent for everyone to see.

Enthusiasm

If teachers want pupils to embrace the concept of learning across more than one subject they need to be enthusiastic themselves and the pupils need to see that during their lessons. This enthusiasm is on a number of levels – enthusiasm for the subject and a desire to impart that knowledge and enjoyment to pupils; enthusiasm for teaching; interest and enthusiasm for trying something new. Enthusiasm is contagious and once pupils (and other colleagues) have seen the success and enjoyment that come from teaching and learning in this way, they will start to consider the approach themselves. Science suffers from being seen as difficult, boring and irrelevant. Teaching it with other subjects that often would not be associated with it can change opinion radically.

Subject knowledge

Before embarking on the demands of teaching in a cross-curricular manner, every teacher needs to feel secure in their own subject knowledge. This is because not only are they going to be teaching pupils, they are also going to have to work with teachers from disciplines very different from their own and be able to use their own subject knowledge in the planning process for a very different way of teaching. Even the most dull and boring topic within any subject can be enlivened by an enthusiastic speaker/teacher and if pupils find themselves being taught by a number of teachers from different subjects, all equally enthusiastic about their individual subject, their attitudes to the subjects and learning will change.

In addition, the concept of subject knowledge is linked to the idea of cross-departmental collaboration. For many teachers, keeping up to date with the latest developments in their own subject area can be difficult enough; however, if cross-curricular delivery has been undertaken by a teacher on their own, this may call for an up-to-date understanding of other subjects too. If however, cross-curricular teaching is planned alongside colleagues from other, relevant departments then each individual teacher can come to the table with their own expertise. This can ensure accurate content and guarantee each subject is being integrated sympathetically in relation to content, techniques, skills and approaches.

Management support

The best ideas can only work in an institution like a school if the classroom teacher has the support of management. In Tate's (1994) study of cross-curricular initiatives in secondary schools a significant number of her interviewees suggested that to be successful, subject integration (on any scale) requires the support of the school's Senior Management Team (SMT). It was suggested that by allocating a senior member of staff to be in charge of all cross-curricular activity across the school, other members of staff felt encouraged to experiment with new approaches.

> Cross-curricular work has to be given some sort of precedence and value, otherwise, being non-examinable, it takes a low priority. A named post helps.
>
> (Teacher response quoted in Tate 1994: 39)

Thinking back to Case Study 3.1 (Chapter 3) of Grenoside Primary School's thematic teaching, SMT support was mentioned on a number of different occasions, as were peer collaboration and cooperation. Recognition was also seen as an important element in delivering successful integrated ventures. Again, this is related to both SMT and other members of teaching staff – with recognition required from both camps. This is all very easy to understand. Pushing forward with any new and/or innovative approach to teaching without support from colleagues and management can be soul destroying. It can feel like treading water when you are trying to revitalise and stimulate your own teaching if those around you are disinterested or worse still – disapproving. In the case of the school's SMT, it is of course also an issue of time. Diversifying your teaching approaches can be a long process that requires a little initial *trial and error*. For successful cross-curricular teaching and learning in any school there has to be a full understanding and commitment from senior leaders in the school. This can be in the form of support for the occasional collapsed timetable day as described in Chapter 3, to agreement to change Schemes of Work and timetabling to accommodate interdepartmental teaching. A starting point can be some interdepartmental training or even just some time for departments and teachers to meet to discuss possibilities. A well-formed argument as to why this would be a good teaching and learning approach to adopt needs to be developed and then put to the senior leaders at the school.

Constraints on teachers

As has been expressed throughout this chapter and throughout this book, there are potential constraints as well as mechanisms of facilitation in regards to any cross-curricular undertaking. Drawing on Tate's (1994) interviews with teachers who have completed some degree of integrated delivery, let us first look at the potential constraints.

National Curriculum pressures

The significant demands placed on teachers by the National Curriculum requirements often leave little lesson (or preparation) time for more experimental delivery approaches.

The ever-looming reality of assessment, exams and league tables can make cross-curricular teaching a very low priority.

Lack of funding

Many teachers associate dynamic, cross-curricular delivery with the need for expensive, high-quality materials. Equally, for many, the idea of exploring an integrated approach must be preceded by intensive CPD or support from specialised staff with an expertise in cross-curricular teaching and learning – all of which carries a cost.

Low status or priority of cross-curricular work within the school

Often this refers to recognition and support from senior management within the school. Without this SMT encouragement many teachers do not believe cross-curricular work is realistic or sustainable. This can also be true of teaching colleagues who may view it as a 'soft option' or a 'filler' (Tate 1994: 55).

Departmental structures

A lack of interdepartmental communication can lead to a misunderstanding of what a cross-curricular venture may be aiming to achieve. As such, other departments may be resistant to involvement for fear of increased workloads and a dilution of their own subject areas.

Staff resistance

As seen in Case Study 3.3 (Chapter 3) involving the collapsed timetable day, if involvement in a cross-curricular project is made compulsory by senior management, this can lead to resistance and even staff resentment.

Despite a somewhat dreary picture, most of these constraints can be overcome. In terms of the National Curriculum pressures it is of course an issue of manageability, particularly for any teacher at the beginning of their cross-curricular journey. The pressures are an unavoidable reality, but careful planning and a realistic attitude should keep any cross-curricular project from impeding National Curriculum linked targets. With regard to funding, it is misleading to correlate cross-curricular work with high resource costs. Many of the activities in this book carry no cost at all and this is also true of many other cross-curricular activities that can be found in this series. While costs may be an issue if a teacher is keen to attend a cross-curricular CPD course, this may only be an issue if the school SMT is unsupportive of the approach, which leads to the notion of low status and priority connected to cross-curricular work. It is more often than not the case that an unsupportive management team can be won over if they can see the benefits to the school as a whole. This is can also be true of obstructive or resistant colleagues. To support the development of a positive argument *for* cross-curricular work we will go on shortly to further summarise the benefits of cross-curricular teaching.

Facilitating cross-curricular teaching and learning

Let us now consider the mechanisms for facilitation as explored by Tate (1994).

External support

This support can be in the form of Local Authorities (LAs) or external networks such as the National Science Learning Centres.

Support of headteacher and senior management team

As explored above, an unsupportive SMT can halt any cross-curricular delivery so it stands to reason that in contrast, a highly supportive SMT (as seen at Grenoside Primary School – see Case Study 3.1) can facilitate exciting and dynamic cross-curricular work. Tate's research draws out some specific kinds of support valued by the teachers interviewed. These included:

- Being allowed a 'free hand' and autonomy for decision making
- Equipment
- Resources, e.g. footing the bill for printing; cover
- Time on timetable for development and for meetings
- Keeping the profile of cross-curricular work high: for example, making sure that Academic Board and Heads of Department meetings has the issue on their agenda as a major item
- Active participation.

(Tate 1994: 56)

High-status posts

This relates to the issue of recognition within school. It is suggested that if a member of staff within the school who has a high status post is placed in charge of cross-curricular work then the approach has a stable and lasting power base and will therefore be maintained.

Ability and experience of post-holders

Following on from the status of the staff in charge of cross-curricular delivery, experience is also viewed as useful in the successful delivery of an integrated curriculum.
We add to Tate's list the following:

- Enthusiasm
- Cross-departmental partnerships

Enthusiasm

Experience working with teachers undertaking integrated initiatives has shown the authors of this book that one of the main factors enabling successful and lasting cross-curricular work is teacher enthusiasm. As seen above, exploring this form of teaching can be time consuming and require a degree of flexibility in regards to content, delivery, planning and the involvement of colleagues. If the teacher undertaking this challenge is not enthusiastic about the approach, and the potential benefits, then the endeavour will undoubtedly struggle.

Cross-departmental partnerships

Cross-curricular work can call upon many skills held within the teacher's arsenal, one of which is unquestionably teamwork. As has been explored throughout this book, exciting and meaningful activities can often involve members of staff from across two or more different subject departments. This adds an authenticity to the work but requires a supportive and open cross-departmental partnership. In Chapter 7, the partnership between the science teacher and the history teacher at Brinsworth Comprehensive illustrates this kind of cooperative collaboration.

As has been seen, there are various factors that can constrain or enable successful cross-curricular work. These can relate to the teacher as an individual or the teacher as a valuable member of a subject department and school. For Rowley and Cooper (2009) this has implications on the way in which any one teacher is feasibly able to embark on an integrated approach:

> Clearly cross-curricular planning raises real issues for many teachers, particularly in finding a balance between teacher-led perceptions of how subjects link and others' understanding of those links. On the one hand, there has to be individual appraisal and choice based on the teacher's professional judgment; on the other hand, the school itself needs to have whole-school policies that enable long-term tracking and assessment for learning.
>
> (Rowley and Cooper 2009: 2)

Benefits

These potential issues, hurdles and challenges make it all the more important that we fully understand the purposes and goals of cross-curricular learning, and of course, as seen above, the various benefits. This brings us back to the ways in which integrated teaching learning can support knowledge and skills development (for both teachers and pupils) as explored in the introductory chapter. To further summarise these benefits let us break it down into benefits to pupils and benefits to teachers.

Benefits to pupils

- Skills development – these can include PLTS, transferable and functional skills as well as subject specific skills.

- Cognitive and meta-cognitive understanding – context-rich, cross-curricular teaching can allow for greater understanding of concepts through a meaningful exploration of different learning approaches.

- The retention of information – as above, the use of real-world and creative contexts can help some pupils to better retain information.

- An increased awareness of societal issues – the use of cross-curricular delivery can help to prepare young people for what is a rapidly changing cross-curricular world. This can support young people to become active citizens capable of both engagement in society and sympathetic decision-making. This can be particularly important in relation to science. Scientific literacy is an important quality for young people who need to be equipped to confidently interrogate scientific evidence, understand the wider issues surrounding scientific advancements and question the media's representation of science in the news.

- A preparation for the world of work – the integrated learning approach and the development of pupils' transferable skills can support workforce readiness.

- The utilisation of creativity in science – this can allow some pupils to better understand a concept. This is particularly significant for those pupils who learn better in a creative environment or by applying creative techniques.

Benefits to teachers

- Supporting the delivery of the National Curriculum requirements – teachers are required as part of the National Curriculum to 'make links between science and other subjects and areas of the curriculum' (QCA 2007a).

- Skills development – along with the skills development seen in pupils, cross-curricular activity can impact on teachers' personal and professional skills, which can in turn impact on performance.

- Cross-departmental partnerships – as stated at the beginning of this book, the forming of cross-departmental partnerships can be an invaluable and exciting process. It can allow teachers to share their teaching experience with other colleagues, which can build confidence. It can also provide an opportunity to learn new approaches, techniques and procedures from colleagues based in a different school department where delivery may require a different approach. This sharing of good practice allows for a form of in-house CPD and can be incredibly insightful for all involved.

- Variety – as seen in Case Study 3.1, designing, developing and delivering cross-curricular teaching can spark enthusiasm in teachers and provide a fresh new perceptive in the classroom.

- Creativity – while the planning of cross-curricular activities can be time-consuming it can also be an engaging process which can trigger untapped creativity.

- Widely accepted form of documentable professional progression – in terms of teacher CPD, demonstrating a variety of teaching approaches (including cross-curricular work) can support professional progression.

This book has aimed to put forward arguments for cross-curricular teaching and learning by highlighting the potential advantages and benefits. It is hoped that by gaining a better understanding of the reasoning behind cross-curricular work, your own cross-curricular undertakings will be supported and improved. As such it is now important to reflect on your own relationship with cross-curricular delivery.

Personal reflection

Much of our work as teachers is about personal reflection. To improve our practice we must stand back and contemplate our work and in the case of cross-curricular accomplishments this can be particularly useful. The broad scope of integrated teaching in terms of both delivery and content allows for experimentation in the classroom. It also creates a notion of personal preference with some aspects appealing to certain teaching styles while others feel awkward or inappropriate. As such there is no right way of approaching cross–curricular teaching; it is a personal journey that will influence professional practice and development. This book has offered a starting point at which you can begin your journey by introducing useful definitions, contexts, framework and activities. Using the book as a preparatory foundation in cross–curricular concepts it is time to now develop your own style and approach. Having explored some of the discussion and arguments presented in this book, it is important to reflect on the aspects of the approach that best suit you and your own teaching techniques. We hope that you have now tried some form of cross–curricular teaching on which you can reflect. Having completed the objectives table in Chapter 1 prior to undertaking your teaching, it is now time to reflect on your achievements in relation to those objectives.

Reflective task

Evaluation

Use the model below to reflect on your own personal, departmental and teaching achievements in relation to your cross-curricular activity. Did you achieve all of your objectives? If not, what could you do in the future to ensure you do?

Personal achievements	Departmental achievements	Teaching achievements
What do you feel you have achieved personally?	What do you feel you have achieved for your department?	What do you feel you have achieved for your pupils?

As illustrated above, cross-curricular delivery is a highly personal endeavour. While the core principles of the concept must remain, the practical approaches you may adopt can be varied. Bear in mind that the core principles of cross-curricular teaching and learning should include:

- A sensitivity towards other subject areas
- A synthesis of knowledge that refrains from undermining techniques and concepts familiar to other subjects
- A focus on knowledge and/or skills.

Reflective task

Jot down any aspects of cross-curricular teaching that you feel are not appropriate to your style of teaching. While this may appear at first to be a slightly negative activity, much like our experience with bad service in a restaurant as opposed to good, it is often easier to remember what you dislike as opposed to what you like.

Now follow this up by making a list of all the aspects of cross-curricular teaching you have enjoyed. This will help you to begin to see what features of the method you would like to use again in the future.

Concluding thoughts

Young people today are growing up in a new and exciting digital age. Social networking, smart phones, the breadth and depth of information available on the Internet and the increased computerisation of public services all combine to create a new global community. Social networking devices such as Facebook and Twitter can instantly connect people across the globe and in the process the world is seemingly getting smaller. This increased connectivity is accompanied by an increased cross-curricularity. Using Twitter to illustrate this point – on the same day, at the same minute, across the globe, topics as diverse as war, political uprisings, rioting and Justin Bieber can all be *trending* on the social networking site, and young people have instant access to all of this. While a complete fusion of academic disciplines is definitely not advised in this book, it is unwise to ignore the fact that young people's lives are bombarded with information that spans the divisions put in place by separate school subjects. As mentioned previously, this is not to suggest a complete merger of all school subjects, because that would in fact undermine each discipline regardless of weight within a new amalgamated curriculum; it is, however, to emphasise the importance of cross-curricularity *when* and *where* appropriate to support a more holistic education that better reflects the modern world. And at its very core, cross-curricular work is about supporting pupils to better process, understand and retain information so as to improve both their knowledge and skills. To do so as a teacher requires time, flexibility, innovation and imagination. The generation of any integrated project necessitates creativity, which can be used to inspire creativity.

So to end this book it is important to re-emphasise that cross-curricular science education is about creativity. Above all else, the application of creativity can generate exciting and engaging integrated learning. In the context of cross-curricular teaching and learning creativity can (and will) apply to the way the teacher delivers the lesson, the nature of the links devised or the new way pupils can view science when they themselves are allowed to get creative. Oliver (2006) in her work on creativity in science describes the creative teacher as one who:

- Provides imaginative activities
- Varies methods of teaching
- Explains in ways to engage thinking, including modelling
- Plans for pupils to use their own initiative
- Is flexible in pursuing ideas
- Responds to unplanned opportunities
- Challenges thinking
- Values the exchange of ideas

(Oliver 2006: 3)

It would be difficult to not link all of the above descriptors to cross-curricular teaching. And while this book does not suggest integrated learning is the only answer to the many and complex problems facing modern science education, it can go some way to spark pupils' imagination and begin to open the subject up to exciting teacher creativity.

Other resources that could be useful

- Further support for cross-curricular teaching and learning specific to science can be found at the National Science Learning Centres which runs regular courses for teachers covering various aspects of creative, cross-curricular planning and delivery. See www. sciencelearningcentres.org.uk

References

Adams, P. E. and Krockover, G. H. (1997), Concerns and perceptions of beginning secondary science and mathematics teachers. *Science Education*, 81 (1): 29–50

Akerson, V. L. and Young, T. A. (2005), Science the 'write' way. *Science and Children*, 43 (3): 38–41

Al-Alwani, A. (2005), Barriers to integrating information technology in Saudi Arabia. Doctoral dissertation, University of Kansas, Kansas, USA

Alexander, J., Walsh, P., Jarman, R. and McClune, B. (2008), From rhetoric to reality: Advancing literacy by cross-curricular means. *Curriculum Journal*, 19 (1): 23–35

Alexander, R. (2004), Still no pedagogy? Principle, pragmatism and compliance in primary education. *Cambridge Journal of Education*, 34 (1): 7–33

Alexander, R. (ed.) (2010), *Children, Their World, Their Education: Final Report and Recommendations of the Cambridge Primary Review*. Abingdon: Routledge

Archer, L., Dewitt, J., Osborne, J., Dillon, J., Willis, B. and Wong, B. (2010), 'Doing science' versus 'being' a scientist: Examining 10/11 year old school children's constructions of science through the lens of identity. *Science Education*, 94 (4): 617–639

Arends, B. and Thackara, D. (eds) (2003), *Experiment: Conversations in Art and Science*. Wellcome Trust: London

Bailey, S. and Watson, R. (1998), Establishing basic ecological understanding in younger pupils: A pilot evaluation of a strategy based on drama/role play. *International Journal of Science Education*, 20: 139–152

Ball, D. L. (1990), Prospective elementary and secondary teachers' understanding of division. *Journal for Research in Mathematics Education*, 21: 132–144

Ball, P. (2012) *The Music Instinct: How Music Works and Why We Can't Do Without It*. www.economist.com/node/15450498 (accessed February 2012)

Ball, S. (1993), Education policy, power relations and teachers' work. *British Journal of Education Studies*, 41 (2): 106–121

Balnaskat, A., Blamire, R. and Kefala, S. (2006), *A Review of Studies of ICT Impact on Schools in Europe*. European Schoolnet

Bamberg, S. and Möser, G. (2007) Twenty years after Hines, Hungerford, and Tomera: A new meta-analysis of psycho-social determinants of pro- environmental behaviour. *Journal of Environmental Psychology*, 27 (1):14–25.

Barnes, J. (2007), *Cross-Curricular Learning 3–14*. London: Paul Chapman Publishing

Barnes, J. and Shirley, I. (2007), Strangely familiar: Cross-curricular and creative thinking in teacher education. *Improving Schools*, 10 (2): 162–179

Barnett, J. and Hodson, D. (2001), Pedagogical context knowledge: Toward a fuller understanding of what good science teachers know. *Science Education*, 85 (4): 426–453

BBC Today Programme (2009), *'Binary* divide' of the Two Cultures. http://news.bbc.co.uk/today/hi/today/newsid_8033000/8033344.stm (accessed August 2011)

Bean, J. A. (1995), Curriculum integration and the disciplines of knowledge. *Phi Delta Kappan*, 76 (8): 616–622

Bennet, J. (2003), *Teaching and Learning Science: A Guide to Recent Research and Its Applications.* London: Continuum

Berlin, D. F. (1991), *Integrating science and mathematics teaching and learning: A bibliography* (School Science and Mathematics Topics for Teachers, No. 6). Columbus, Ohio: ERIC Clearinghouse for Science, Mathematics and Environmental Education

Berlin, D. F. & White, A. L. (1994), The Berlin-White Integrated Science and Mathematics Model. *School Science and Mathematics*, 94 (1), pp 2 –4

Berlin, D. F. & White, A. L. (1995), Connecting school science and mathematics. In P.A. Coxford (Ed), *Connecting mathematics across the curriculum.* Reston, VA: National Council for Teachers of Mathematics

Bernstein, B. (1971), On the classification and framing of educational knowledge. In M. D. Young (ed.), *Knowledge and Control.* London: Collier_MacMillan, 47–69

Bevins, S., Brodie, E. and Brodie, M. (2005), *UK Secondary School Pupils' Perceptions of Science and Engineering.* A report submitted to the Engineering and Physical Sciences Research Council and the Particle Physics and Astronomy Research Council

Bevins, S., Brodie, M. and Byrne, E. (2011), English Secondary School Students' Perceptions of School Science and Science and Engineering. *Science Education International*, 22 (4): 255–265

Black, P. and William, D. (1998), Assessment and classroom learning. *Assessment in Education*, 5 (1): 7–73

Black, P. and William, D. (2006) *Inside the Black Box: v.1: Raising Standards Through Classroom Assessment.* London: Kings College

Bourdieu, P. (1985), The social space and genesis of groups. *Theory and Society*, 14: 723–744

Bourdieu, P. and Wacquant, L. J. D. (1992), *An Invitation to Reflexive Sociology.* Cambridge: Polity Press

Bransford, J., Brown, A. L. and Cocking, R. R. (eds) (2000), *How People Learn: Brain, Mind, Experience and School* (2nd edn). Washington, DC: National Academy Press

Brighouse, T. (2006), Essential pieces: The jigsaw of a successful school. Conference paper, International Design and Technology Conference 2006

British Educational Communications and Technology Agency (BECTA) (2003), *Primary Schools – ICT and Standards.* http.//dera.ioe.ac.uk/1700/ (accessed August 2011)

British Educational Communications and Technology Agency (BECTA) (2004), http://www.e-learningcentre.co.uk/Resource/CMS/Assets/5c10130e-6a9f-102c-a0be-003005bbceb4/form_uploads/Literature_review___barriers_to_the_uptake_of_ICT_by_teachers.pdf (accessed August 2011)

Brodsky, L. (2008), The use of mathematics in KS3/KS4 science classes. *Proceedings of the British Society for Research into Learning Mathematics*, 28 (3): 7–12

Brown, V. and Pleydell, S. (1999), *The Dramatic Difference: Drama in Preschool and Kindergarten Classroom.* Portsmouth, NH: Heinemann

Burg, J. and Lüttringhaus, K. (2006), Entertaining with science, educating with dance. *Computers in Entertainment*, 4 (2): 7

Calkins, L. and Parsons, S. (2003), *Poetry: Powerful Thoughts in Tiny Packages.* Portsmouth, NH: First Hand

Clarke, K. (1991), *Primary Education: A Statement by the Secretary of Education.* London: Department of Education and Science

Cobb, P. (2000), The importance of a situated view of learning to the design of research and instruction. In J. Boaler (ed.), *Multiple Perspectives on Mathematics Teaching and Learning.* Westport, CA: Greenwood Publishing

Cobb, P., Boufi, A., McClain, K. and Whitenack, J. (1997), Reflective discourse and collective reflection. *Journal of Research in Mathematics Education,* 28 (3): 258–277

Cobb, P. and Bowers, J. S. (1999), Cognitive and situated learning perspectives in theory and practice. *Educational Researcher,* 28 (4): 4–15

Csikszentmihalyi, M. (2004), *Good Business.* New York: Viking

Davies, F. and Greene, T. (1984), *Reading for Learning in the Sciences.* Edinburgh: Oliver and Boyd

Dawes, L. (2001), What stops teachers using new technology? In M. Leask (ed.), *Issues in Teaching Using ICT.*London: Routledge, 61–79

Dawkins, R. (2008), *The God Delusion.* New York: Mariner Books

Department for Education and Skills (2003), *Excellence and Enjoyment – a Strategy for Primary Schools.* London: DfES

Department for Education and Skills (2004), *Putting the World into World-Class Education, An international strategy for education, skills and children's services: A supporting paper for head teachers.* London: DfES

Department of Education and Science (1987), *The National Curriculum 5–16: A Consultation Document.* London: HMSO

Department for Education and Skills (DfES) (2006) *The Science, Technology, Engineering and Mathematics (STEM) Report.* London: DfES

Department for Children, Schools anD Families (DCSF) (2010) *Functional Skills Support Programme: Developing functional skills in science.* London, HMSO

Dewey, J. (1916), *Democracy and Education.* New York: Free Press

Diamond, I. (2010), *Science Education in Schools: Issues, Evidence and Proposals.* A Commentary by the Teaching and Learning Research Programme. London: TLRP, Institute of Education, University of London

Donnelly, J. (2005), Reforming science in the school curriculum. *Oxford Review of Education,* 31 (2): 293–309

Driver, R., Asoko, H., Leach, J., Mortimer, E. and Scott, P. (1994), Constructing scientific knowledge in the classroom. *Educational Researcher,* 23: 5–12

Duit, R., Goldberg, F. and Nidderer, H. (1991), *Research in Physics Learning: Theoretical Issues and Empirical Studies.* Kiel: IPN-University of Kiel

Ede, S. (2005), *Art and Science.* London: I. B. Taurus

Eliot, C. (1898), *Educational Reform.* New York: Century

Erduran, S., Simon, S. and Osborne, J. (2004), TAPping into argumentation: developments in the application of Toulmin's argument pattern for studying science discourse. *Science Education,* 88 (6): 915–933

Erduran, S., Simon, S. & Osborne, J. (2004), TAPping into argumentation: developments in the application of Toulmin's argument pattern for studying science discourse, *Science Education,* 88 (6), pp 915–933

Erduran, S., Osborne, J. F. and Simon, S. (2004), 'Enhancing the quality of argument in school science' *Journal of Research in Science Teaching,* 41(10), 994–1020

Foucault, M (1977) *Discipline and Punish.* London, Tavistock

Franklin, A., Drivonikou, G. V., Bevis, L., Davies, I. R. L., Kay, P. and Regier, T. (2008), Catergorical perception of color is lateralized to the right hemisphere in infants, but to the left in adults. *PNAS,* 105 (9): 3221–3225

Freud, S. (1965) *New Introductory Lectures on Psychoanalysis.* Norton: New York

Frykholm, J. A. (1998), Beyond supervision: Learning to teach mathematics in community. *Teaching and Teacher Education,* 14 (3): 305–322

Frykholm, J. and Glasson, G. (2005), Connecting science and mathematics instruction: Pedagogical knowledge for teachers. *School Science and Mathematics*, 105 (3): 127–141

Gardner, H. (2004), *Changing Minds: The Art and Science of Changing our Own and Other People's Minds*. Boston, MA: Harvard Business School

Gillespie, H. (2006), *Unlocking Learning and Teaching with ICT: Identifying and Overcoming Barriers*. London: David Fulton

Glennan, S. (2009), Whose science and whose religion? Reflections on the relations between scientific and religious worldviews. *Science and Education*, 18: 797–812

Goldberg, A., Russell, M. and Cook, A. (2003), The effect of computers on student writing: A meta-analysis of studies 1992–2002. *Journal of Technology, Learning and Assessment*, 2 (1); 1–52. Available from http://www.jtla.org (accessed August 2011)

Goleman, D. (1999), *Working with Emotional Intelligence*. New York: Bantam

Gomes, C. (2005), Integration of ICT in science teaching: a study performed in Azores, Portugal. *Recent Research Developments in Learning Technologies*

Goodrum, D., Hackling, M. and Rennie, L. (2001), *The Status and Quality of Teaching and Learning Science in Australian Schools*. Canberra: Commonwealth Department of Education, Training and Youth Affairs

Gove, M. (2010), Secretary of State for Education: Speech to the National College for School Leadership Annual Conference, Birmingham

Grabe, M. and Grabe, C. (2007), *Integrating Technology for Meaningful Learning* (5th edn). New York, NY: Houghton Mifflin

Gräber, W. and Bolte, C. (eds) (1997), *Scientific Literacy: An Annual Symposium IPN 154*, Kiel Institut für die Pädagogik der Naturwissenschaften an der Universität Kiel

Hand, B. M., Alvermann, D. E., Gee, J., Guzzetti, B. J., Norris, S. P., Phillips, L. M., Prain, V. and Yore, L. D. (2003), Message from the 'Island Group': What is literacy in science literacy? *Journal of Research in Science Teaching*, 40: 607–615

Hardy, G.H. (1940) *A Mathematician's Apology*. Cambridge: Cambridge University Press

Hargreaves, A., Earl, L., Moore. and Manning, S. (2001), *Learning to Change: Beyond Subjects and Standards*. San Francisco, CA: Jossey-Bass

Harris, E. (2010), Is science teaching undermined by religious instruction in faith schools?, www.guardian.co.uk/science/political-science/2010/aug/27/science-teaching-religious-education-re (accessed August 2011)

Haste, H. (2004), *Science in My Future: A Study of Values and Beliefs in Relation to Science and Technology amongst 11–21 year olds*. London: Nestlé Social Research Programme

Hayes, D. (2010), The seductive charms of a cross-curricular approach. *Education 3-13*, 38 (4): 381–387

Hayward, G. and Fernandez, R. M. (2004), From core skills to key skills: Fast forward or back to the future? *Oxford Review of Education*, 30 (1): 117–145

Higgins, S. and Moseley, D. (2001), Teachers' thinking about ICT and learning: Beliefs and outcomes. *Teacher Development*, 33 (3): 345–347

Higgins, S., Baumfield, V., Lin, M., Mosely, D., Butterworth, M., Downey, G., Gregson, M., Oberski, I., Rockett, M. and Thacker, D. (2004), *Thinking Skill Approaches to Effective Teaching and Learning: What is the Evidence for Impact on Learners*. Research Evidence in Education Library. London: EPPI-Centre, Social Science Research Unit, Institute of Education, University of London

Higgins, S., Hall, E., Baumfield, V. and Mosely, D. (2005), *A Meta-analysis of the Impact of the Implementation of Thinking Skills Approaches on Pupils*. London: EPPI-Centre, Social Science Research Unit, Institute of Education, University of London

Hollenbeck, J. E. (2007), Integration of mathematics and science: Doing it correctly for once. *Bulgarian Journal of Science and Education Policy*, 1 (1): 77–81

House of Commons Science and Technology Committee (2002), *Science Education from 14 to 19*: the House of Commons London: The Stationary Office Limited. Volume HC 508-1

Iding, M., Crosby, M. E. and Speital, T. (2002), Teachers and technology: Beliefs and practices. *International Journal of Instructional Media*, 29 (2): 153–171

Johnson, S. (2001), *The Teaching of Thinking Skills*. London: PESGB

Jones, J. (2008), Why don't art and science mix? www.guardian.co.uk/artanddesign/jonathanjonesblog/2008/sep/02/darwinscanopy (accessed August 2011)

Kind, P. M. and Kind, V. (2007), Creativity in science education: Perspectives and challenges for developing school science. *Studies in Science Education*, 43: 1–37

Lave, J. and Wenger, E. (1991), *Situated Learning: Legitimate Peripheral Participation*. Cambridge: Cambridge University Press

Lederman, N. G., Gess-Newsome, J. and Latz, M. S. (1994), The nature and development of pre-service science teachers' conceptions of subject matter and pedagogy. *Journal of Research in Science Teaching*, 31 (2): 129–146

Lefebvre, S., Deaudelin, D. and Loiselle, J. (2006), *ICT implementation stages of primary teachers: The practices and conceptions of teaching and learning*. Paper presented at the Australian Association for Research in Education National Conference, 27–30 November, Adelaide, Australia,

Lotto, R. B. and Purves, D. (2005) *Perceiving Colour*. Colour Dyes Review, Purves Lab. www.purveslab.net/publications/Perceiving%20colour.pdf (accessed February 2012)

Lumpe, A. T., Haney, J. and Czerniak, C. (2000), Assessing teachers' beliefs about their science teaching context. *Journal of Research in Science Teaching*, 37 (3): 123–145

Lyotard, J. F. (1984) *The Post-Modern Condition: A Report on Knowledge*. Manchester, Manchester University Press

McGuinness, C. (1999), *From Thinking Skills to Thinking Classrooms: A Review and Evaluation of Approaches for Developing Pupils' Thinking*. Nottingham: DfEE

McKinney, J. and Hademenos, G. (2009), Learning as they write: An assignment to explain physics concepts. *The Physics Teacher*, 47: 290–294

Meijer, J., Elshout-Mohr, M. and van Hout-Wolters, B. (2001), An instrument for the assessment of cross-curricular skills. *Education Research and Evaluation*, 7 (1): 79–107

Metcalfe, R. J. A., Abbott, S., Bray, P., Exley, J. and Wisnia, D. (1984), Teaching science through drama: An empirical investigation. *Research in Science and Technological Education*, 2: 77–81

Millar, R. and Osborne, J. (eds) (1998), *Beyond 2000: Science Education for the Future*. London: King's College London, School of Education

Morrison, K. (1994), *Implementing Cross-Curricular Themes*. London, David Fulton Publishers

Mortimer, E. F. and Scott, P. H. (2003), *Meaning Making in Secondary Science Classrooms*. Buckingham: Open University Press

Murphy, C., Beggs, J., Russell, H. and Melton, L. (2005) *Primary Horizons: Starting Out in Science*. London, Wellcome Trust

Murray, I. and Reiss, M. (2003), *Student Review of the Science Curriculum*. London: Planet Science, Institute of Education, Science Museum

National Academy of Sciences (1984), *Science and Creationism*. Washington, DC: National Academy Press, 4–6

National Advisory Committee on Creative and Cultural Education (NACCCE) (1999) *All Our Futures: Creativity, Culture and Education*. London: DFEE

National Curriculum Council (1989), *A Curriculum for All: Curricular Guidance*. York: NCC

National Science Foundation (NSF) (1965), *Science Education in the Schools of the United States*. Report to the Committee on Science and Astronautics, US Congress, Washington, DC: US Government Printing Office

Newton, L. and Rogers, L. (2003), Thinking frameworks for planning ICT in science lessons. *School Science Review*, 84 (309):113–119

Niederhauser, D. S. and Stoddart, T. (2001), Teachers' instructional perspectives and use of educational software. *Teaching and Teacher Education*, 17 (1): 15–31

Nord, W. A. (1999), Science, religion, and education. *Phi Delta Kappan*, 81 (1): 28–33

Ødegaard, M. (2003), Dramatic science: A critical review of drama in science education. *Studies in Science Education*, 39: 75–101

Ogborn, J., Kress, G., Martins, I. and McGillicuddy, K. (1996), *Explaining Science in the Classroom*. Buckingham: Open University Press

Oliver, A. (2006) *Creative Teaching Science in the Early Years and Primary Classroom*. Abingdon: David Fulton Publishers

Osborne, J. (2007), *Engaging Young People with Science: Thoughts about Future Direction of Science Education*. Proceedings of the Linnaeus Tercentenary Symposium held at Uppsala University, Uppsala, Sweden. 28–29 May

Osborne, J. and Collins, S. (2000), *Pupils' and Parents' Views of the School Science Curriculum*. London: King's College London

Osborne, J., Duschi, R. and Fairbrother, B. (2002), *Breaking the Mould? Teaching Science for Public Understanding*. London: School of Education, King's College London

Osborne, J. and Hennessy, S. (2003), *Literature Review in Science Education and the Role of ICT: Promise, Problems and Future Directions*. London: Futurelab

Osborne, J. F., Simon, S. and Collins, S. (2003), Attitudes towards science: A review of the literature and its implications. *International Journal of Science Education*, 25: 1049–1079

Osborne, J., Erduran, S. and Simon, S. (2004) Enhancing the quality of argumentation in school science. *Journal of Research in Science Teaching*, 41 (10): 994–1020.

Oulton, C., Dillon, J. and Grace, M. (2004), Reconceptualising the teaching of controversial issues. *International Journal of Science Education*, 26: 441–467

Özden, M. (2007), Problems with science and technology education in Turkey. *Eurasia Journal of Mathematics, Science and Technology Education*, 3 (2): 157–161

Peterson, S. S. (2005), *Writing across the Curriculum: Because All Teachers Teach Writing*. Winnepeg, MB: Portage and Main

Piaget J (1974). The principles of genetic epistemology. Routledge: London, UK

Pickersgill, D. (2003), Effective use of the Internet in science teaching. *School Science Review*, 84 (309): 77–86

Pressley, M. and McCormick, C. B. (1995), *Advanced Educational Psychology*. New York: HarperCollins

Puttnam, R. and Borko, H. (2000), What do new views of knowledge and thinking have to say about research on teacher thinking? *Educational Researcher*, 29 (1): 4–15

QCA (2007a), *The National Curriculum 2007: Statutory Requirements for Key Stage 3 and 4*. London, QCA. Extended version with additional guidance online, available at http://curriculum.qcda.gov.uk/key-stages-3-and-4/ (accessed August 2011)

QCA (2007b) *Science: Programme of Study for Key Stage 3 and Attainment Targets*. www.qca.org.uk/curriculum (accessed August 2011)

QCA (2007c) *Citizenship: Programme of Study for Key Stage 3 and Attainment Targets*. www.qca.org.uk/curriculum (accessed August 2011)

QCA (2007d) *Programme of Study for Key Stage 3 and Attainment Target: Art and Design*. www.qca.org.uk/curriculum (accessed August 2011)

Qualification and Curriculum Authority (QCA) (2009) *Cross curricular dimensions: A planning guide for schools*. Available at http://schoolsonline.britishcouncil.org/sites/default/files/el/98919.pdf (accessed February 2012)

Reiss, M. J. (2005), The importance of affect in science education. In S. Alsop (ed.), *The Affective Dimensions of Cognition: Studies from Education in the Sciences*. Dordrecht: Kluwer, 17–25

Reiss, M. J. (2008), Should science educators deal with the science/religion issue? *Studies in Science Education*, 44: 157–186

Reiss, M. J. (2010), Science and religion: Implications for science educators. *Cultural Studies of Science Education*, 5: 91–101

Rigden, J. S. (2005), The mystique of physics: Relumine the enlightenment. Millikan Award Speech, *American Journal of Physics*, 73: 1094–1098

Romeo, G. I. (2006), Engage, empower, enable: Developing a shared vision for technology in education. In M. S. Khine (ed.), *Engaged Learning and Emerging Technologies*. The Netherlands: Springer Science

Roth, W-M. & Bowen (1994), Mathematization of experience in a grade 8 open-inquiry environment: An introduction to the representational practices of science. *Journal of Research in Science Teaching*, 31 (3), pp 293–318

Roth, W. M. and McGinn, M. K. (1998), Knowing, researching and reporting science education: Lessons from science and technology studies. *Journal of Research in Science Teaching*, 35 (2): 213–235

Rowley, C. and Cooper, H. (2009) Cross-curricular learning and the development of values. In C. Rowley and H. Cooper (eds), *Cross-Curricular Approaches to Teaching and Learning*. London, Sage

The Royal Society (2010) *Royal Society State of the Nation Report: Science and Mathematics Education, 5–14*. London: The Royal Society

The Royal Society (2011), *Royal Society State of the Nation Report: Increasing the Size of the Pool*. London: The Royal Society

Sampson, G. (1921), (1970 edition), *English for the English: A Chapter on National Education*. Cambridge University Press: Cambridge

Savage, J. (2011) *Cross-curricular teaching and learning in the secondary school*. London, Routledge

Schoepp, K. (2005), Barriers to technology integration in a technology-rich environment. *Learning and Teaching in Higher Education: Gulf Perspectives*, 2 (1): 1–24

Scott, J. (ed.) (1993), *Science and Language Links: Classroom Implications*. Portsmouth, NH: Heinemann

Seals, M. A. (2010), Teaching students to think critically about science and origins. *Cultural Studies of Science Education*, 5: 251–255

Shamatha, J. H., Peressini, D. and Meymaris, K. (2004), Technology-supported mathematics activities situated within an effective learning environment theoretical framework. *Contemporary Issues in Technology and Teacher Education*, 3 (4): 362–381

Shepherd, J. (2011), A-level choices: The sharp contrast between private schools and comprehensives – get the data. www.guardian.co.uk/news/datablog/2011/jun/15/a-level-subjects-preferred-by-universities-by-private-school-and-comprehensive (accessed August 2011)

Shoemaker, B. J. E. (1989), Integrative education: A curriculum review for the twenty-first century. *OSSC Bulletin* 33 (2). Oregon ED: Oregon School Study Council

Shulman, L. S. (1986), Those who understand: Knowledge growth in teaching. *Educational Researcher*, 15: 4–14

Simon, S. (2003), Students' attitudes towards science. In M. Monk and J. Osborne (eds), *Good Practice in Science Teaching*. Berkshire: Open University Press

Sjøberg, S., Schreiner, C. and Stefánsson, K. (2004), *The Voice of the Learners: International Perspectives on S and T based on the ROSE Project*. Paper presented at the XI Symposium of the International Organisation for Science and Technology Education, Marie Curie-Sladowska University, Lublin, Poland, 25–30 July

Skinner, N. C. and Preece, P. F. W. (2003), The use of information and communications technology to support the teaching of science in primary schools. *International Journal of Science Education*, 25 (2): 205–219

Tamir, E. (2010), Capital, power and the struggle over teacher certification. *Educational Policy*, 24 (3): 465–499

Tate, A. (1994), *Core Skills and Cross-Curricular Initiatives in Secondary Schools*. Berkshire: National Foundation for Educational Research (NFER)

Thomson, P. (2010) Headteacher autonomy: a sketch of a Bourdieuian field analysis of position and practice. *Critical Studies in Education*, 51 (1) 5–20

Trier, U. P. (1991), Non-curriculum bound outcomes. Presented at the OECD/INES/Network A meeting, Paris

Tvieta, J. (1998), Can untraditional learning methods used in physics help girls to be more interested and achieve more in this subject? In E. Torracca (ed.), *Research in Science Education in Europe*. Dordrecht: Kluwer, 1–7

Uitto, A., Juuti, K., Lavonen, J., Byman, R., and Meisalo, V. (2011), Secondary school students' interests, attitudes and values concerning school science related to environmental issues in Finland. *Environmental Education Research*, 17 (2): 167–186

Vasagar, J. (2011), A-levels boom in maths and science credited to 'Brian Cox effect'. www.guardian.co.uk/education/2011/aug/18/a-levels-boom-maths-science (accessed August 2011)

Venville, G., Wallace, J., Rennie, L. and Malone, J. (1998), The integration of science, mathematics and technology in a discipline-based culture. *School of Science and Mathematics*, 98 (6): 294–302

Verma, G.K. & Pumfrey, P. (Ed.) (1993) *Cultural diversity and the curriculum. Vol.2, Cross-curricular contexts, themes and dimensions in secondary schools*. London, Falmer

Vygotsky, L.S. (1978), *Mind in Society: The Development of Higher Psychological Processes*. Cambridge, MA: Harvard University Press

Ward-Penny, R. (2011), *Cross-Curricular Teaching and Learning in the Secondary School: Mathematics*. London, Routledge

Wellcome Trust (2010), *Leading Debate: 21 Years of the National Curriculum for Science*. London: Wellcome Trust

White, J. (2002), *The Child's Mind*. London: RoutledgeFalmer

Will.i.am (2011), Science is rock'n roll and technology is recession proof. The Huffington Post. http://www.huffingtonpost.com/william/science-education_b_920125.html (accessed August 2011)

Wilson, V. (2000), Educational forum on teaching thinking skills. In V. Wilson, *Can Thinking Skills Be Taught?* Spotlight: Scottish Council for Research in Education, Edinburgh

Wong, A. F. L., Quek, C.-L., Divaharan, S., Liu, W.-C., Peer, J. and Williams, M. D. (2006), Singapore students' and teachers' perceptions of computer-supported project work classroom learning environments. *Journal of Research in Technology Education*, 38 (4): 449–479

Woolnough, B. (1998), Authentic science in schools, to develop personal knowledge. In J. Wellington (ed.) *Practical Work in School: Which Way Now?* London: Routledge: 109–125

Yackel, E. and Cobb, P. (1996), Sociomathematical norms, argumentation and autonomy in mathematics. *Journal of Research in Mathematics Education*, 27: 458–477

Yelland, N. (2001), *Teaching and Learning with Information and Communications Technologies (ICT) for Numeracy in the Early Childhood and Primary Years of Schooling*. Australia: Department of Education, Training and Youth Affairs

Yorks, P. and Follo, E. (1993) *Engagement Rates during Thematic and Traditional Instruction*. ERIC ED363412

Index